GRANITE LEGENDS

Aberdeen's Sporting Heroes

DEDICATION

To Coral, Finlay and Mia.

The Press and Journal

GRANITE LEGENDS

Aberdeen's Sporting Heroes

Paul Smith

First published in Great Britain in 2010 by The Derby Books Publishing Company Limited, 3 The Parker Centre, Derby, DE21 4SZ.

ACKNOWLEDGEMENTS

My thanks go to the many people who played a major role in bringing *Granite Legends* to fruition, in particular to Dave McDonald and the Aberdeen Sports Council members for their vision in creating a sporting hall of fame for the city, and Susan McKay of Aberdeen Journals for in turn driving forward the plans to detail the project in print. Alex Morton and the team at DB Publishing deserve praise for their creativity in pulling the book together, while Colin MacLeod's attention to detail was vital throughout the process. My appreciation also goes to the countless others who provided input to the project at every stage. Last but certainly not least, my thanks to Coral, Finlay and Mia for their support, encouragement and inspiration.

ISBN 978-1-85983-789-4
Printed and bound by Cromwell Press Group, Trowbridge, Wiltshire

CONTENTS

INTRODUCTION

When the ribbon was cut to declare the multi-million pound Aberdeen Sport Village officially open in March 2010 it was with a sense of hope and anticipation. The centre, on the eastern edge of the city, was created to address the pressing need for top-class facilities to match the potential of the north-east sporting talent in every sphere. From the staples of football and rugby to the niche pursuits, the Granite City is home to a thriving group of young sportsmen and women who are being pushed to make the most of their raw ability.

As they tread the path towards international recognition, each and every one can look towards a hero for inspiration. The Aberdeen Sports Village will house the city's recently established sporting hall of fame, an initiative spearheaded by the Aberdeen Sports Council and designed to recognise some of the most influential figures in the area's rich past.

When the hall of fame was founded in 2006, the Sports Council inducted 21 inaugural members, a number chosen to commemorate the organisation's 21st anniversary. As part of the process *Press and Journal* readers were asked to nominate sporting figures worthy of a place on the esteemed list and from those suggestions a judging panel selected the first batch of names to form the hall of fame. All 21 were Aberdeen-born, a strict criteria for the first intake but one which has since been relaxed to ensure that those from outwith the city who are intrinsically linked with the area are not ignored.

The 21 Aberdonians selected in 2006 were: Harry Bannerman (golf), Bill Berry (judo), Anne Robb Boyle (skiing), Martin Buchan (football), David Carry (swimming), Neil Cochran (swimming), Chris Cusiter (rugby), Tony Dawson (badminton), Elaine Farquharson-Black (golf), Stephanie Forrester (athletics), Denis Hay (hockey), Donny Innes (rugby), Denis Law (football), Paul Lawrie (golf), Graham Leggat (football), Linda Lesperance (curling), Ian McCrae (rugby), Sandy Pirie (golf), Frank Robertson (cricket), Colin Smith (cricket) and D.W.C. Smith (rugby).

Granite Legends profiles all 21 of those great names, as well as some of the nominees who did not make the initial list but are sure to feature as the hall of fame grows in the years ahead. It is far from a definitive tribute to Aberdeen's sporting greats, however, and it would be easy to fill a second volume with tales of the many characters not featured in the pages of this book.

However, the 50 profiles selected are designed to give a flavour of Aberdeen's proud and diverse history, a city which has bred generation after generation of sporting stars. From Olympians to Scottish champions and European stars to Commonwealth heroes, the Granite City has given birth to some of sport's most talented and devoted sportsmen and women. It is a group to be remembered, revered and celebrated as the next generation seek to emulate those wonderful achievements.

Paul Smith, 2010

Paul Lawrie

The Granite City has produced many fine golfers through the decades. From the formation of the Society of Golfers in Aberdeen in 1780 through to the modern day there has been a marvellous love affair with the sport – but it took more than 200 years for the dream of the founding fathers of that organisation to be realised and for an Aberdonian to claim his place at the head of sport's top table. In 1999 it happened, the city finally had a Major champion to call its own.

Paul Lawrie was the man who made it happen, the individual with the determination and guts to go all the way. His victory in the Open at Carnoustie in 1999 marked an unforgettable moment in his home town's sporting history. He produced a 10-shot comeback to earn a play-off place and eventually clinch the Claret Jug in a shoot-out against Frenchman Jean Van de Velde, who crumbled in the face of his Scottish opponent's relentless 67-shot charge on the final day. In doing so, Lawrie set a Major Championship record for overturning a fourth-round deficit which remains unmatched.

His penultimate shot during the tense play-off, an exquisite four iron arrowed straight at the pin to leave a three-foot putt, was worthy of victory on any course. It just so happened that Lawrie's moment of glory came in front of a home audience, and the triumph was lapped up by an appreciative Carnoustie crowd.

Paul Lawrie on home soil in the north-east in 2006, set against the dramatic backdrop at Murcar Links (Picture by Raymond Besant).

Paul Lawrie with the famous Claret Jug following the Open win in 1999 (Picture by Colin Rennie).

He had experienced the rush of victory three years earlier when he claimed his maiden European Tour victory at the Catalan Open, but that success paled into insignificance in comparison to his landmark Open win.

It was a life-changing moment for the quiet yet assured Aberdonian. Overnight he became one of the game's highest-profile players, with his Major achievement not equalled by a European player until Padraig Harrington sampled the sweet taste of success in 2007.

After a steady and studied climb through the ranks, Lawrie instantly had superstar status. With the rewards came intense scrutiny and media attention, but through the press and television scrum the proud Aberdonian kept his feet on the ground and his roots firmly planted in the north-east.

Lawrie, who has become one of Aberdeen Football Club's most high-profile supporters, admits his first sporting love was the beautiful game rather than the game of golf, which soon became his burning passion and lucrative career.

The seeds of his life in the sport were sown early, however, with the gift of a set of clubs as an eight-year-old. He honed his skills as a teenager and, despite not competing at the top level as an amateur, his talent shone through and he was spotted by Banchory Golf Club professional Doug Smart.

Smart, who had lost assistant Fraser Mann to Ballater, invited the 17-year-old Lawrie to have a trial spell on his staff. Lawrie, who joined the Banchory payroll in April 1986, took to the role instantly and took advantage of the opportunities the professional game presented.

In his first tournament as a pro, less than two months after accepting Smart's job offer, he won £300 when he pipped Murcar's Peter Smith to the Moray Seafoods title at Buckpool. For an enthusiastic young golfer who had his heart set on one day establishing himself as a club professional, it was a significant victory. All of a sudden a career as a tournament player opened up in front of him.

The youngster from Kemnay served a thorough and rock-solid apprenticeship in his native north-east over the next four years, moving up a gear in 1990. In April that year a storming final-day performance in the Scottish Assistants' Championship at Cruden Bay brought him a £1,000 cheque and underlined the big-hitting 21-year-old's potential. In the summer of that year he switched from Banchory to the Kings Links Golf Centre, where Bruce Davidson was establishing a formidable pool of talent at Aberdeen's new driving range.

By the end of the 1990 season the Aberdeenshire lad had taken his winnings to more than £17,000 on the Tartan Tour, in addition to winning the coveted Scottish Alliance Championship and Scottish Under-25 Championship, and decided to move up a level by bidding for a place in the European Tour qualifying school final.

He headed for Spain with young hopefuls from across the world intent on winning a place on the Continent's premier circuit, but missed his target. Undaunted, he returned to the Kings Links and spent hours on the practice range with coach and colleague David Thomson.

At the end of 1991, following another successful Tartan Tour campaign in which the prize money continued to flow and he topped the money list, the young gun earned his big ticket through six gruelling rounds of the European Tour qualifying school. At the age of 22 he was about to join the big boys of the global game.

Consolidation is always the key for any European Tour rookie, but for Lawrie that goal was met rapidly. Just four months after making his debut on the tour in 1992 he had smashed through the £30,000 barrier, the magic figure required to secure a card for the following season.

With that pressure lifted from his shoulders the Aberdonian went from strength to strength during his maiden season at the top level, winning more than £55,000 in European events alone. He was crowned European Under-25 champion, won the Scottish professional title and made his Open debut at Muirfield – lighting up the tournament with a cool and accomplished performance, finishing tied for 22nd and ahead of former champions Mark Calcavecchia and Lee Trevino in the field.

Lawrie, accompanied on tour by his wife Marian throughout his rookie year, coped admirably with the demands of the worldwide programme and laid the foundation stones of a long and fruitful career.

The rising star, who turned to St Andrews-based coach Jim Farmer in preparation for his second season on the European Tour, was at the centre of an expanding Kings Links team. He was joined by Adam Hunter and Craig Cassells on the top tour, while prolific Tartan Tour player Kenny Walker was also part of Bruce Davidson's empire at the links centre, complemented by teaching professionals David Thomson and Paul Girvan.

Success became a given for the Kings Links squad, but it was Lawrie who set the pace. In 1993 he marked his second appearance at the Open by finishing sixth in the star-studded field at Royal St George. Already a very special relationship with the world's greatest tournament was forming, with the consistent young Scot leading the event in the clubhouse for a lengthy spell before Greg Norman came through to lift the Claret Jug. Lawrie's time would come, however, and he continued to work on the game with the same vigour which led the late Doug Smart to earmark him for success at the very start of his journey.

'Chippie', as Lawrie had been tagged since his teenage days, vowed not to let success change him and even when his career as a pro was in its infancy he remained dedicated to his home patch. He supported tournaments for north-east professionals and continued to make appearances on the Alliance circuit, always quick to highlight the role that particular competition had played in building his confidence and skill as a tournament player.

Paul Lawrie with wife Marian and children Craig (right) and Michael in 1999 (Picture by Colin Rennie).

His win in the Catalan Open in 1996 was followed in the same season by a runners'-up place in the Volvo PGA Championship. A smattering of top 10 finishes in the following two years led to the 1999 campaign, culminating in the Open triumph but also featuring a winner's cheque at the Qatar Masters.

His outstanding form that year also clinched a place in the 1999 Ryder Cup at Brookline and the new recruit did not disappoint, finishing joint leading points scorer despite his team's agonising 14½–13½ defeat overall.

Lawrie played with distinction in a hostile environment, partnering Colin Montgomerie in both the foursomes and four-ball to emerge with a win and a half. The Scottish pair fell to defeat in their second foursomes tie, but recovered by defeating Tiger Woods and Steve Pate in the final four-ball. That set him up for the singles, where Lawrie stormed to a 4 and 3 win over Jeff Maggert. The effort could not help Europe to victory, but demonstrated that the Major-winning star's Open heroics were representative of his ability.

The Dunhill Links Championship win in 2001, which brought with it a bounty of close to 900,000 Euros, took Lawrie's annual prize fund past the one million Euro mark for the first time in his career, but the Open Championship, and the string of endorsements that followed, had already secured his future.

His winning run continued at the Wales Open in 2002 and he has remained a consistent performer on the European Tour while developing his off-course activities, which include course design and his charity work through the Paul Lawrie Foundation.

Richie Ramsay

European and British golf endured barren years at the very highest level following Paul Lawrie's win at the Open in 1999. Padraig Harrington was the man who officially broke the drought when he won the Open Championship in 2007, but arguably it was Aberdeen's very own Richie Ramsay who led the way.

Richie Ramsay has quickly become established as one to watch on the European Tour.

When Ramsay brushed aside a long line of home favourites to win the US Amateur Championship in 2006 it was a shot across the bows of the Stateside stars. No longer could they expect to have it all their own way – the Europeans were back in the driving seat.

Ramsay is part of the next generation of continental players, a group justifiably confident of making a big impact on the sport. He has belief to match his ability and a burning desire to do well: all the ingredients needed to succeed in a game which with every passing year makes new and increased physical and mental demands on its participants. A keen fitness enthusiast, Ramsay epitomises the modern player with his attention to detail in his preparation and practice.

His qualities brought him the US amateur title at the age of 23. The magnitude of the Scot's achievement is best demonstrated by the length of time which had elapsed between his momentous victory and that of the nation's last winner in the tournament – a whopping 108 years.

Findlay S. Douglas was his eminent predecessor, winning the prestigious title in 1898 when the competition was still very much in its formative years. In between a who's who of golf stepped forward to lift the trophy. Past winners include Arnold Palmer, Jack Nicklaus, Craig Stadler, Mark O'Meara and, in more recent times, Justin Leonard and a certain Tiger Woods.

What is notable from the winners' roll of honour is the dominance of the Americans in their own back yard. It takes skill to win the US Amateur Championship, as the star-studded list proves, but for an outsider to upset the odds and take the prize out of the country it also requires resilience and sheer determination.

Ramsay, with a reputation for a heart-on-sleeve approach on the course, which belies his easy-going nature outside of the game, has those qualities in abundance and

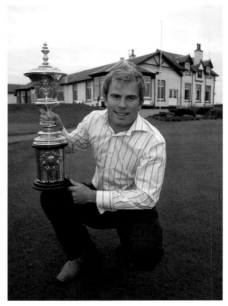

they were on full show in 2006 when he stormed to the greatest achievement of his career to date.

He faced Canadian player Mark Leone, Finland's Antti Ahokas and the American trio of Kyle Davis, Rickie Fowler and Webb Simpson on his way to a Final showdown against Missouri starlet John Kelly. The common theme throughout his run to the last tie was the visitor's command in every match – establishing a lead on the front nine on each occasion and holding it with a vice-like grip to sail to the showpiece game in the fiercely contested match play event.

Kelly had a vocal backing for the Final, with the crowd at the Hazeltine National Golf Club in Minnesota rooting for a home win. Ramsay had other ideas and produced a sparkling display to put himself three up through the first 13 holes of the two-round contest, holding on to eventually come through 4 and 2.

Hazeltine was a fitting venue for such a memorable occasion. Regarded as one of the country's finest courses, the Robert Trent Jones design was opened in 1962 and hosted the US Open as recently as 1991, when Payne Stewart was the man who withstood the test of the long and demanding set-up, and the US PGA Championship, just four years prior to Ramsay's amateur win over the same turf. The PGA event returned to the Minnesota club in 2009 and in 2016 the course will host the Ryder Cup. Could the stage be set for a dramatic return to familiar surroundings for Ramsay? Time will tell.

The 2006 celebration was the Royal Aberdeen amateur's finest hour in golf, although he was no stranger by then to the big occasion. Aged 23 when he won at Hazeltine, Ramsay had been a mainstay of the Scottish team for two years.

His first cap came in 2004, the year in which Ramsay's potential truly shone through. It was the year in which he was crowned Scottish universities champion, Scottish stroke play champion and clinched the East of Scotland title.

In 2005 the Stirling University student won the Irish Amateur Championship and also made his Walker Cup debut as part of the Great Britain and Ireland team which fell to a single-point defeat against the Americans at the Chicago Golf Club.

His victory the following year in the US Championship propelled Ramsay to the head of the world amateur rankings and he maintained pole position for more than four months. In that time he was named Scotland's golfer of the year and inevitably took the decision to turn professional in 2007, having sampled the best the paid game had to offer as an amateur guest at the Masters, Open and US Open on the back of his Hazeltine glory.

Mentored by Scottish national coach Ian Rae since 2000, Ramsay's profile soared in the aftermath of his US Amateur win in 2006. When he lined up in the Masters the following year, his first Major experience, he was alongside Tiger Woods. Ramsay did not look out of place in such exalted company and it stood him in good stead in the years ahead.

So many young hopefuls have strained under the weight of pro status, finding the transition from amateur to the big money world of the paid ranks too hard to handle. Ramsay was an exception, never once faltering after taking the plunge and dedicating his life to the game following the completion of his university studies.

He dipped his toe into the European Challenge Tour pool and found it welcoming, recording five top-12 finishes in his first nine events to secure a full card for the circuit in 2008.

He took full advantage of the opportunity, clinching his first tournament win as a professional when he charged to the head of the pack at the Vodafone Challenge in Düsseldorf. Ramsay produced five birdies and an eagle in his final round to win the title by a single shot, an inspired and gutsy performance typical of the fiery Scot's character.

He followed that victory up with another title at the Toulouse Open and his form on his first full Challenge Tour season, earning more than 100,000 Euro in prize money alone, won him the prize every aspiring young player craves – a European Tour card.

Ramsay stepped up to the elite circuit in 2009 and settled quickly, coming close to his first title when he challenged for first prize at the star-studded Alfred Dunhill Links Championship over familiar tracks in Fife, just a short hop down the east coast from his links education at Balgownie. He eventually had to settle for a share of fourth spot, but it hinted that the best is yet to come for the Granite City's latest golfing export as he duelled with eventual winner Simon Dyson on the final day of the tournament.

The event, played over Carnoustie, Kingsbarns and St Andrews, where it concluded, was blighted by high winds which forced one round to be postponed, and saw Ramsay card a five under par final round of 67 – but Dyson went two better at St Andrews, producing seven birdies, to give himself a four-shot cushion over Ramsay and a three-shot lead over joint runners-up Rory McIlroy and Oliver Wilson. It was a week for tough characters and the Aberdonian was one of the stars of the show, playing in a field packed with celebrities from the world of film and sport as part of the event's pro, celebrity and amateur mix.

The Dunhill performance was his best and most lucrative display, carrying a 150,000 Euro prize, but was far from the only highlight of a debut European Tour season. Consolidation was the obvious aim, but Ramsay surpassed that with a clutch of top-25

Richie Ramsay signing autographs during the Open at Carnoustie in 2007 (Picture by Colin Rennie).

Richie Ramsay with his winning medal from the South African Open in 2009 (Picture by Kenny Elrick).

finishes, including taking 10th place at the Wales Open and 18th at the European Open.

He did even better at the start of the 2009–10 season, winning the South African Open in December 2009 to get the new campaign off to a rip-roaring start and give him his first European Tour title.

His life now revolves around international travel, but Ramsay remains true to his north-east upbringing, ignoring the logistical nightmare and maintaining Aberdeen as his touring base. It was in his home city that Ramsay learnt the ropes as a golfer, having been introduced to the game even before he had begun primary school. He soon showed promise with a club in his hand.

A keen footballer in his youth, Ramsay represented his school team at Airyhall primary, but golf became the sport of choice in his teenage years as a Hazlehead Academy pupil. His studies took him south to Stirling, and also to Texas for a stint on a golf scholarship, but Royal Aberdeen remained Ramsay's home club throughout a glittering amateur career. When he turned professional, Ramsay boasted a handicap of +4 and an armoury of shots perfectly suited to the step up. His grounding in the amateur game, with skills honed on the rugged links courses of the north-east, are the foundation for what promises to be a long and illustrious professional career.

Harry Bannerman

The glamour and glitz of the Ryder Cup on American soil is as far removed from the biting cold and howling winds of north-east links golf as it is possible to imagine. For Harry Bannerman, the two worlds came together in glorious fashion in 1971 as the Aberdonian lad went head to head with the finest the US had to offer and strode away with his head held high.

For Bannerman, the Granite City's most successful golfing export prior to Paul Lawrie's heroics in the 1990s, the Ryder Cup match that year proved to be a defining moment in a long career as a club and tournament professional.

Injury problems curtailed his top-level involvement soon after the match against the US at St Louis in Missouri, but by then he had already savoured life on one of the biggest stages of all. He had won a place in captain

Harry Bannerman on the Royal Aberdeen track in 1972.

Harry Bannerman in his heyday.

Eric Brown's British team for the Ryder Cup on the back of his most impressive season on the European Tour, finishing fourth in the PGA Order of Merit to become an automatic pick for the trip across the Atlantic.

He was joined by Neil Coles, Christy O'Connor, Peter Townsend, Peter Oosterhuis, Brian Huggett, Tony Jacklin, Maurice Bembridge, Peter Butler, Bernard Gallacher, Brian Barnes and John Garner. Bannerman and Jacklin raised the stakes in the warm-up to the tournament by placing wagers during practice sessions, with the Scot shelling out $100 after his English colleague's hole in one effort.

Even among illustrious names such as Jacklin and Gallacher, it was cup rookie Bannerman who stole the show for the visiting party as one of three newcomers. Garner and Oosterhuis were the other debutants, but it was the Aberdonian who captured the imagination of an entire nation with his performance at Old Warson. The exclusive country club was still developing, built in 1954 to a Robert Trent Jones design. The course features rolling terrain, tree-lined fairways and large undulating greens, but held no fears for Scottish visitors.

Bannerman made his debut as Gallacher's partner in a 2 and 1 win over Billy Casper and Miller Barber but, partnering Townsend, lost out in two four-ball ties. Breaking the successful partnership with Gallacher appeared an unusual choice, but there was method in the skipper's decision. Bannerman and Townsend were close friends off the course and had even teamed up as bridge partners, so the pairing was nothing new to them.

It was in the singles, with the pressure at its most intense, that Bannerman came into his own. He faced the formidable prospect of tackling the legendary Arnold Palmer in his first match and did not falter – even in the face of 10,000 fervent Palmer supporters tramping the fairways behind the duo.

Harry Bannerman played at the highest level, at home and abroad.

It was during that match and in that cauldron that Bannerman produced what he maintains is the best play of his life. It was on the eighth hole of the Old Warson Country Club, a four-iron approach made all the more testing by a bunker situated directly in front of the pin and the green tucked behind an overhanging branch. Bannerman opted to be brave and fired a perfect iron shot which flew towards the target, fading perfectly to fizz within inches of the hole. Palmer graciously conceded the hole and the pair could not be separated as the round drew to a close. A proud Banchory Golf Club member was in the gallery and captured the moment on cine film for Bannerman to cherish.

After the satisfaction of his draw against Palmer, Bannerman had to collect his thoughts and prepare for his final tie against Gardner Dickson. His opponent did not have the lasting kudos of Palmer, but Dickson did retire from the game with a Ryder Cup record of played 10, won nine and lost just one. That single reverse came at the hands of a certain Harry Bannerman, who defeated the American 2 and 1 at the end of a hard-fought encounter in which the home player did his best to knock his British adversary off his stride.

The Ryder Cup thrust Bannerman into the international limelight, but by then he was no stranger to attention closer to home. He had first hit the headlines in 1959 when he was called into the Scotland boys international team. He was an Ellon Academy pupil who had made a big impact locally, playing out of Murcar and gaining a reputation as a keen student of the game.

Bannerman would take the opportunity to caddie in local tournaments when not competing himself, soaking up every piece of information he could about the courses and competitors on his home patch. In 1957 he had won the Hands Across the Sea Trophy, the junior prize in the Aberdeen Links Championship, and he continued to progress at pace as he added the North of Scotland boys title to his growing collection.

The teenage prospect went on to become a star of the amateur game in the north-east, winning his club title and going on to win the Scottish Alliance Championship in 1965. He was 23 years old when he claimed that significant victory and it proved to be the spur needed to propel Bannerman into the paid ranks.

In November 1965 he relinquished his amateur status, turning his back on a career as a lab technician at the Rowett Institute to concentrate on his sporting passion. He was appointed assistant professional at Royal Aberdeen and received backing from a consortium of local businessmen who were adamant the young player would go right to the top. Hugh McDermott, Jack Hall and Bobby Morrison dug deep to give Bannerman the financial backing required to test the water at the top level.

When Bannerman, whose mastery of the short game brought him many admirers, won the Scottish Professional Championship at Montrose and Northern Open at Dornoch in 1967 he began to repay that faith. He was bold and confident, willing to take calculated risks on the course to great effect – not surprising, given his part-time work as a croupier at an Aberdeen gaming club during his formative years as a golf pro.

In 1969 the confident and charismatic player was appointed as club professional at Banchory and this new-found stability off the course brought rewards on the fairways, as he returned to form on the British tournament scene, building towards the impressive 1971 campaign, which brought him fame and fortune.

That year Bannerman recorded a string of impressive performances, not the least of which was his 11th place finish in the Open at Royal Birkdale, and rose to fourth in the PGA Order of Merit after hoovering up in excess of £5,000 in prize money.

More important than the financial rewards, however, was the biggest prize of all – a Ryder Cup place. His standing on the merit list was enough to earn an automatic place in the Great Britain and Ireland team for the 1971 tournament, and it is that achievement which has defined the career of one of Aberdeen's greatest-ever golfers.

The Ryder Cup appearance brought Bannerman recognition locally, with a civic reception staged in Banchory to mark his return, but also opened up international doors. The following year he toured in the Caribbean and also played in American events. The highlight was his 33rd place finish in the US Masters at Augusta, beating the cut to last the distance.

Yet he did not forget his roots. In 1972 he turned out in several tournaments on home soil and won the Scottish Professional Championship for a second time, emerging victorious at Strathaven to repeat his 1967 triumph, as well as winning the 1972 Northern Open to make it a hat-trick in that event.

Bannerman stepped down from his Banchory post in 1974 to immerse himself in tournament golf, basing himself in Yorkshire but travelling far and wide. Postings included stints on the African golf scene but, after being hindered by recurring back problems, the lure of the north-east was too strong to resist and in 1976 the wanderer returned to become a professional at Cruden Bay so that he and his wife could settle with their young family.

The golf bug bit the Bannerman brood, with the Ryder Cup star's daughter Jackie married to a prolific amateur player and son David a former Cruden Bay champion. Stuart, the son who completes the Bannerman family, is a golf professional based in Germany.

Bannerman spent more than a decade with the village club before the globetrotting instinct returned in the late 1980s, when he moved to the Continent with his wife Hazel to embark on another intriguing adventure. The couple became immersed in

Harry Bannerman, pictured in 2003, remains a popular figure in north-east golf.

German golf, with Harry helping establish the Schloss Mainsondheim Golf Club and his wife handling the administrative side of the business.

Out of sight did not mean Bannerman was out of mind in golfing circles, and in 1992 he was tempted out of playing retirement to lend his profile to the inaugural European Seniors Tour. The Scot held his own, finishing 24th on the money list as over-50s golf hit the Continent for the first time.

The Bannermans returned to their roots once and for all in 2003 when Harry accepted an invitation to become a teaching professional at the newly-opened Aspire Golf Centre on Deeside, setting up home back in Banchory.

John Chillas

When John Chillas made his European Tour debut in 1973 he could hardly have imagined that he would have to wait 30 years to collect his first trophy. The talented Aberdonian's moment of glory came at Wentworth when he claimed the Senior Masters title in 2003, as part of the increasingly high-profile European Seniors Tour programme, and it marked an incredible comeback perfectly.

Chillas had spent the best part of three decades on the outside looking in, taking the decision at a young age to turn his back on life on the road and throw his heart and soul into life as a club professional and golf coach.

In that time he became recognised as one of the game's great teachers, but the competitive instinct had been subdued rather than extinguished and in 2001, on his 50th birthday, a whole new world of opportunity opened up in front of the veteran campaigner.

The milestone triggered his qualification for the senior game and he attacked the challenge with relish, returning to the big time with great aplomb and soon establishing himself as a key player on the scene.

John Chillas in action in 1984.

Gary Player and John Chillas (right) practising at the Senior British Open at Royal Aberdeen (Picture by Raymond Besant).

A compact and powerful player, he waited just two years for his first tournament victory and climbed to fourth in the rankings in 2003 on the back of the Senior Masters triumph, in which he pipped Irish veteran Eamon Darcy to the big prize.

That ranking finish was usurped by his third place the following year courtesy of another tournament win in the Estoril Seniors Tour Championship and four runners'-up prizes as the wily Aberdonian proved he could practise what he preached to his many pupils.

Chillas won the Scandinavian Senior Open in 2007, after a four-hole play-off against England's Glen Ralph, to maintain his impressive run of results on the immensely competitive circuit, which has been graced by some of the best-known names in the game and has begun to attract the audiences and financial backing the regular tour has come to expect.

He was a top-10 player in each of his first four seasons on the circuit and has become known as one of the players to watch, with a stylish game befitting a man who spent years passing on his wisdom and expertise to the Scottish game's rising stars.

He was able to teach youngsters from his own experiences as a player making his way in the game. From a young age the talents of John Chillas were clear for all to see. As a teenage Inverurie Academy pupil, playing out of Huntly Golf Club, he was a regular winner in junior tournaments throughout the north-east and his prize haul included the Hands Across the Sea trophy at the Aberdeen Links Championship in 1967. Sporting prowess ran deep in the Chillas genes. His bank manager father, Bill, was a Scottish international bowler.

John opted to turn professional as a 19-year-old in 1971, by which time he was working as a bank clerk. Chillas took the brave decision to turn his back on the comfort and familiarity of the financial sector and accepted the offer of an assistant pro job at Dalmahoy.

He had been representing Royal Aberdeen, having joined the Balgownie club in 1966 when the family moved from Huntly to the city, but competed sparingly on the amateur circuit due to his work commitments.

The move to the paid game came as a surprise to most in the golfing world but it was a calculated move by a young player confident that he had what it took to make a living from the game. He wore the Deeside badge as a touring professional for 18 months but, with the European Tour still developing, he faced a battle for survival as he paid his way around the world in the hope of winning big. From Germany to the Netherlands and from France to Italy and Spain, Chillas made his share of cuts but soon came to the conclusion that the European Tour road was not paved with gold.

John Chillas tees off at the 16th in the Senior British Open at Royal Aberdeen in 2005 (Picture by Kevin Emslie).

His best result had been a respectable tie for 39th in the German Open of 1973 and the reward was a £122 share of the prize pot. A handful of additional top-50 finishes helped to offset the mounting travel costs, but within two years of joining the paid ranks he decided on a change of direction and landed his first job as a head professional, recruited by Ballater to become the club's first pro as the Aberdeenshire club expanded its operation. The level-headed Chillas took the decision to put his competitive ambitions on the back burner as he concentrated on establishing himself in the club role, allowing younger brother David to take centre stage with his European Tour exploits.

In 1975 Ballater began the search for a new professional after Chillas was headhunted by Crow Wood Golf Club in Lanarkshire. The central base was more conducive to tournament golf and the following year Chillas celebrated a glorious double as he was crowned Scottish Alliance champion at Hilton Park after first claiming the Scottish Professional Championship. He celebrated the 25th anniversary of his Scottish pro win in 2001 by winning the title again – earning an £8,000 cheque as opposed to the £750 his first win had brought.

In the 1976 event he held off a strong challenge by Ryder Cup star Bernard Gallacher, but Chillas insisted it would not alter his decision to step back from the European Tour. His mind was made up and the intention was to focus on his club commitments, moving to Stirling Golf Club in 1979 and then on to Glenbervie as he carved out a reputation as a fine coach. Most notably he steered Stirling University's brightest talents on the path to stardom and has been credited with a major role in establishing the university as one of higher education's sporting centres of excellence.

His protégés included women's stars Catriona Matthew and Alison Rose, both of whom hold the distinction of clinching both the Scottish and British Amateur

Championships, but Chillas was always careful to keep his own hand in by picking and choosing Tartan Tour events to compete in. By his own admission, Chillas cherished his time on the range as much as he did his hours on the course and viewed practice as a pleasure rather than a chore throughout his career.

When he turned 50 in 2001 and became eligible for the European Seniors Tour that maintenance regime proved to be worth its weight in gold as he slipped effortlessly into life as a touring player – a life he had waved farewell to almost three decades earlier but one he embraced wholeheartedly after getting his second wind on the lucrative and high-profile senior circuit. Amid a who's who of the golfing glitterati, Chillas has established himself as one of the most consistent and talented players of his generation.

When he first made his breakthrough in the 1970s he laid the path for his younger brother David to follow. David Chillas quickly succeeded in surpassing his esteemed brother's golfing achievements. While John won the Hands Across the Sea Trophy once, David claimed the prestigious prize twice in consecutive years from 1968. The younger of the two brothers was also capped by Scotland at boys, youth and amateur level, as well as representing Britain.

In 1971, at the age of 18 and a year after being crowned Scottish boys stroke play champion, David turned professional as assistant at Royal Aberdeen and then tournament pro at Turnberry and set off on a global adventure which took him to Nigeria and South Africa within his first few months as a pro. The former Aberdeen Grammar School pupil was named best young player in Europe and Britain in 1974, having broken into the top 20 on the PGA money list, and was a man in demand as a string of agents and management companies beat a path to his door in a bid to secure the services of one of the game's brightest prospects.

Appointed as touring professional by Royal Aberdeen in 1976, David flew the flag for Aberdeen across the world throughout the 1970s with his best finishes including a third place at the Dunlop Masters in 1974 as well as fourth and fifth place finishes in the Spanish and French Opens that year and the Northern Open title in 1976 at Balgownie. His 1974 prize haul of £7,500 represented his most profitable year and he was by far and away the best rewarded rookie during that campaign as he flirted with title success.

David spent 10 years on the tour, including a spell representing the Ben Mhor Hotel in Grantown on Spey, before concentrating on business commitments which now include the Pine Warehouse in his home city.

David returned to the competitive scene in 2003 when he joined his elder brother on the European Seniors Tour for three seasons, but it was John who claimed family bragging rights with his series of championship wins.

David Chillas putts on the 18th green at Murcar Links in 2005 (Picture by Kevin Emslie).

Sandy Pirie

The green green grass of home can have a big bearing on a sportsman's development and, in the case of Alexander Kemp Pirie, his upbringing on the fairways and greens of Hazlehead proved to be an education that has stayed with him throughout his life. The grand old course, the undoubted jewel in the Granite City's golfing crown, is embedded deep within amateur star Pirie's soul.

The classic Alister MacKenzie blueprint may not have the same worldwide profile as the Scottish designer's best-known creation at the Augusta National, but for generations of Aberdonians it remains a special place.

Pirie's connection to the tree-lined course is stronger than most. Established in 1928, one of Hazlehead's first head greenkeepers was his father. It meant Sandy junior spent every day of his life at the course, and it was during that time that his passion for the game began to take over.

He went on to become head greenkeeper in his own right before being promoted to the role of district superintendent, taking responsibility for all of the area's municipal courses, in 1977. His career path changed dramatically a year later when Pirie embarked on a long association with the licensed trade, buying a pub and beginning life as a landlord.

Sandy Pirie plays his approach shot to the fourth green in the Quaich final at Hazlehead in 1970.

By then the dogged Pirie was already a legend in amateur golf. He won title after title in the north-east and across the country – but it is his service with Scotland that brings Pirie the greatest pride.

The pinnacle was his Walker Cup appearance in 1967. He was part of a British team pipped to the prize by America at Royal St George's in Kent, but earned wonderful plaudits. Singles opponent Bob Dickson claimed his Scottish adversary had one of the finest short games he had ever seen, something any Aberdeen golf fan could have told him.

Hazlehead regulars knew of Pirie's ability from a very young age. The first sign for outsiders was his impressive victory in the Hands Across the Sea Trophy at the Aberdeen Links Championship in 1956, when he won the boys event at the age of 14.

Within five years he had his name etched on the Douglas Philip Trophy, making him Aberdeen's unofficial match play champion, and word of his ball control, coupled with precision with the putter, was spreading. He went on to dominate the open scene in Aberdeenshire and Aberdeen in his early 20s and won Scotland Under-25 honours in 1966, when he produced a typically clinical display against a British universities select side.

That helped bring the Hazlehead and Victoria club champion to the attention of a wider audience, and when he was called-up for the international matches at Porthcawl in 1966 he ended the event as the leading Scot.

Pirie, who was the north-east's only scratch golfer during his heyday, was invited to attend Walker Cup trials in 1967 along with compatriots Ronnie Shade and Gordon Cosh. He withstood the pressure superbly, finishing third after losing just three matches in a gruelling 13-game programme to win a place in the team for the showdown.

He became the first player from the Granite City ever to play in the Walker Cup. The city did have historic links to the revered tournament, however, with Aberdeen University graduate Dr William Tweddell, an Englishman, captaining Britain in 1928 and 1936 to fly the flag for Royal Aberdeen and Murcar.

The tournament began life after World War One. The opening match was contested in 1921 when the US Golf Association and Royal & Ancient joined forces to launch the event, with USGA president George Herbert Walker lending his name to what would become one of the most cherished prizes in the game and presenting it for the first time when the Americans won the inaugural meeting 9–3 at Hoylake. It was played annually for the first three years before becoming a biennial event, taking in some of the finest courses in the world and establishing a reputation for great sportsmanship coupled with intense rivalry.

The US, with a far greater pool of amateur talent to delve into, have dominated the Walker Cup. Britain's first win was in 1938 and when Pirie competed in 1967 there had not been another success, though the Brits had come close on the previous occasion. The 1965 match had finished deadlocked at 11–11 after a nip-and-tuck affair at St Andrews. That close-run thing gave Pirie and his teammates great hope for the challenge facing them.

When Pirie returned to Hazlehead following his successful trial he was welcomed by a standing ovation from the proud members waiting to greet him. What he did not

Hazlehead Golf Club presented Sandy Pirie with a silver tray to mark his achievements at the top of amateur golf in 1974.

know was that his club mates had been planning the party long before he received confirmation of his Walker Cup place. In their view there was no doubt that the club's young star would stand up against the best the UK had to offer.

When the big occasion rolled around at Royal St George's, Pirie was not blessed with the best of luck. He played solid golf throughout his three ties, but emerged with just half a point after cruel breaks. He was not only up against an immensely talented pack of visiting players, but also a hugely testing course. The undulating links course at Sandwich in Kent has a pedigree to rival the biggest and best in world golf. Prior to the Open Championship's return in 2011, the club hosted the event 13 times between 1894 and 2003. Only three winners recorded scores under par, hinting at the severity of the set-up. Pirie coped admirably with everything Royal St George's could throw at him, but missed out on the breaks required to turn over the Americans.

In his singles match against New York champion Don Allen he led by two holes as they teed up on the 17th, but was pegged back to all square at the end of the round. Against the 6ft 6in hulk Bob Dickson, from Oklahoma, he fell to a 4 and 3 defeat despite a spirited fight and lost in his foursomes tie, partnered by Forfar's Sandy Saddler, after falling victim to a sublime wedge shot by US player Bill Campbell at the 18th.

The Walker Cup experience could not tempt Pirie to turn his back on the amateur game, even if former north-east rival Harry Bannerman had taken the plunge and entered the pro ranks. He later represented Scotland's amateurs against their pro peers and came out on top.

Instead of going for prize money, he continued to wow the galleries at venues close to home, and his talents were recognised far and wide. He was made an honorary member at Cruden Bay in recognition of his ambassadorial role for the area in the aftermath of his Royal St George's experience, an award already made to him by Hazlehead officials.

The following year he was confirmed as successor to his father as head greenkeeper at his west end club, the same year in which he won the Aberdeen Links Championship for the first time. In 1969 he and Hugh Stuart set a first for north golf when they had their handicaps set at +1. Other distinctions for Pirie included his place as course record-holder at his home course, at Orkney Golf Club and at Cruden Bay.

In 1970 Pirie continued to break the mould, becoming the first amateur to win the sought-after Northern Open prize since Dick Walker at Deeside in 1936. Pirie hit top form to triumph by a single shot over former amateur rival Bannerman, who by then was the professional at Banchory and on his way towards Ryder Cup stardom.

He equalled his own course record thanks to some heavenly iron play in the final round to ensure the Northern Open trophy joined his collection of silverware, taking advantage of the excellent knowledge of the coastal course amassed during his regular practice rounds over a track which was his home from home.

Representative honours flowed thick and fast, with the big occasions including Scotland duty in the European Team Championship in Hamburg in 1969 and a Great Britain and Ireland cap for the St Andrews Trophy match against Europe in 1970. That same year he was part of the Scottish team which won the Home Amateur International Championship at Royal Porthcawl.

A winner of the Phillips Trophy and Aberdeen Quaich with almost monotonous regularity throughout his peak years, Pirie added the course record at Balnagask and the Kings Links to his list of accomplishments in the early 1970s. His success was not limited to home soil, with international glory including the Catalonian Championship in Spain in 1974.

His move into the pub trade in 1978, when he bought the Golf Inn at Montrose, curtailed Pirie's exploits with club in hand. He spent five years building his business in Angus before selling up and embarking on a new project when he and his wife took on the Strathspey Hotel in Grantown. He remained in the Highlands until 1989 and the following year snapped up the Red Lion bar in Aberdeen, remaining the landlord at the Spital hostelry until his retirement in 2002.

Aberdeen golfing legend Sandy Pirie pictured in 2001.

Elaine Farquharson-Black

Glaswegian golfer Helen Holm was the pace setter in the women's game north of the border, winning her first Scottish Championship in 1930 and claiming the title a further four times over the next two decades to become immortalised in her home country. The legend lives on through the Helen Holm Trophy, and for every ambitious player in the land it is a prize which means more than any other on the country's packed calendar of female tournaments.

Elaine Farquharson-Black is one of the select band to have held the silverware aloft, and for the Aberdonian it remains one of the proudest moments in a prolific career at home and abroad.

Holm's home course, Royal Troon, created the trophy in her honour in 1973 and it quickly became established as the nation's premier women's stroke play test. Farquharson-Black was a 19-year-old law student when she sailed through the examination in style during the spring of 1987, defeating Swedish challenger Malin Landehag by one shot after three rounds of enthralling golf in the Ayrshire sunshine. In doing so she became the first player ever to win the prestigious prize before gaining a full international cap.

Elaine Farquharson-Black displays the prize she received for winning the Helen Holm Trophy in 1987.

The former Cults Academy pupil was already accustomed to success after a flawless junior career, but the Helen Holm Trophy triumph proved the teenager had what it took to transfer her talents to the senior game.

When she confidently negotiated her way around Royal Troon in April 1987, Farquharson-Black became the first player ever to win the prestigious prize before gaining a full international cap. Despite her inexperience at the very highest level, the rookie made her victory look easy. The competitors had opened the event with two rounds over Troon Portland and it was the Scandinavian starlet Landehag, herself only 19, who set the pace with two matching par rounds of 74.

Farquharson-Black was just one shot off the pace after 36 holes, opening with a one under par 73 before carding a 76 in her second round, and went into the finale over the monstrous Royal Troon links track poised to overhaul the leader.

The Scottish hopeful, whose excellent form had lowered her handicap to +1, produced a controlled and inspired front nine performance to reach the turn in par thanks to some wonderful approach shots. Nerves began to tell on the back nine, but the Granite City golfer held firm, finishing three over par for the round and four over for the tournament to clinch the trophy ahead of a chasing pack full of experienced campaigners from Scotland, England and the Continent.

Troon, which received its Royal status during its centenary year in 1978 and has hosted the Open eight times, is widely recognised as one of the most demanding of all the championship courses. With its rugged features and dramatic backdrop, the inward half in particular has tripped up some of the most renowned performers ever to swing a club. Farquharson tamed the beastly back nine to join an illustrious list of champions crowned at the famous venue.

Golf was the number-one interest though, having been in the new Helen Holm Trophy holder's blood. The daughter of respected golf and sports writer Colin Farquharson, a former sports editor of the *Press and Journal*, she was hooked on the game of golf as a seven-year-old. Her mother Ethel also has strong ties to the game as a former chairwoman of the SLGA and organiser of the Aberdeenshire Girls' tournament.

Elaine showed an instinctive understanding of the mechanics of the game and within years had translated that natural ability into tournament wins. At the age of 12 the Bieldside girl became the youngest winner of the North of Scotland Girls' Championship in 1980 and at 16 already had a hat-trick of Deeside Women's Club Championship victories under her belt.

As a teenager her dedication to the game shone through, with the youngster often to be found on the Deeside practice ground at 7am, to squeeze in some fine tuning of her swing before the school day at Cults Academy began.

That commitment brought many rewards, including Scotland recognition as the baby of the Scotland team for the Under-18 girls internationals at Edzell and the Scottish schoolgirls team to face the English at Allerton in 1982. Within two years she was part of the Scotland Under-22 set-up and in 1987 made her full international debut.

Farquharson-Black's joy was not confined to her home district, where she had set a number of new club records, and in 1985 she took her talents to a national audience

Elaine Farquharson-Black celebrates her Curtis Cup call-up in 1992.

when she clinched the Scottish Under-18 Stroke Play Championship, the Under-18 Scottish Match Play Championship and was a beaten finalist in the British girls' event. She was also a finalist in the British a year later.

As a senior player she continued to hold an Indian sign over her Scottish rivals, underlining her claim to be one of the finest players of her generation when she reached the semi-final of the Scottish Ladies Amateur Championship in 1989 at Lossiemouth and won it the following year at Machrihanish.

In that Final she eased past defending champion Shirley Huggan 3 and 2, having defeated Catriona Lambert, better known now by her married name Catriona Matthew, as a star of the professional game, and Kathryn Imrie on her way to the showdown with US-based Huggan. Farquharson-Black was the beaten finalist in 1992 on home turf at Royal Aberdeen, Janice Moodie, now a Solheim Cup player, winning on that occasion.

All of the individual success, which included glory in the Women's World Four-ball Championship with Helen Dobson in Brazil in 1989, also brought international honours in abundance. She had been defeated by Dobson in the 1989 British Ladies Amateur Championship at Hoylake.

Farquharson-Black made her Scotland senior debut in the 1987 home internationals and became a fixture in the national side, earning a six wins from six ties record on her European Championship debut in 1989 to help the country to the semi-finals. She had a matching record when the home international honours were clinched in 1990 and was part of the winning side in 1991 – the last time the title was won by Scotland.

The north-east star also represented team GB with distinction. She was part of the British team that won the Commonwealth Championship at Newcastle in 1991 and made it a double with success in the Vagliano Trophy, against continental Europe at Nairn, in the same year. She had already savoured Vagliano success in 1989 in Venice, but even greater recognition would soon follow on the international stage.

Farquharson-Black played in two Curtis Cup matches against the Americans, becoming the first Aberdonian to play in the tournament since Muriel Thomson in

1978 when she made her debut in 1990 in the event. The US won on that occasion, but two years later the solicitor gained justice, winning the cup at Hoylake.

The decision about whether to pursue a career in the legal profession or to look towards the world of professional golf was a difficult one. There was unfinished business in the amateur game, as Farquharson-Black had come close to British Championship success as a runner-up in the girls' event at that level in 1984 and 1985 as well as being beaten in the Final of the women's British Amateur Open in 1989. But the lure of the professional tour was strong and in the end Farquharson-Black, who married Jonathan Black in 1993, compromised and opted for pro status while continuing to work with city solicitors, Paull and Williamsons.

She made the leap into the paid game in 1992 but found it impossible to keep pace with peers who were playing full-time on the European Women's Tour, opting to take a step back two years later and applying to have her amateur status reinstated.

Those achievements had led to an honorary membership at Deeside, but could not fast-track the process of reinstatement. It was not until 1997 that she was able to turn out as an amateur again, quickly regaining her place in the Scotland team after displaying the type of form that had made her a star in the first place. She set course records of 9 and 10 under par at Braemar and Lossiemouth, before retiring from her international playing career with the birth of her first son, Nicholas.

Farquharson-Black was appointed captain of the Scottish women's team in 2001 to mark a fresh chapter in her golfing career and led them again in 2002 and 2003 – the last occasion falling just weeks before the birth of her second son, Michael. Farquharson-Black also captained the Scottish team in the European Team Championships in Sweden in 2005.

Perhaps captaining the British team is the only accolade left to be won.

Elaine Farquharson-Black in her role as a solicitor in Aberdeen (Picture courtesy of Fifth Ring).

Scott Henderson

The roll call for past winners of the Sir Henry Cotton Rookie of the Year Award reads like a *Who's Who* of professional golf. From Tony Jacklin back in 1963 through to Sam Torrance, Nick Faldo and Sandy Lyle in the 1970s, the list bounds through the following decade taking in luminaries such as Jose Maria Olazabal and Colin Montgomerie before the more recent additions of Thomas Bjorn, Sergio Garcia and Ian Poulter. Sandwiched between those world-famous players is Scott Henderson, a man who earned his place in such esteemed company courtesy of a phenomenal introduction to life among the elite of the European Tour.

For Henderson the year of reckoning was 1997, when he made his debut on the circuit at the age of 27. He was a latecomer to the professional game, having taken the gamble to leave behind a promising and comfortable career as an engineer in the North Sea oil industry to stake his future on making it big in the unpredictable world of sport. Within months this spin of the roulette wheel had paid off in dramatic fashion as the talented Aberdonian slipped effortlessly into life on the tour and briskly set about climbing up the rankings, ending the season well inside the top 50 on the intensely competitive European Tour and coming within an ace of landing a maiden championship win. It was a performance far beyond the young Scot's wildest dreams, and one which clearly caught the eye of the selection panel responsible for handing out the end-of-season awards, with the prestigious Cotton prize handed to Henderson in recognition of his heroics. Awarded in honour of three-time Open champion Sir Henry Cotton, Henderson succeeded Bjorn and had lifted his profile to a whole new level with an accomplished first year in such a high-pressure environment.

Although the unknown's arrival on the world stage had taken the European Tour establishment by

Scott Henderson at the Kings Links after turning pro in the 1990s.

Scott Henderson tackles the first hole at Murcar Links during the
Scottish Challenge in 2006 (Picture by Colin Rennie).

Scott Henderson tackles the first hole at Murcar Links during the
Scottish Challenge in 2006 (Picture by Colin Rennie).

surprise, it was no shock to those who had watched a teenage Henderson star closer to home. His golfing dream was sparked into life in 1983 when he travelled to Royal Birkdale with his father Brian to sample the drama and excitement of the Open first hand. He travelled back to the north-east with a new passion for the game and started playing seriously that summer, as his 14th birthday loomed.

Within three years his dedication had produced its first tangible reward when Henderson was crowned the North-east boys' champion in 1986. He had won the junior championship at his home club Bon Accord the previous year, honing his skills on the testing Kings Links after a spell playing out of the more forgiving Hazlehead, and by the age of 17 he had reduced his handicap to three as well as reaching the final of the club's senior championship.

His ability was quickly noted by the Scottish Golf Union, who supported Henderson with coaching as a teenager, and the selectors of the North-east boys' team. The Dyce Academy pupil embarked on an engineering apprenticeship upon completing his school studies, but continued to make strides in golf, winning the Hands Across the Sea Trophy at the Aberdeen Links Championship in 1987. That victory propelled Henderson, who was still only 17 at that stage, onto the international scene and he made his debut for the Scotland boys' team at Kilmarnock Barassie that summer.

Making the leap from outstanding junior to a major contender in the man's game is always the great test and for Henderson the transition was slow and sure. It was in 1991 that the clear signs of his progress shone through with a superb victory in the North of Scotland Open at Royal Dornoch, a tournament in which he blew away personal concerns about his putting ability and built a new-found confidence on the greens which would stand him in good stead for the future. The following season he added the West of Scotland Open at Cardross to his CV and locally became the first Bon Accord player to win the coveted Phillips Trophy title in the summer of 1992.

Henderson had been called to the fringes of the senior Scotland squad as a reserve on the back of that strong form when he was invited to turn professional by Bruce Davidson at the rapidly expanding Kings Links Golf Centre in Aberdeen. At the age of 22 and with a handicap of +2, he had the game to make an impact in the paid ranks and the desire to go with it. He worked as an assistant under Davidson at the seaside driving range as he set about earning playing rights as a tour player, with David Thomson also instrumental in coaching Henderson during his formative years as a pro.

On his first season outside of the amateur game he finished fifth in the assistants' Order of Merit and raked in a respectable £7,000 bounty from early forays into Tartan Tour events. It won him the Scottish Rookie of the Year award in 1993 and a reputation for being one to watch.

In 1994 Henderson's ascent continued when he claimed the Scottish Assistants' Championship at Newmachar, and the following year he spread his wings by sampling South African golf, firstly on the domestic circuit and then as a guest at the European Tour's South African PGA Championship in Johannesburg.

A full European Tour card was always the target, but it was a long and expensive journey for Henderson, as he returned year after year for the arduous qualifying school. Persistence finally paid off at the end of 1996, when he came through the gruelling process in Spain.

Henderson had spent the year taking in some of golf's outposts on the European Challenge Tour – a satellite circuit which took in Kenya, the Ivory Coast, Finland, Norway and Russia among other destinations – and that experience was vital as he battled through the qualifying school. He also went into the qualifiers as a winner, having claimed the Northern Open at Cruden Bay earlier in the year on his way to topping the Tartan Tour's money list with a season's haul of £25,628. All of this ensured that his confidence was high and Henderson carried those high spirits into qualifying as he reached the Final of the tour school and finished 22nd to earn one of the 45 cards on offer. At the third time of asking, he had won the dream ticket to the big time.

As he began the 1997 season as a fully-fledged European Tour player, the assured pro from the Granite City was a 27-year-old with a solid grounding. He was ready to make his mark at the top level and did it in style. He survived the cut on 10 occasions during his debut season and, more importantly, recorded three top-10 finishes. The first was when he tied for ninth in the TPC of Europe in Hamburg, the next when he clinched fourth spot at the European Grand Prix at Slaley Hall in his next outing and the last, but far from least, was when he stormed to the runner-up's spot at the European Masters in Switzerland. Italian star Costantino Rocca pipped his Scottish rival to the title by a single shot over the

Scott Henderson in action at Newmachar (Picture by Kevin Emslie).

stunning Crans-sur-Sierre course, with the winner carding a dramatic final round of 62 to set a target that could not be matched. Henderson came close to forcing a play-off when his birdie putt to draw level with the clubhouse leader lipped out on the last – but the disappointment of missing out by a single stroke was tempered by a cheque for more than £69,000. All in all he won £147,000 on his first year on the European Tour, finishing 42nd in the rankings table to guarantee his place as the stand-out rookie in the class of '97.

The following year Henderson, with earnings of £94,000 and a 68th-place finish in the rankings, retained his card but went on to suffer the familiar vagaries of life as a professional golfer as the putts stopped dropping and the results began to fade. In 2000 Henderson returned to his roots on the Challenge Tour and Tartan Tour, gaining invitations to a select band of European Tour events to keep his hand in as well as regular excursions to play and practice in the US at mentor Bruce Davidson's club at River Oaks in Texas.

His career has dovetailed with that of fellow Aberdonian golfer Greig Hutcheon, who has been a notable player on the Challenge Tour and Tartan Tour. Hutcheon won elevation to the European Tour in 1999, the highlight of a pro career launched in 1995. After his brief time on the elite circuit, Hutcheon has thrived on home soil and was crowned Scotland's Order of Merit winner in 2006 and 2007 to confirm his place as one of the domestic game's most consistent and talented performers.

Hutcheon, who grew up on Deeside and now represents Peterculter Golf Club, is bidding for a permanent return to the European Tour stage and a late push for glory in the all-star company his friend and peer Henderson impressed among in the 1990s.

THE OLYMPIANS

Katherine Grainger

In the eyes of most observers Katherine Grainger could retire a happy woman following her success at the Beijing Olympics in 2008. The Aberdeen rower won silver in the quadruple sculls to add to the runner-up prizes she claimed at the summer games in 2004 and 2000, to confirm her place as the most resilient woman in the history of British sport – the only lady to have medalled at three Olympics.

Katherine Grainger celebrates Olympic success during homecoming celebrations in Edinburgh in 2008 (Picture courtesy of snspix.com).

That impressive track record also confirms Grainger's status as team GB's most decorated oarswoman and assures her of legendary status. Having celebrated her 33rd birthday months after returning from China, the option to bow out on a high could have been tempting. Instead, Grainger announced her intention to return to the rigours of training and start preparing for one final push for Olympic gold at the 2012 games in London.

The decision was the result of a summer spent soul-searching. Having broken down in tears at the end of the Olympic Final, after a late surge by pre-race favourites China had robbed the British boat of gold, Grainger returned to a hero's welcome in Edinburgh along with her fellow Scottish medal-winners before flying out to South Africa to reflect on what direction to take at this most crucial crossroads of her career.

She took advice from friends, family and colleagues in the rowing world before committing to another four years of lung-bursting training, agonising gym work and the sacrifice associated with total dedication to the pursuit of Olympic excellence. For Grainger, approaching the twilight of her competitive life, there is no guarantee that a place in the team for 2012 will be open to her – but with her determination, inner strength and talent it would take a brave person to bet against her lining up in London.

Rowing is renowned as one of the most physically demanding sports on the programme, but it was the mental demands rather than those on her body that were the crux of the matter for the enthusiastic athlete. She had to be sure that the passion to train and compete still burned bright but the time out, away from the hubbub and hysteria surrounding every British medal in Beijing, convinced her that was the case. She went through the same process after Athens in 2004 and came back with the same answer. In her own words: 'There is still a gold to be won.'

Grainger is one of Aberdeen's adopted sports stars, having been born and educated in Glasgow, at primary and secondary school in Bearsden, before relocating to Maryculter on the outskirts of the Granite City with her parents Peter and Liz. She divided her time between the north-east and her university studies in Edinburgh, but nobody can question the impact the Granite City had on her sporting development.

Her love of water was first fostered during trips to visit her grandparents in Aberdeen, swimming in the chilly waters of the North Sea, while she cites the 'Dons victory in the European Cup-Winners' Cup Final in 1983 as one of her most vivid sporting memories.

Grainger's first competitive rowing outing was made in the silvery shadow of her adopted city's riverside buildings, as she took to the Dee not long after being introduced to the sport on the Union Canal in Edinburgh. It was an eventful regatta, with the rookie taking an unscheduled dip in the river during the course of the day and being tracked by a playful seal during her maiden races.

The athletic student, who boasted a black belt in karate gained during her school days and also showed promise as a runner and high jumper in her early years, quickly found her rhythm and emerged as a force to be reckoned with. She rapidly rose to become captain of Edinburgh University's rowing team and won the Eva Bailey Trophy, awarded to the university's most outstanding female athlete, in both 1996 and 1997.

Just four years after taking up the sport she struck gold at the 1997 World Under-23 Championships, racing in the coxless pairs, and later in the year collected a bronze from the women's eight at the Senior World Championship. She was already well on

Katherine Grainger in action.

her way to Olympic recognition and by the time the British team was named for Sydney in 2000 she was assured of a place.

She joined forces with Scottish compatriot Gillian Lindsay, a veteran of the 1992 games in Barcelona, and sisters Miriam and Guin Batten to compete in the quadruple sculls in Australia and came home second to land the first Olympic medal of what would become a very impressive collection.

In 2003, in partnership with new coxless pairs partner Cath Bishop, she became a world champion. An amazing burst of energy in the closing stages of the Final in Milan took the British duo past the highly-fancied Romanian boat to upset the applecart in glorious fashion.

It was a signal that the 2004 Olympics in Athens would bring more drama for the Glaswegian medal hopeful, and the Greek games did not disappoint. Both she and Bishop had insisted that it would be their last shot at glory at the highest level and their endearing partnership was one of the stories of the event.

Grainger brought the analytical nous, combined with a feisty will to win, while Bishop's incredible power married perfectly to create a team the British coaching team hoped would prove unbeatable. In the end it was the Romanians who crossed the line first, but the gutsy display by Grainger and Bishop did not go unnoticed by an admiring rowing public.

Rather than retiring as had been hinted at, Grainger returned to regroup and focus her considerable efforts on the quadruple sculls. What followed was a glittering array of prizes, with gold in the World Championships for three successive years from 2005 to 2007. A matching medal at the 2008 Olympics would have provided the perfect

Olympic medallist Kath Grainger at the family home on the outskirts of Aberdeen.

collectors' set, but instead the Brits had to settle for silver after China's four rose to the challenge in front of their home crowd.

In the build-up to Beijing, Grainger and her British colleagues had been pushed to breaking point. They were taken to Germany for a training camp which tested their physical and mental strength in a way they had never experienced, a masochistic exercise in which the thrill was derived from surviving the gruelling programme in one piece. Grainger, a survivor by nature, came through unscathed, but admits they were two of the toughest weeks of her life. She and her boat were one of the few British crews to complete the workload set out on the Continent. By opting to continue through to 2012 she has signed up for much more of the same in the years ahead.

When the squad returned to serious action at the turn of 2009, it was the most experienced woman who led the way in the single sculls time trials. It is the solo boat that Grainger is being pushed towards for the 2012 effort, although much will depend on how her experiences of racing in the singles pan out in the years between Beijing and the UK games.

She has long since left Scotland behind, choosing to set up home in Marlow near to the British rowing squad's base near Reading, but she remains patriotic and lists the Caledonian Canal in Inverness as her favourite rowing venue. That could all change if Eton Dorney, the Olympic lake currently being refined in time for the visit from the world's elite, is the setting for gold medal triumph. The facility will be able to house 30,000 spectators and the Brits among the crowd will be willing Grainger to realise her greatest ambition.

Honoured with an MBE in recognition of her services to rowing in 2006, the rowing star has used her studies as a welcome distraction from the stress and strain of competition at the top level. She completed a degree in law during her Edinburgh University days and a masters in medical law at Glasgow University before embarking on her most recent academic challenge – a PhD in the study of homicide.

The murderous pursuit, just like the karate black belt, is just one of the many quirks of the Grainger tale. It is an intriguing story with unexpected twists and one that most in the rowing fraternity expect will wind its way to the top step of the Olympic podium in London. Medal or no medal, in 2012 Grainger will be able to look back on the games with the satisfaction of knowing she has become one of Britain's true sporting greats.

David Florence

With the rapids flowing fast and the gates looming large, Aberdonian paddler David Florence kept his nerve to join the list of Olympic medal-winning legends with a blistering run in the Final of the 2008 canoe slalom event at the Beijing games. In 178.61 seconds over the Chinese course he had fulfilled the dream that had been bubbling below the surface from the moment he first took to the water as a teenager. Just two seconds separated Florence and winner Michael Martikan, but a silver medal helped compensate for that narrow miss.

David Florence will go for gold in the 2012 London Olympics.

It was Britain's first medal in the slalom since 1992 and sparked huge celebrations in the British camp and among the GB followers who formed a vocal support within the impressive Shunyi rowing and canoe park on the Chaobai River. For the first time in the history of the games, the hosts had chosen to stage the flat water rowing events and the white water canoe competitions at the same complex. The venue was designed to hold 37,000 spectators and it took canoeing to a whole new level, providing an added incentive for the athletes tasked with taming the daunting man-made course. Florence had celebrated his 26th birthday on the day of the Beijing opening ceremony and returned to Scotland with the ideal birthday present in his luggage in the shape of a gleaming silver medal.

It was Edinburgh rather than Aberdeen which provided the homecoming for the Olympic hero, with Florence moving to the capital during his school days. Born in Aberdeen, he attended Mile End School before his family's move south. He went on to study at Stewart Melville's College and took up canoeing as a 14-year-old, learning his skills on the Union Canal in Edinburgh with the Forth Canoe Club. He still represents the club on the international stage.

Despite being one of Aberdeen's select few Olympic medal-winners, bizarrely Florence cannot even lay claim to being the most famous Olympian on his own street in Edinburgh. He grew up a few doors away from Sir Chris Hoy in Haymarket, ensuring he will forever be destined to finish runner-up in the neighbourhood game of medal trumps.

While Aberdeen and Edinburgh can both claim a share in Florence's success, it was Nottingham that the canoeist called home when he crossed the finish line in Beijing to secure his place in Scotland's sporting annals. He moved to the Midlands at the age of 18 to study physics at university and take advantage of the city's excellent watersports training facilities.

The thrill-seeker is nothing if not ambitious, having failed in an audacious bid to win a place on the European space programme's team of trainee astronauts before winning his place on the Olympic team for 2008. With his physics credentials in the bag and his physical ability not in question, Florence's downfall was a lack of fluency in the Russian language – although he does boast French, German and a good understanding of Mandarin, having studied the language for a year in preparation for the Olympics. Fortunately for the British team he was not chosen from among the 10,000 applicants for the space programme, and was left to concentrate on his competitive efforts.

Having begun taking part in canoe events recreationally in 1996, within a year he was taking part in organised competitions. By 2001 he had won a place in the British senior team and in 2006 claimed his first major international title, World Cup gold in the German town of Augsburg. After a bronze in the World Team Championship that year, the World Cup win signalled that Florence had come of age as a paddler and there was further success around the corner.

In 2007 he clinched bronze in the World Championships in Prague and gained a matching medal at the World Cup Final back in Augsburg. Gold in the Pan Am Team Championship in Brazil in the same year suggested the fast-approaching Olympics would bring success for Florence and his teammates.

The Scot went into the games expecting to do well, being one of around 10 slalom competitors who were rated as genuine medal contenders. He was fourth fastest going

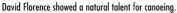
David Florence showed a natural talent for canoeing.

into the Final, but found an extra gear on the last run to ensure a place on the podium. In a punishing discipline, where one tiny mistake can have drastic consequences, he held firm to overcome raging torrents at the testing Chinese venue to claw his way into the medal positions. Proud parents George and Jill, resplendent in T-shirts bearing images of their son in action, were there to soak up the moment. The clean lines of the slalom centre were a far cry from the surroundings in which George won the Scottish Championship in his sporting heyday, but the basics were the same. Interestingly Florence junior did not find out about his father's own white water pedigree until after he had taken up the sport himself, relying on his own drive and attention to detail rather than any family ties to reach the top.

Even the presence of his father's old canoe, stored at the side of the family's Edinburgh home, did not spark curiosity until he reached his teens. One day Florence persuaded his uncle to take him out on the water in the family relic and the rest is history. His interest snowballed, the family pedigree was revealed and the quest for perfection was off and running.

Even as the final strains of *God Save the Queen* were fading away, Florence was already thinking of ways to improve and turn silver into gold. London 2012 is his main focus, with the lure of success in front of a British crowd providing an extra spur during the long hard training sessions come rain or shine. By then he will be at his peak and he is planning to become the first British canoeist to win a double Olympic gold as he plots a twin-pronged podium assault, aiming for success in both the single and doubles disciplines. He teamed up with Richard Hounslow at the European Championships in 2009 to sample the demands of the dual role and is determined to carry it through to 2012, despite the additional physical and mental demands it will place upon him.

Florence will travel to London flying the flag not just for Britain, but also for Scotland, Edinburgh and the city of his birth. In 2009 he was named Aberdeen's Sports Personality of the Year and, despite leaving the north-east as a seven-year-old, he was proud to accept the award.

He could be joined in the squad for 2012 by fellow Aberdeen canoeist Tim Baillie. The Westhill competitor and his C2 partner Etienne Stott narrowly missed out on a place on the plane for the Beijing games, but are mounting a final push for a berth at London. Baillie will be 32 when the greatest sporting show on earth rolls into the UK and he knows it will represent his best chance of glory on that stage.

Baillie, who represents Aberdeen Kayak Club but is based in Nottingham, won bronze at the European Championships in Nottingham in 2009. At the same meeting he joined Florence for the team competition and the Granite City pair helped Britain to silver, just one second behind the winners from the Czech Republic.

Buoyed by their success, both will be going for gold in London. Florence has been an inspiration to all around him in the close-knit canoe community at the national centre in Nottingham and in 2009 he continued to set the pace in events across the world. He finished the year as series champion in the World Cup, having won in Canada as well as taking bronze at Pau in France and recording top-10 finishes in the other two rounds.

David Florence with the silver medal he won in the slalom canoeing final at the Shunyi white water park at the Olympics in Beijing in 2008.

While Florence was climbing to the top of the rankings, construction gathered pace at the Broxbourne White Water Canoe Centre in Hertfordshire as Olympic chiefs attempt to create a setting befitting a squad packed with medal potential. The new complex will feature two slalom courses, a 300m competition run and a 160m training facility nestled on the edge of the River Lee Country Park. Florence and his elite colleagues will get the chance to try the new set-up in 2011 and uniquely the public will also have the opportunity to use the new complex before the games take place, the only purpose-built Olympic venue that will be accessible in the build-up to the games. Given Florence's swift rise from recreational paddler to Olympic medal-winning hero, the Broxbourne facility could well help to unearth a new hero to thrill British fans. Before then, Florence and Baillie hope to put Aberdeen's stamp on that corner of England.

Ian Black

Swimming sensation Ian Black became a household name overnight. When the 17-year-old travelled from his Aberdeen home to take his place on the guest list for the BBC Sports Personality of the Year awards in 1958 he did not realise he would return from the London sojourn with the famous trophy in his grasp, beating shortlisted football stars Bobby Charlton and Nat Lofthouse to the prize after receiving a flood of support from Scotland when the public vote began.

The bashful teenager gracefully accepted his award in front of the great and good of the sporting world at the plush Grosvenor Hotel – not to mention a television audience of eight million viewers. The award had been established four years earlier and has stood the test of time, with the presentation to Ryan Giggs in 2009

Ian Black with his BBC Personality of the Year award in 1958 and the Sportsman of the Year prize he received from a national newspaper in the same year.

the latest in a long line of popular choices. The success Black enjoyed more than half a century earlier was well received as the underdog came through to pip the more established sporting celebrities to the crown.

The announcement by the BBC that Black had triumphed sparked celebrations throughout the north-east, with various functions interrupted to break the news that the area's best-loved sporting son had gained national recognition. There were celebrations too in the Black family home on Mastrick Drive, where his parents and brother watched on television as their boy continued his sublime journey.

The story began in Inverness, the city of Black's birth. Widely regarded as an Aberdonian through and through, the up-and-coming swimmer had already demonstrated his potential before he moved from Inverness. He learnt to swim in the Highland capital's Corporation Baths and, as a nine-year-old pupil of Central School in Inverness, he became the youngest person ever to swim the Kessock ferry route.

Soon after this his association with Aberdeen began when he moved with his family to the north-east in 1953, enrolling at Robert Gordon's College and coming under the wing of renowned swim coach Andy Robb at the city centre school. Robb had been alerted to Black's natural ability by those who had tutored him in Inverness, and he made it his mission to ensure the stylish and versatile young pupil did not waste his talent.

Robb's philosophy was simple and effective: 'Think big and you will accomplish more, think small and you will accomplish less'. It was a attitude Black took to heart and one he carried with him throughout his swimming career and later life in the teaching profession.

By the age of 14, under Robb's guidance, he had won selection for the Scottish international team. That cap, against England in Blackpool in 1956, made him the youngest ever to appear for the national squad in a senior meet and came on the back of sparkling performances in the Northern District Championships, in which he scored a hat-trick of titles, and record-breaking performances at school level.

In 1956 he was also awarded the Nancy Riach Trophy, a prize reserved for the athlete who has done most for Scottish swimming. It was the first of four times that the name Ian Black would be etched onto that particular trophy and happened in the year he set a new Scottish record in the 200 yards butterfly and won a quartet of Scottish Championship prizes as he confidently touched home first in the 100 and 200 yards freestyle, 100 yards breast-stroke and the 100 yards butterfly.

He also became the first swimmer from Aberdeen to win a British ASA Championship title when he claimed the 110 yards butterfly honours, earning a GB cap in the process and lining up in a challenge against Spain, Portugal and Hungary. During that international he set his first British record in the 110 yards butterfly, and it was the first of a long line of fastest times shattered by the impressive Scotsman during his short but emphatic career. In a single 110 yards butterfly swim in Dundee in 1957 the youngster broke eight different records: the British senior, British junior, Scottish open, Scottish native and the same four records for his split time at the 100-yard mark.

Ian Black in action.

It was a good year for Black – but nothing in comparison to 1958. The Commonwealth Games, or Empire Games as they were known at that time, in Cardiff provided an international platform befitting a swimmer of his outstanding ability. He rose to the occasion, winning gold in the 220 yards butterfly and silvers in the 440 yards freestyle and the relay. It was a sensational debut, but the glory was not reserved for the games in Wales. A hat-trick of gold medals at the European Championships in Budapest were also added to the Black trophy cabinet and five British titles strengthened the collection even further.

It was this immense haul of precious metal that made the bashful young swimmer from Aberdeen a celebrity in British sport and captured the imagination of the viewing public. It also won the admiration of the written press, who voted Black the Sportsman of the Year award, presented by the British Sports Writers' Association.

Black had set the bar high, but he continued to impress the following year, setting world records in the 400m and 440 yards individual medley and securing a place in the British team for the 1960 Olympics in Rome.

The Italian showpiece presented him with the opportunity to shine – but the experience did not go to plan. As a committed student, swimming had to take its chances alongside the Highlander's school work and as a result he arrived in Rome expressing concern about his ability to match the conditioning of the full-time swimmers on the international scene.

Black, who was appointed captain of the swim team for the games, opted to drop his traditionally strong butterfly events after linking up with the GB team on the Continent and it looked a wise move for such a young head when he broke British, European and Olympic records in the 400m heats. A medal looked to be guaranteed as the Final loomed, but nothing in Olympic sport is predictable. The 19-year-old

Ian Black rose to become headteacher at Robert Gordon's College in Aberdeen.

swam what appeared to be a race good enough to earn a podium place but, to the dismay of the millions of Brits watching on television back home, the crucial third spot was awarded to Australian rival John Konrads. Replays suggested it was Black who touched home marginally ahead of Konrads, but the records show it was the Aussie who won bronze.

It was a crushing blow for a competitor who until that point had known nothing but triumph, and he opted to take time out to regroup and devote himself to his university studies. Black returned in 1962 and normal service resumed, with four British records tumbling as he set about rediscovering his peerless form.

With the Commonwealth Games just around the corner, Black had news about his future plans to announce. On 26 June 1962, on the eve of his 21st birthday, he dropped the bombshell that he was retiring from competitive swimming with immediate effect. The burning desire which had taken him to the very top of the sport had faded and without total commitment to the cause there was no justification for continuing.

Free from the training schedule which had been part of day-to-day existence for his entire adult life, the Aberdeen University graduate could concentrate on life after sport. Black found his niche in teaching and, after spells working in schools overseas, with postings in Canada as well as Hong Kong and Bahrain, he settled back in Scotland and rose to become a headteacher in Moray during the mid-1970s before eventually winding his way back to his roots when he was appointed head of the junior school at Robert Gordon's College in 1990.

Black held that post until his retirement and, having doubled as a swim coach throughout his teaching career, used his expertise and experience to help foster the next generation of Gordon's pool stars. Among those to fall under his wing was David Carry, who would go on to replicate his Commonwealth heroics and share in the Olympic adventures.

Many have followed in Black's wake, but it was he who firmly established the Granite City on swimming's international map with his dominant displays in the 1950s. For that alone the Invernessian deserves his place as an honorary Aberdonian, representing his adopted home on the international stage with great aplomb and carving his place in the college's proud sporting history to serve as an inspiration to every budding sportsman and woman who passes through its gates.

Neil Cochran

The 1984 Olympic Games opened in typically grand style as the American organisers treated the watching world to the spectacle of a futuristic jet pack pilot's dramatic entrance to the sprawling Coliseum stadium in Los Angeles. Just as the US daredevil made his own impression on the event, a young Scot by the name of Neil Cochran was patiently biding his time, waiting to make his own mark on the biggest sporting stage of all.

The newly-constructed open-air aquatic stadium at the University of Southern California was the venue for the talented and single-minded swimmer's biggest moments as he powered to bronze medals in both the 200m individual medley and the freestyle relay to earn his place among the legends of British swimming. He was a 19-year-old who had enjoyed a meteoric rise, and the '84 games proved to be his time to shine.

Cochran, born in Torphins, began swimming competitively as a 10-year-old with the Aberdeen Dolphins club before moving to Aberdeen Swimming Club and working under coach Wally Lord. As a pupil of Robert Gordon's College, he was mentored by former Olympic swimmer Ian Black in his role as head of the junior school. Cochran grew up in Cults at the heart of a sporting family, with father Gordon playing cricket for Aberdeenshire and serving as president of the Mannofield club. His mother Jill, an all-round sportswoman, was president of the North District Swimming Association while

Neil Cochran displays his Olympic medals in 1985. AJL Archive.

younger sister Jill was a Scottish swimming record holder in her own right.

In his mid-teens Cochran began to make a big impact. In 1980 he returned from a French international meet with two golds, two silvers and a bronze. The following year the young Aberdeen Swimming Club member swept the boards at the prestigious Geneva Youth International. He claimed two individual golds and a matching pair in the relays, breaking the Scottish junior long course record in the 200 individual medley. That performance was in January and six months later Cochran, still only 16 years old, won promotion to the full British team to face Italy in Blackpool.

He was part of the Scotland squad for the Commonwealth Games in Brisbane in 1982 and showed great potential when he reached the Final of the 200m backstroke, finishing sixth to prove he could compete at international level. He collected his first major medal with a team bronze in the Australian games.

At the age of 17, in 1983, Cochran began to lay plans to complete a chemistry degree. He was accepted to courses at Cardiff and Edinburgh universities but found American institutions clamouring to lure him across the Atlantic. Santa Barbara University in California and Iowa both courted the talented teen, but it was Arizona State University which won the day.

British swimmers had mixed results after accepting scholarships to study in America. Duncan Goodhew returned early after a disappointing experience overseas, but David Wilkie prospered. Cochran took the bold decision to follow the trail blazed by previous swimmers and settled immediately.

He worked under respected coach Ron Johnston and joined a team knocking on the door of the top five American swim teams. His form after moving to Arizona clinched a place in the British team for the European Championships in Rome in 1983. This led him to the Olympic trials in Coventry in May 1984, where he excelled. He returned from America to show just what he had been working towards while in the States, and cemented his place in the British team with some thrilling displays.

While overseas he had risen dramatically up the world rankings, becoming the third fastest on the planet in the 200m individual medley after slicing almost six seconds off his personal best time in the space of a year. A competitor who thought he might struggle to make the team suddenly found himself ranked among the country's best medal prospects for the adventure in California.

Cochran was quietly confident going into the Olympics and the belief proved justified when he swam the first leg of the 4x200m freestyle relay, helping the Brits to a bronze medal behind the United States and West Germany. Teenager Paul Howe, who had his own north-east connection through his family's move to Kemnay prior to the games, was in the team along with Paul Easter and Andy Astbury. Cochran, aged 19 when he took to the water in Los Angeles, produced his fastest-ever time to do his bit for the medal-winning effort.

There was no time for the teenager to catch his breath or reflect on his podium place. Instead he returned to action in the 200m backstroke, finishing third in his heat but just missing out on a place in the Final.

Days later he was back in the spotlight with a storming swim in the 200 individual medley final. He had set a new Olympic record in the heats, before seeing that time eclipsed by fellow Scottish competitor Robin Brew and then Canadian star Alex Baumann, and continued his form in the Final when he battled to pip Brew, who was the British captain, to the bronze medal as they chased winner Baumann and home favourite Pablo Morales down the final length. He was the only British male to win two medals and his achievements were a huge bonus for the team, sparking celebrations in the Granite City and leading to a civic reception for the latest sporting celebrity.

Early in 1985, on the back of his LA success, Cochran was presented with the Nancy Riach Memorial Medal by the Scottish Amateur Swimming Association. It was Scottish swimming's highest honour and the last north district winner had been a certain Ian Black. It was the same year in which Cochran set a new British 200m individual medley record while competing at the US Open in Texas.

He warmed up for the 1986 Commonwealth Games by winning two silver medals in the Golden Cup in Strasbourg. He knew he had his work cut out to challenge world record holder Baumann, but looked to be hitting form at the right time as he joined Aberdeen's Duncan Cruickshank and Inverurie's Neil Hudghton in the Scottish aquatics team.

Cochran had infuriated the British coaching team by putting the brake on his training schedule in 1985, but he argued that he was resting in preparation for a major push in 1986.

A brave swim in the 200m individual medley in Edinburgh, as he took on the intimidating Baumann stroke for stroke, ended in disappointment as Cochran had to settle for bronze. Baumann, recognised as the finest all-rounder of his generation, held on for victory and, after a conservative race, Australian challenger Robert Woodhouse nipped in to take silver after taking advantage of Cochran's lung-bursting attempt to beat the favourite. A sixth place finish in the World Championships in Madrid followed before the curtain fell on 1986.

Neil Cochran (right) with fellow Olympian Paul Howe in Aberdeen.

Cochran regrouped and continued to excel, setting a new British 100m butterfly record in 1987 on his way to a gold and three bronzes at the Vancouver international meet. That was a precursor to the European Championships in Strasbourg, where he added to an already impressive CV with a silver as part of a 4x100m medley relay team featuring Adrian Moorhouse.

In March 1988 he smashed the British 200m individual medley record during the American indoor championships in Florida and rounded off his preparations by clinching the Scottish Open titles at East Kilbride in the 100m butterfly and 200m individual medley as well as the British Championship over the 200m individual medley and 100m backstroke.

Cochran had always been a versatile competitor. For the Seoul Olympics in 1988 he represented Britain at the 100m butterfly and backstroke as well as in the 200m individual medley. He had the pedigree to reflect his selection, holding the British medley record as well as Scottish bests in the two 100m events.

The South Korean games proved to be a heartbreaking experience for the Aberdonian. He had gone into the Olympics as a hot tip for a podium place in the 200 individual medley, but failed to reach the Final, an outcome which led to months of soul-searching. Cochran had had high hopes of bowing out at the top, but could not deliver the performance he believed was waiting to be unleashed. In his heat everything that could have gone wrong did, with the Scot spluttering his way through a key turn after gulping down water by mistake. Even before that unfortunate moment he had felt that something was not right and, in a sport in which the margins are miniscule, his hopes of glory quickly evaporated.

Cochran made the decision to quit the sport completely and concentrate on building a career in the US, combining his work as an industrial engineer with a passion for golf. When he retired from top-class swimming he settled in the US, marrying his American wife Eileen Brennan in 1993 after setting up home in Denver, Colorado.

David Carry

Some are born great; some achieve greatness. In the case of David Carry the truth lies somewhere in between, after a lifetime spent devotedly honing the natural ability he demonstrated from the moment he first took to the water. As a Commonwealth Games gold medal-winning hero, Carry ranks as one of the greatest aquatic talents ever to be produced in Aberdeen.

The key to his success was a refusal to rest on his laurels and every challenge in his sporting life has been met with a steely determination to improve on his past performances. The approach has taken the consummate professional across the globe and thrust him into an ambassadorial role, flying the flag for the Granite City in exemplary fashion and winning as many friends as he has medals and awards during more than a decade in senior competition.

Even in the face of adversity his attitude has never faltered and Carry has become a role model for a new generation of north-east swimmers, returning to his home

David Carry in action.

town at every opportunity and always willing to impart his experience and expertise to those following in his wake.

He knows exactly what it takes to become a star, having worked morning, noon and night to realise his ambitions. Carry showed promise from an early age, becoming the youngest ever person to represent the Scottish schools team when he was selected as a 12-year-old. He was a regular member of the Scottish youth squad as early as 1996 as he began to underline his star quality by smashing a succession of records at local and national level. He had taken his first swimming lesson as a three-year-old before representing the Aberdeen Dolphins and then Aberdeen Swimming Club.

Early in 1998, at the age of 16, Carry was named as Scotland's best swimmer at the Speedo Schools International as the accolades began to pour in. It was the year in which he set four north district bests – with the 200m backstroke and 200m individual medley times previously set in 1982 by Olympic star Neil Cochran. That, more than anything, was the indication that Carry was ready to join Aberdeen's elite club of top-level swimmers. He was already Scottish junior record holder in the 50m backstroke and British junior champion in the same discipline, but the bar continued to rise as the teenager set about demolishing the competition.

At the 1999 British Championships he claimed five gold medals in five different events at Pondsforge in Sheffield. The 50m, 100m and 200m backstroke treble was followed by success in the 200m and 400m individual medleys. That glorious run earned recognition closer to home in the shape of the Chris Anderson medal, awarded annually to the north-east's most promising young athlete.

By then he had completed his studies at Robert Gordon's College and enrolled at Robert Gordon University, studying business administration, as he fitted life as a student around a rigorous training schedule which included eight sessions every week under the watchful eye of Eileen Adams.

Adams, the woman responsible for developing a string of world-class swimmers in the Granite City, had a major role in Carry's career as he broke onto the international stage, but he had a far earlier influence. As a pupil at Gordon's in the city centre he had Ian Black as his headmaster.

Carry first caught the attention of his school's swimming doyen as a raw 10-year-old, who even at that age did enough to convince Black that his latest protégé had the ability to go to the very top in the sport. After one gala in Primary 6, Black took the opportunity to address parents and assure them that they had witnessed swimmers with the potential to swim for Britain. He did not name names for fear of embarrassment, but in later years he could candidly admit that a certain Master Carry was the star in their midst that he had been referring to.

The youngster did not disappoint and in 2001 he continued his rapid rise when he won two titles at the British Championships at Crystal Palace. The 100m backstroke title was one and the 200m freestyle was another – an event which brought with it the George Rope Trophy, a prize dating back to 1895. When Carry took a closer look at the base of the cup he noticed a familiar name etched upon it – Ian Black, winner in 1958.

In 2002 Carry qualified for the Commonwealth Games in Manchester, a championship which proved to be the foundation for years of competition against the finest aquatic talents in the world. He did not win a medal in England, but did hold his own against a raft of stronger and more experienced campaigners, laying down a marker. In the aftermath he decided to put his heart and soul into swimming, taking a break from his university studies and leaving the comfort of the family home in Bieldside to strike out on his own at the British offshore training centre in Australia.

Commonwealth gold medal-winner David Carry makes a guest of honour appearance at Robert Gordon's College (Picture by Kevin Emslie).

David Carry makes a triumphant return to Aberdeen after his Commonwealth heroics.

This gruelling Queensland stint brought Carry to a new level and in the build-up to the 2004 Olympics in Athens, while back training at Northfield pool in Aberdeen and his adopted home base of Loughborough University in England, the dedication and determination began to pay dividends as the Greek games loomed. Carry set a new personal best of 1 minute 48.04 seconds as the anchor in the British 200m freestyle relay team at the French Championships and was targeting a repeat when the same group of swimmers went into action in the Olympics.

With Ross Davenport, Gavin Meadows and Simon Burnett he stormed into the Final of the 4x200m freestyle event as the British quartet touched home second in their heat and fourth fastest overall. Carry looked set to join Aberdeen's Olympic medal-winning heroes until a shock decision robbed him of the opportunity. Having swum in every one of the previous rounds, Carry was dropped for the Final in favour of Stirling's David O'Brien. Without the Aberdonian in the pool, the team finished just outside the medal places.

Despite the heartbreak in Athens, the diplomatic pool star refused to be critical of the team management. Instead, he quietly set about proving himself all over again and set bold targets for the 2006 Commonwealth Games in Melbourne. Adamant he had what it took to rival the incredibly strong group of athletes pulled together by the host nation, Carry was confident of returning with a medal.

Even he could not have predicted the scale of his achievements in the 2006 games. It began when he powered to the 400m freestyle gold in a personal best time of 3 minutes 48.17 seconds, a victory which prompted joyous scenes in the north-east as the Carry family celebrated in style. With father Peter a partner in the Jamieson and Carry jewellers business in Aberdeen city centre, the family had experience of precious metal – but nothing could compare to the gold brought back from Melbourne that year for sheer sentimental value.

Carry had become the first Scotsman to win gold at the Commonwealths since David Wilkie in 1974 and back home his home town was wakening up to the size of his accomplishment as plans were laid for a civic reception and hero's welcome.

Then came gold number two, in the 400m individual medley. Silver in the 4x200m relay Final capped a memorable time in Australia and a rewarding year, with a European Championship relay silver medal added to the collection.

Carry teamed up with fellow Aberdonian Robbie Renwick as well as Ross Davenport and Andrew Hunter to win silver in the 4x200m World Short-course Championship in Manchester in 2008 as he worked towards the Beijing Olympics. He freely admits that in the wake of his Olympic debut in Greece he had been 70–30 in favour of quitting the sport. He had taken time to seek advice from friends, family and fellow swimmers before deciding to work on to try and fulfill his ultimate dream.

He went into the Chinese games as the reigning British freestyle champion over 400m, confident that he was in peak form. He did not reach the Olympic podium, but did enough to convince himself that the 2012 games in London represented a realistic target and he has since switched to the Stockport Metro team in Manchester in a bid to freshen his regime and ramp up his training for the UK spectacle and the 2010 Commonwealth Games in Delhi.

Robbie Renwick and Hannah Miley

When the bookmakers draw up odds for medal contenders for the 2012 Olympics in London the likelihood is that two emerging aquatics stars will be near the top of the list. The first is Robbie Renwick and the second is Hannah Miley, two veterans of the summer games despite their tender years.

Neither was born in Aberdeen, but both have become entwined with the city's push for sporting glory and, after cutting their teeth in the shadow of the famous rings in Beijing in 2008, both will be hoping to return to the north-east from the spectacular south of the border with medals to show for their efforts.

Renwick's passport shows his birthplace as the United Arab Emirates, but his heart is in the Granite City, where he first made a splash as a medal-winner for Cults primary at the Scottish Schools Championship in 2000.

Miley is a Swindon lady by birth but Inverurie is her home patch, a product of the Garioch Amateur Swimming Club and an ambassador for Aberdeenshire thanks to her efforts in the pool.

Both sampled competition at Olympic level in China and at the Commonwealth

Swimmer Robbie Renwick is one of Scottish swimming's rising stars.

Games in Manchester in 2006, with Renwick savouring the sweet taste of medal success. The City of Aberdeen swim team member was part of the 4x200m relay squad for the Manchester event and collected a silver medal alongside David Carry.

It proved to be a rewarding year for the north-east teenager, who won gold in the 200m freestyle at the European Junior Championships as well as bronze in the 4x100 medley relay and silver in the 4x100 freestyle relay to add to the silver he had won the previous year in the 400m freestyle at the same meet.

He had launched onto the international medal trail in 2004 as a member of the Scottish squad for the Commonwealth Youth Games in Bendigo, Australia, as a Cults Academy pupil and under the tutelage of coach Eileen Adams displayed all the signs of going right to the top. Sporting excellence is nothing new to the family, with the young swimmer the nephew of former Scotland rugby international Lindsay Renwick.

While the Commonwealth medal in Manchester was a significant step forward, the springboard was pointing in the direction of the Olympics. Renwick is working flat out to perfect his preparation for the 2012 games in London, the window of opportunity he believes presents him with his best chance of striking gold.

The practice run was in Beijing in 2008, when Renwick won his place in team GB in great style. When he finished third in the 400m freestyle at the World Short-course Championships in 2008, to match the bronze he won over the same distance at the British Championship in 2006, he highlighted his ability – but it was his record-breaking 200m freestyle race at the British Championships in 2008 that clinched his Olympic place for China. In the process of winning silver he set a new British best to cement his place in the British relay team.

Although the hotly-tipped side failed to bring home a medal, Renwick's typically cool yet ruthlessly efficient contribution to the cause won him praise from swim chiefs. With the experience of competing in front of 15,000 at the futuristic Water Cube under his belt, Renwick returned to the UK primed for a huge push towards 2012.

For the Aberdeen swimmer, that determination to peak in London forced some difficult decisions. As Aberdeen City Council and the sports bodies in the north-east dithered over plans for a 50m pool to give its world-class performers and rising stars a decent training base, Renwick had to look south to find a home befitting his status as an Olympian. The road led to Glasgow and the Tolcross pool, which has become his new base, and he was followed south by trusted coach Eileen Adams.

The issue of Aberdeen's lack of an Olympic-size pool has been bubbling away for decades. Plans are in place for a £23 million facility, but finding the funds to turn the blueprint into reality is a thorny issue in times of swingeing cuts to local authority spending in key areas. Aberdeenshire Council has refused an invitation from its city neighbour to contribute towards the start-up costs, although there is the compromise offer of a £134,000 annual cash injection to help meet running costs, and until a financial package can be secured there will be no solution. Until then, the area's finest have the option of the 50m outdoor recreational pool at Stonehaven, a non-starter for top-level athletes, or the long haul to the next nearest venue at Stirling.

More often than not, the outcome is the decision to uproot completely. David Carry chose England as the best location to further his career, while Renwick has opted to stay closer to home by choosing the west coast. His swimming schedule has been married to a study timetable at Strathclyde University, where he began a four-year sports engineering degree in 2009.

Already Renwick believes he is reaping the rewards of daily access to 50m lanes and that testimony is supported by results, with the student teaming up with Carry in 2009 for a new British record time in the 4x200m relay at the World Championships in Rome. The team did not make the podium, but the impressive performance hints at great things to come. Renwick was selected to compete against America in the high-profile Duel in the Pool event in Manchester in December 2009, joined in the British select by his peer Hannah Miley.

She went into the exhibition meeting on a high, having just returned from the European Short-course Championships in Istanbul with two medals – a gold from the 400m individual medley and silver from the 200m Final. Having won silver in the 2008 World Championship event over 400m and bronze in the 200m competition at the same gathering, the victory in Turkey was further evidence of progress. Days later, during the Duel in the Pool, the Inverurie racer set a new European record on her way to third spot in her 400m individual medley contest against strong competition from the US.

For Miley, who will be just 22 when she bids for medals at the 2012 Olympics, there have been the same age-old training issues to contend with while on her home territory in Inverurie. Even the town's 25m pool was out of bounds at the start of 2010 due to refurbishment work, leading to a swift alteration of the training schedule by her father and coach Patrick Miley. It is her dad, who combines his role as the Garioch club's head coach with his job as a helicopter pilot in Aberdeen, who has been the greatest single influence on the youngster's career to date. As a former triathlete who swam competitively for the army in his younger days, he has been instrumental in his

Hannah Miley going to Istanbul, Turkey, for the European Short Course Championships (Picture by Jim Irvine).

daughter's success so far and would not let the small matter of a closed pool get in the way of their carefully orchestrated programme.

The solution was to rise even earlier than usual to make the trip to Aberdeen to use the facilities at Robert Gordon University, where Miley is a student, but like all of her colleagues in the city she has to make do with short-course work. This has not prevented the former Inverurie Academy pupil from dominating the domestic and European scene, winning her first international recognition when she claimed a silver medal in the 400m individual medley at the European Junior Championships in 2005.

By then Miley was already a Scottish champion, having claimed gold in the 200m butterfly and 400m individual medley as a 14-year-old in 2003, and a bronze at British Championship level in her favoured medley following a smooth performance in 2005.

She upgraded to a British gold in the 400m individual medley in 2006 and won the title again in 2008 and 2009, adding golds in the 200m individual medley in 2008 and 2009 as well as gold in the 200m breaststroke and silver in the 200m butterfly in the latter event. She would surely have won a medal at the Commonwealth Games in Manchester in 2006 had it not been for a vicious virus that struck her down in the weeks leading up to the competition, leaving her preparations in tatters.

Those health worries are in the past and both Miley and Renwick began their Olympic countdown in earnest as the bells chimed to ring in 2010, with the hard yards to be covered in the two years leading up to the games deemed a necessary part of the plan to win podium places when the start buzzer sounds at the stunning aquatics centre in London's new complex. With its wave-like roof and clean lines, the centre will be the base for some of Britain's best medal hopes. With seating for 17,500 around the pool, Miley and Renwick will be guaranteed enthusiastic home support as they hit the water for their moment of Olympic destiny.

Athole Still

An Olympian, scholar, opera singer and international sports agent to some of the biggest names on the planet. Athole Still, once a starry-eyed young hopeful in Aberdeen, has made his mark many times over in a long and varied career in and out of the sporting sphere.

Still became a pin-up personality in the Silver City during the golden era of the 1950s as he emerged as an international swimming star. It opened doors that led to opportunities he could never have dreamt of, and before long he set off on a path which drew him to the bright lights of London and an incredible journey.

In recent years Still has become best known for his role in some of world football's most high-profile soap operas. As agent to Swedish coach Sven-Goran Eriksson, Still was at the Scandinavian's side for the roller-coaster ride he endured as manager of the English national team. Eriksson's colourful personal life ensured his representative earned his corn.

That involvement highlighted Still's central role in modern sport, but it was his beginnings in his home town that laid the foundations for all he has achieved as a

Athole Still after receiving an honorary degree in Aberdeen.

competitor, artist and businessman. His education began at King Street School and continued at Robert Gordon's College, where his aquatic ability was quickly spotted by renowned instructor Andy Robb. Still was 11 when he moved to the city-centre school and he became part of an elite group coached by Robb, going on to set north district records over the 50, 100, 220, 400 and 440-yard distances.

Gordon's already had a proud swimming heritage, but it was the class of 1947, with Still at the centre of the action, which claimed the Sladen Trophy for the first time. The prize was awarded to the winning team at the Scottish Schoolboys Championship. The following year Still and his classmates became the unofficial British title-winners when they defeated a hand-picked selection of English champions in Sunderland.

Not surprisingly, the Aberdonian teenager's exploits in school competitions and in national meets led to a call-up to the Scotland team in 1950. It elevated Still to a new level but, with his reputation as a sprint specialist growing, he proved up to the task and helped his country to the Bologna Trophy in his debut season at the top level.

The Bologna Trophy was contested by Scotland, England and Wales on an annual basis and the Granite City had a big part to play in the 1950 success. Ian Spence, another of the Robert Gordon's College production line of swimmers, joined Still in the line up.

Still was accepted by Aberdeen University to study French and German when he completed his school studies, but the move to higher education did not halt his progress in sport. Despite having his individual hopes of Scottish titles thwarted by the incredible form of Motherwell twins Jack and Bert Wardrop, who dominated the national scene in the 1950s, the team glory continued to flow thick and fast.

In 1952 the energetic Still became part of the Aberdeen University team which took the British Universities Swimming Championship back to Scotland for the first time, with his form in the event giving great hope as the Olympic trials loomed. With a place in the team for the summer games in Helsinki at stake, the 18-year-old north-east swimmer came good. He cruised to first place in his 110yd freestyle trial and touched home in second place in the 220yd freestyle. His inexperience was a concern, but selectors could not ignore the Aberdonian's potential and included him in the final cut for the Olympic squad, including him as reserve for the 4x200m relay quartet.

Still, one of eight Scottish stars in the 22-strong swimming team, did not get the chance to test himself competitively at the games, but lapped up the experience of being part of the British set-up. He trained hard in Finland with his fellow Brits and

Athole Still pictured in 1959.

his style and pace drew many admirers, including American coach Mike Peppe.

Peppe offered Still the opportunity to move to the United States and study at Ohio State University by taking advantage of the scholarship system. The Scot was tempted, particularly given Ohio's six-strong contingent in the US team in Helsinki. His old adversaries, the Wardrops, had already beaten a path to Michigan University, but Still was not convinced, believing a degree from his home city's university would be worth far more in the long run than one from a Stateside institution.

What Still did do was accept the training schedule proffered by the respected Peppe and set about implementing his suggestions immediately. The Olympic adventure had begun with a reception hosted by the Queen at Buckingham Palace and ended with a leisurely cup of coffee with Harry Llewellyn, the showjumper who claimed Britain's only gold medal in 1952. It had been a whirlwind for the young rookie but one he would be able to look back on with fondness for the rest of his life.

On his return to more familiar surroundings, Still was presented with a silver medal bearing Aberdeen's coat of arms by the town council. A matching trinket was also awarded to Dr Quita Shivas, who had competed in the women's 100m sprint in Helsinki. Dr Shivas was a student of Aberdeen University at the time, although she ran under the English flag. Still's other modest Olympic bonus was the decision by the Aberdeen Links and Parks Committee to award him unlimited and free access to the swimming pond at Justice Mill Lane.

He continued to combine studying with swimming for a further two years, graduating from Aberdeen with a Master of Arts degree in the summer of 1954. His life was reaching a crossroads, but Still continued to excel in the pool, setting a new competition record on his way to a 100yd freestyle win in the Bologna Trophy when the prestigious event was held in familiar surroundings at the Bon Accord Baths in 1955.

He won further British honours that year when he was part of the first UK team to swim competitively in Russia, travelling to Moscow to take on the hosts alongside the Netherlands, Hungary, France and Sweden.

In 1958 Still warmed up for the Commonwealth Games by clinching the Scottish Championship over 100 yards at Coatbridge, pipping emerging Robert Gordon's

College talent Ian Black to first place. Black could console himself with the five gold medals he bagged at the event.

Cardiff hosted the Commonwealths and it gave Still, who was at his peak, the chance to star as an international. In the same team as Black, he won silver as part of the 4x220yd relay team to etch his place on Aberdeen's roll of games medal-winners. Five years later Black served as best man at Still's wedding to Isobel Cordiner at East and Belmont Church.

By the time he was married, Still had completed a unique sporting double. In 1960, he became the first post-war swimmer to earn Scotland recognition as a water polo player, adding another feather to his sporting cap. He was diversifying away from the pool too, with his full-time teaching job flexible enough to allow him to carve out a niche as a television presenter and commentator for both the BBC and Grampian TV.

Then came an unexpected twist in the tale. Just months after their wedding, the couple were packing their bags at the family home in Strachan and heading for London. Swimming was in the past – now it was time for opera to take Still's full focus. In July 1963 he announced his intention to quit teaching and train as an operatic singer, having been tutored for the previous two years by Aberdeen University's director of music.

He carved out a successful career, going on to spend more than a year studying opera in Naples during the early 1970s after landing a lucrative scholarship. Still also had the chance to play to a home audience, starring in productions for Grampian TV and on stage in Aberdeen at His Majesty's Theatre and the city's Arts Centre.

Still's expertise led him to establish an opera and concert agency with New Zealander Haydn Rawstron in the 1980s, with the duo building a successful business together. Among their clients was Still's fellow Robert Gordon's former pupil Brian Kemp, who with Still's guidance made a big impression on the opera scene in Britain.

Having retained an interest in swimming through his continued commentary work, it was natural for Still to expand his role as an agent to sport. Football became a key area for Athole Still International, the management company formed in 1988 as he struck out on his own.

Opera remains a core part of the business, but sport has been a lucrative part of the model, with a string of high-profile clients including John Barnes and Brian McClair, as well as Gianluca Vialli during his Chelsea days and, more recently, Middlesbrough manager Gordon Strachan.

Athole Still prepares to take to the stage at the Aberdeen Arts Centre while part of the Scottish Opera cast for the 1975 production of *The Barber of Seville*.

Denis Hay

Denis Hay was a world-class hockey player with an impressive track record at the highest level. He starred locally, nationally and internationally, but came into his own when his playing career ended and his life as a coach began. It was as boss of the British women's team that Hay went on to live the dream and become an Olympic medal-winner in Barcelona in 1992 to cement his place in the bedrock of Aberdeen's sporting history and help propel his game of choice into the limelight thanks to the heroics of his charges.

Under the experienced Aberdonian, the British women claimed a bronze medal in only the second Olympics the ladies had contested. The team had never even qualified for the games until Hay took the helm in 1985 and transformed their fortunes in the most spectacular fashion.

The female competition made its first appearance on the calendar at the 1980 games, initially as a 10-team tournament before its expansion to 12 nations in 2008. Before Hay's appointment there had been nothing but disappointment in the British ranks as the ladies failed to land a spot in the 1980 and 1984 events. That all changed when the Scot arrived.

First he led them to the 1988 Olympics in Seoul, when fittingly it was Scottish player Moira McLeod who scored the first-ever women's goal on the biggest stage of all. Team GB went from rank outsiders to mainstays of the sport at the highest level as they charged through the group stages. They were only just edged out of the medal positions, finishing fourth. The British ladies had announced their arrival and were ready to embark on the next leg of their trip to the top, a journey which would take them all the way to the podium when they made their next attempt in 1992.

The Barcelona games of 1992 were the first in three decades to be held without a boycott by a single country. The unified Soviet states were there, the South Africans had banished apartheid in time to compete and for the first time ever the Germans were on the medal table as a single unified nation. In short, competition at the Olympics had never been more comprehensive. With so many major nations challenging for medals, Britain's chances appeared to be substantially reduced. To succeed the UK athletes would need spirit and organisation in equal measure – two qualities Hay brought to his squad in abundance.

While it was the Catalan capital that hosted the summer games in Spain, the hockey stars were billeted outside of the main Olympic zone in the neighbouring city of Terrassa. Located less than 20 miles from Barcelona, Terrassa is steeped in hockey heritage and has produced generation after generation of leading players for the Spanish national team.

To celebrate the sport's homecoming, the facilities were comprehensively overhauled and the renamed Olympic Stadium lived up to its billing to provide an inspiring setting for the drama which was about to unfold for the UK women.

Hay and his side were paired with dark horses Korea, the highly-fancied 1990 World Cup winners from the Netherlands and New Zealand in the group stages. Having finished runners-up to Germany in the qualifiers, the Kiwis were expected to progress alongside the Dutch. However, the pool was turned on its head, with only goal difference separating the top three sides after a fiercely contested series of games. It was Korea who took top spot with Great Britain second to clinch a berth in the knock-out stage. The Netherlands were the unlucky side dumped out of the competition on goal difference, while New Zealand lost all three of their matches to return home humbled.

Germany, who had emerged unbeaten from a gruelling group featuring hosts Spain and the mighty Australians, were the team awaiting the Brits in the semi-finals. After a gallant fight, the Germans nudged their way into the Final with a 2–1 win before falling to Spain in the Final. That left Hay's troops to face Korea in the play-off for the remaining medal and they did not let their wily coach down, carving out a 4–3 victory to earn their podium place and ensure the union flag was once again raised in the Spanish sunshine.

The squad assembled by the Aberdonian mentor was a mix of part-time players from all walks of life. They went head to head with full-time professionals from nations who had thrown resources at domestic and international hockey, but gave every team they encountered a run for their money and nobody could grudge the plucky UK outfit their medals.

It proved to be the pinnacle of Hay's career, as he chose to bow out at the top and retired from international hockey in the months following the success in Barcelona, having been named as Scottish Sports Coach of the Year on the back of his Olympic contribution.

The seeds of Hay's finest hour had been sown decades earlier as a schoolboy hockey player at Aberdeen Grammar School. He went on to represent Grammar former pupils on the domestic scene and was quickly elevated to the Scotland team.

He came from a family steeped in the traditions of the sport, with his father J.G. Hay himself a former Grammar player and then an umpire in the north district. Brothers Ian, Arthur and Kenneth were all notable players in their own right in the 1960s as the family made a significant mark on hockey north of the border.

Scotland caps led to a wider audience for Hay and the British selectors sat up and took note of his ability in the right-half position. Life as part of team GB was not all a bed of roses for the Aberdonian, with one of his earliest experiences of touring with

Dennis Hay was an inspirational coach for Great Britain.

the elite side creating some painful memories. During the 1966 adventure in Australia, Hay was well on his way to establishing himself as one of the stars of the British side when he smashed his finger during only the second game of the tour – breaking the bone in three places and ensuring he was confined to a spectator's role for the remainder of the trip.

The British team of the late 1960s and early 1970s was dominated by Englishmen, but there was room for a select band of Scots. Having moved from his native north-east to Edinburgh, Hay represented Inverleith Hockey Club by the time he boarded the plane for Munich in 1972 to compete in the Olympics. He was joined in the pool for Germany by Peter Ewles of the Edinburgh Civil Service club, both men having cemented their places by starring during tours to West Germany and India the previous year as well as when the national side took on Australia during the build-up to the big event.

The Munich games will forever be remembered for the tragic deaths of 11 members of the Israeli team during a terrorist attack by a group of Palestinians. The event was suspended for a period as the world came to terms with the shocking attack. Although the competitive action resumed, a black cloud hung over the entire programme. The British men's hockey team came within an ace of winning a place in the semi-finals, finishing third in their eight-team group, and finished in sixth place after the play-off matches were completed.

Hay was approaching his 32nd birthday when the Munich games concluded, ensuring the experience would be his last as an Olympic player. He continued to star at club level and began to embark on a coaching career which saw him progress from leading the Scottish schoolboys side to the men's national side and then Scotland's women. He led the ladies through two World Cup campaigns before in March 1985 the call from Great Britain came.

Hay, a teacher by profession, quickly established a reputation as a master tactician and he was tasked with transferring that analytical approach to the UK women's squad. It was a break with tradition to appoint a man to the top job, but it proved an inspired decision. The Aberdonian created a playing system far removed from anything being used by any of the home nations, but one which proved perfectly suited to blending the best of British into one coherent unit.

The English bias associated with hockey at that level disappeared, with five Scottish players promoted on merit to Hay's side and strong representation from Wales and Ireland also a feature of his evolving squad. It took Hay time to stamp his authority on British hockey, but the results in 1988 and 1992 helped him leave an indelible mark.

Alistair McGregor

When goalkeeper Alistair McGregor was presented with British hockey's Player of the Year award in 2008 he confirmed his status as an Olympic star. McGregor was part of the GB team for the summer games in Beijing and grabbed the opportunity with both hands to stake his claim to be one of the finest players of his generation.

Ali McGregor training at Countesswells in 2006.

He had been instrumental in ensuring Britain had a place in the Chinese competition, having produced a string of world-class performances in the qualifying tournament in Chile just months before the Asian adventure. A place in the games proper was by no means guaranteed and the Brits had to show true spirit to reach the Final and defeat India to book their seat at hockey's top table. McGregor insisted he was concerned that even after his heroics in Central America he would not make the Beijing-bound squad, but his self-deprecation masked a commendable contribution to the team effort during the qualifiers and his was one of the first names inked on the team sheet by selectors.

The Player of the Year award had been instigated by the British Olympic Association to mark its centenary. Every governing body of the 35 Olympic sports was given a trophy to pass to their leading athlete on an annual basis. The inaugural presentation was made in 2006 when Crista Cullen was honoured and in 2007 it was the turn of Kate Walsh to take centre stage.

In 2008 it was McGregor who shone, a popular choice among his teammates after a successful year. While in Beijing the brilliant form he had displayed in qualifying continued as the men's team embarked on a campaign which ended in the best finish since the gold medal success of 1988, with McGregor and his teammates claiming fifth in a competition won by Germany. Spain were the beaten finalists, falling to a single-goal defeat, with Australia thumping the Netherlands 6–2 in the play-off for the bronze medal. All four of those nations will present major challenges to Britain when they go head to head in London, but confidence among the current squad has never been higher after a decent showing in China.

The performance was beyond all expectations and a string of match-changing stops by the Scottish 'keeper were vital to the progress. His influence off the park has been important too, with his work ethic and leadership qualities leading to the call to captain the side and become the only Scot and the only goalkeeper to have skippered Britain. Team management had such faith in their netminder's ability that they chose him as their sole goalkeeper for the big event.

Jason Lee is the men's head coach charged with taking Britain into the medal places at the 2012 games. He held the position for the Athens event and again in Beijing, ensuring continuity for the bid to secure a podium place. Lee is himself a former Olympic star, having played in the 1992 and 1996 games, but retired in 1998 to concentrate on his coaching ambitions and the task of bringing through the group of players spearheaded by McGregor.

It is not just the coaches that the Ellon star has impressed, with the sport's media followers also joining his unofficial fan club. The respected Hockey Writers' Club voted the Ellon old boy and women's goalkeeping counterpart Beth Storry as male and female Player of the Year early in 2008 after their contribution in the Olympic campaign. It was another feather in the cap for a player who is gathering support at every turn. The most encouraging factor is his age, with the London games falling just after his 31st birthday and ensuring that 2012 need not be his last appearance at that level.

Born in Aberdeen but raised in Aberdeenshire, it was with Ellon Gordon Hockey Club in his home town that he was introduced to the sport with taster sessions as an eager nine-year-old. McGregor, a former Ellon Academy pupil, began life as an outfield player and was only banished to play between the sticks after failing to pass to teammates in a practice match. Coached and spurred on by Colin Gallacher and Gordon McFarlane, he turned out to be a natural and has never looked back, falling under the wing of coach Murray Carnie and appearing for Scotland's Under-15, Under-16 and Under-18 sides before stepping up to the full international side in 2001 and going on to star in the European Championship in 2003 and 2005.

Together with the emerging talents of Mark Ralph and Stephen Dick, McGregor and the new breed of young Scots have helped the country climb to 22nd in the world after a slump in the 1990s. The 'keeper's performances in dark blue caught the eye of British selectors and he joined the GB development squad at the age of 16 in 1998, by which point he was playing his club hockey for MBC.

The 'keeper, who is also an accomplished golfer, represented Scotland at the Junior World Cup in Hobart in 2001 and even scored a penalty flick despite his role between the sticks to add another line to his already well-filled CV.

Ali McGregor in action for Team GB.

Ali McGregor has become a star of British hockey.

The early place in the development squad suggested McGregor was earmarked for a role at the 2004 Olympics, but he had to be patient. The Aberdonian made his debut for Britain as a substitute in a 3–1 defeat against the Netherlands in Eindhoven in 2007, but quickly became an indispensable member of the GB team, notching up 29 caps inside his first year in the side. With more than 80 Scotland caps to his credit, McGregor is one of the most experienced players in the British camp.

Like so many of his sporting peers, McGregor has moved south to continue his development. After qualifying as a teacher, he took up a post in the physical education department of a Leicestershire school in 2006 and combines the role with his playing commitments with Loughborough Students in the English league. The Loughborough club is one of the country's biggest hockey outfits and has a proud tradition of producing international class players.

The students won the National Indoor Championship in 2003, 2004, 2005 and 2008, as well as the European Indoor Challenge in 2004 and bronze in the European Indoor Trophy the following year. Playing at that level week in and week out has been crucial to the former Ellon player's swift promotion to star billing with the GB team.

Many of his British teammates in Beijing were full-time athletes but he has never grudged the dual role, believing the daily routine of work helped make his time on the hockey pitch even more enjoyable.

Of the 16-man hockey squad in China, nine were in full-time employment in the sport either as professional players or as coaches. The odd ones out include a builder, fashion marketing expert, financial adviser, accountant, electrician and marketing manager. The eclectic mix of British players went up against the world's biggest hockey playing nations undaunted, knowing their planning had gone like clockwork.

Pakistan provided the opposition in Britain's opening match in a pool which also included the Netherlands, South Africa, Canada and Australia. A 4–2 win in the opening game got McGregor and his men off to a flying start, but the Dutch brought them back to earth with a 1–0 defeat before a 2–0 win against the Springboks raised hopes of progress. Draws against Canada and Australia, when the games ended 1–1 and 3–3 respectively, clinched third place in a six-team group and earned a play-off against Korea to decide fifth and sixth spot in the tournament. Britain won 5–2 to complete a programme which brought just a single defeat in six games.

It was McGregor's second taste of a global contest, having featured for Scotland in the 2006 Commonwealth Games in Manchester. The national team struggled to make an impact on that occasion, having been pitted against England, Australia, New Zealand and Canada – but the experience was a valuable one for McGregor as he worked towards Beijing two years later.

Now the focus is on building for London 2012, when the hockey stars will run out at a brand new 15,000-capacity stadium on the edge of the Olympic village. Their aim is to replicate the achievement of the 1988 squad and land gold. That team had at its heart a Scottish goalkeeper – Veryan Pappin – something McGregor hopes will prove a lucky omen for the next assault on the Olympic title.

Eric Watt

Eric Watt is Aberdeen's honorary Olympian. As the north-east's most eminent hockey player of the 1950s and 1960s he had to make the agonising decision to reject the opportunity of a lifetime when he was invited to join the squad preparing for the 1964 games in Tokyo.

For a young man making his way in business as well as in sport, the sacrifices involved in joining the travelling party for the Japanese spectacle were simply too great to contemplate and the chance was passed up. While Watt never added his name to the Olympic role of honour, his selection for the squad bears testament to the ability of the Scotland stalwart.

Watt was carving out a career as a fish merchant in the Silver City when he got the call from Britain's selectors as they assembled a group of players to compete in Tokyo. It was the first time the games had been held in Asia and heralded a brave new era, with the Japanese introducing computers to record results for the first time in Olympic history. More than 5,000 athletes from 93 countries took part and, in another first for the games, a global audience was allowed in on the act when links were created to broadcast the action to households throughout the world.

While the prospect of performing on the biggest platform of all was a massive pull for the Aberdonian, the practicalities of becoming part of the bid for Olympic success made it impossible for him to lend his considerable talents to the team effort. The British side was scheduled to meet for regular training weekends in Birmingham in the build-up to the games, as well as fulfilling a busy programme of friendly matches. The logistics presented a nightmare scenario for Watt, who simply could not afford to take three months out from the day job he was working so hard to develop.

Eric Watt of Seatown, Cullen: schoolmaster and international hockey player.

Without the Scot in their ranks, Britain's men finished tied for ninth place, having been placed in a group featuring silver medallists Pakistan and bronze medallists Australia in the pool stages. India won gold.

Hockey remains a rarity in the evolution of the Olympics, with the British team retaining its amateur status even today. While the majority of athletes in the 2008 travelling party were full-time professionals, the bulk of the hockey players had to take sabbaticals from their day jobs to participate. While nations such as South Africa invest heavily in ensuring hockey is the sole focus for their stars, Britain features an eclectic mix including a builder, a financial services analyst, an electrician and a teacher, in among a smattering of players fortunate enough to be able to earn a living from their sport.

The difference for the amateur players now is the support granted to the GB stars, a luxury not afforded in the formative years in the 1960s and one of the reasons Watt had to make the choice between career and his sporting passion. That said, he managed to juggle his commitments at international level for 16 years as he became the nation's most-capped star, with 52 appearances in Scotland colours and two for Great Britain along the way. A.B. Burt of Rutherglen was the previous record holder, turning out 33 times from 1905 to 1921. Along the record-breaking path, Watt became the most prolific player on the British Isles when he overtook Irish player K. Blackmore's previous tally of 42 caps.

It took dedication and commitment to the cause to reach those milestones and demonstrated Watt's loyalty to the cause. His love of field hockey was fostered at Aberdeen Grammar School, where the teenage prospect quickly proved adept with stick in hand. Grammar had only adopted hockey as part of the sporting curriculum during World War Two, but soon made up for lost time, with Watt proving a pioneer.

He was still a pupil at the city-centre school when he made his Scotland debut, selected in 1950 for internationals against Wales, Ireland and England.

His inexperience and tender years did not deter the selectors, who were wowed by Watt's natural ability and youthful enthusiasm.

Watt went on to study at Aberdeen University and played hockey for the varsity side while still in the Scotland fold. He won his first British cap in the 1950s and was one of the Granite City's notable sporting personalities for two decades, collecting the *Press and Journal* Cup awarded to the sportsman of the year in 1961.

After completing his university studies, Watt returned to familiar surroundings when he pulled on the navy blue of Aberdeen Grammar former pupils and represented the club with distinction. He was a key part of the squad who helped mark the club's jubilee year in 1961 with an imperious performance, with the first team as well as the second and third strings all winning their respective leagues. The introduction of the Scottish Cup in the 1962–63 season provided a new target for the Silver City side to aim for and before the decade was out the Grammar boys had bagged the prestigious trophy. With Watt also representing Grammar with aplomb at international level, it was a wonderful period in the history of the former pupils.

Watt was the first Rubislaw star to become a Scotland mainstay, but not the first to appear for the national side. R. Forgan, one of the Grammar hockey club's founder members, appeared pre-war and H.J. Strachan, a product of the club, was another to join the roll of honour, even if he was a Galashiels player when he made his debut in 1934.

Watt was the next to make his mark at the top level in 1950 and blazed a trail for several teammates at around the same time. Sandy Innes is among the former Grammar players to have earned his spurs on Scotland duty, although he was turning out for the city's university side when he was capped in 1954.

Watt announced his retirement from the international game in 1966 but did not fade away from the club scene, quickly becoming a prominent figure on the administration team on his home patch. In 1967 he was appointed vice-president of the North District of the Scottish Hockey Association and four years later was one of the 20 founder members of the Scottish Sports Council. The body had been formed to help promote activities north of the border and had a £500,000 pot of funding to dip into each year.

Watt, who switched profession in later life after qualifying as a teacher, stepped back from first-team duty with Grammar as the 1970s dawned, opting for a more relaxed environment as he lent his experience to the second team at Rubislaw, switching from his traditional full-back berth to a role as an all-action forward. Not surprisingly for a man of his ability and experience, Watt made the transition look easy. By then he had handed over the international mantle to Grammar former pupils colleague Fred Lawson, who was another of the players to roll off the conveyor belt of talent at Rubislaw.

Lawson, a schoolboy international, stepped up to the full Scotland side in 1967 and proved to be a fitting successor to Watt in the national squad as he slotted in beside another Grammarian in Denis Hay as part of a team managed by fellow Aberdonian and Grammar old boy Sandy Innes to keep the school link strong. The influence of Innes, Hay, Watt and Lawson was phenomenal for a club tucked away in the remote north-east and far removed from the traditional hockey heartlands of Edinburgh and the Central Belt.

Lawson, a goal-scoring midfielder who was part of the touring Dominoes hockey side when it was formed in 1969 to travel to South Africa, went on to break through the 50-cap barrier with Scotland before retiring in 1974 at the age of 30. Like Watt before him, Lawson had to work hard to balance work, home life and his considerable commitment to his role as an international sportsman.

While Lawson and Watt bowed out from elite hockey during the 1970s and 60s, both remain inspirational figures for the next generation of young players. Both have been appointed as honorary vice-presidents of Aberdeen Grammar former pupils Hockey Club, being famous names from the past for the forward-thinking city outfit to cite as role models for the players within a set-up which now boasts four men's teams, three women's sides and a youth system fostering players as young as 12. Grammar, with a recently introduced all-weather pitch installed at their traditional home, are rightly looking towards a bright future in Scottish domestic hockey – but the club will always flash a respectful glance towards its rich past and the characters such as Watt and Lawson who helped put the city side well and truly on the map.

Stephanie Forrester

As Stephanie Forrester builds a new career as a triathlon coach, the Aberdonian can reflect on her own achievements and claim with pride: 'I was there'. Forrester was in at the start when her sport finally achieved Olympic status at the 2000 games in Sydney and could hold her head up high after competing with the world's best athletic all-rounders and emerging as the only Brit to complete the strength-sapping course in Australia.

The concept of triathlons is not new, with the format believed to stem from a French race in the 1920s, but it did not become popular until the Americans embraced

Stephanie Forrester's dedication to her sport has led to a coaching role.

the swim, cycle and run format in the mid-1970s. It took a quarter of a century for the Olympic chiefs to recognise the sport and when they did it was adopted with vigour as the Sydney debut was set up as the ultimate test.

The swimming leg took place in the city's iconic harbour, in the shadow of the opera house, while the cycle route took in some of Sydney's other most famous sights. To complete the set, a hilly running course provided a final barrier for the medal hopefuls. Organisers left nothing to chance, with divers shadowing competitors during the swim using devices designed to ward off sharks.

Forrester excelled in the run, recording the fastest time by far, but a disastrous hold-up in the transition between the swim and run due to a stuck wetsuit zip cost her dearly and she had to settle for 15th overall after battling through the field from 43rd at one stage after losing an estimated 40 seconds due to the changing delay. The consolation was her role as leading Brit in a field packed with strong athletes.

Forrester had survived a scare in the weeks before the games, suffering an ankle injury which at one stage doctors feared might have been a stress fracture. A series of scans eased those concerns, but the injury still required rest to heal fully and that disrupted the Scot's training programme, as she was forced to avoid running altogether for close to two months. Instead she put in extra shifts in the swimming pool and on the bike to compensate.

She travelled to Australia as a relative newcomer to the event, having taken part in her first triathlon in 1996 as a 27-year-old. She had excelled as an academic up to that point, progressing from Hazlehead Academy as she grew up in the Mannofield area of her home city and moving to Edinburgh University before continuing her studies at Cambridge, where she completed a PhD in chemical engineering.

It was while in the English university city that she first dabbled in triathlon, having become running partners with a triathlete from New Zealand, and within two years she was competing in international events and in the wake of her Olympic experience recorded several top-five finishes in World Cup events. Domestically she won the British Triathlon Championship in 1998 and won bronze on her European Championship debut in the same year to add to the Scottish title she claimed during that whirlwind period.

Forrester did get to enjoy her champagne moment in 2000, but it was at the World Duathlon Championships rather than the Olympics. She became the first British woman to win the International Triathlon Union's showpiece event when she powered to victory in Calais in an event featuring a cycle sandwiched between two runs. Since then Michelle Dillon and Catriona Morrison, in 2005 and 2006 respectively, have followed in Forrester's footsteps and won the coveted prize, but the breakthrough year was a special one for Forrester given her disappointment about her Olympic result.

She did not agree to take part in the World Championship until late, but was glad she did after completing the 10km run, 40km cycle and final 5km running leg just four seconds ahead of American challenger Siri Lindley.

The world title, coupled with her commendable effort in the Olympics, won Forrester recognition closer to home when she collected the Aberdeen city Sports Personality of the Year award. Having given up her job as a chemical engineer in the

Stephanie Forrester in training.

year leading up to the Sydney games in order to devote her attention to a 30-hour per week training schedule, the appreciation of her efforts was deserved. Up until that point she had worked at the Zeneca plant in the Yorkshire town of Huddersfield and received next to no support from the sporting agencies. The funding problems were an obstacle to overcome, but never dampened the Aberdonian's love of her sport, and a lottery grant, matching her previous salary, enabled her to turn full-time and match the rest of the world's elite athletes in the 1999 season. The cash injection enable her to indulge in warm-weather training in Australia and South Africa, as well as competing on the international triathlon circuit in countries such as Japan.

The resilient athlete, who missed out on a place in the 2004 Olympics in Athens after being struck by a series of injuries in the qualifying period, savoured another first when she made her Commonwealth Games debut in Manchester in 2006. She had had to sit out the 2002 event after suffering an injury on the eve of the race. As an athlete ranked in the world's top 25, the Aberdonian was entitled to accept an automatic place in the Scotland team for the Manchester games – but Forrester has never been one to shirk a challenge and rejected the guaranteed spot. Instead, she chose to do things the hard way and put herself through the qualifying races. Her calculated gamble paid off and she made the team after typically dominant displays in the counting events.

Forrester took her place in the Scotland squad alongside fellow north-east racer Bella Comerford. Although born in Norwich, Comerford spent the bulk of her athletics career racing out of Aberdeenshire. Her first multi-sport experience was in a tetrathlon in Aboyne – a contest which combines running, swimming, shooting and horse riding. She left the family home in Tarland to take up a post as a riding instructor in Edinburgh but, after deciding to focus fully on triathlons, returned to the north-east and settled in Stonehaven to work with Scottish national coach John O'Donovan. She was crowned Aberdeenshire's Sports Personality of the Year in 1999 and the following year received the Scottish Sports Aid Foundation Sports Personality of the Year prize.

The former Aboyne Academy pupil struck gold in the Duathlon World Championship 20–24 age group in 1998 to underline her potential and decided to pursue a career in sport. She won the 20–24 world duathlon title again in 2000 and qualified for the 2002 Commonwealth Games in Manchester, where she finished a respectable 14th. In the wake of the Commonwealth experience she attempted her first triathlon over the extended ironman course and stormed to victory on her debut – leading her to shift focus permanently to the longer distance competitions.

Ironman and powerman events have taken Comerford all around the world, taking titles in Malaysia and Florida among others. The World Ironman Championship in

71

Hawaii, boasting a $100,000 prize fund, has been among her favourite challenges. The event attracts more than 2,000 of the world's top endurance competitors each year for a race featuring a 2.4-mile ocean swim, a 112-mile bike ride and a 26.2-mile marathon to conclude. The ironman series is viewed as the ultimate sporting test of endurance and versatility, but the harsh nature of the discipline does not faze Comerford, who has found her niche in the gruelling competitions.

That practice stood her in good stead for the World Long-distance Triathlon Championship, which she won in Australia in 2006 to match Forrester's achievement in duathlon. In 2007 Comerford was voted Britain's female Triathlete of the Year as she continued to rack up a succession of ironman wins across the world as well as in Britain. In 2008 she married fellow triathlete Stephen Bayliss, adopting her husband's name. She continues to compete globally at the highest level.

Forrester is now employed by Triathlon England as regional talent coach, entrusted with fostering the next generation through one-to-one coaching and by offering the level of support she did not benefit from in the early stages of her own career.

Jackie Lockhart and Linda Lesperance

When Jackie Lockhart stepped onto the ice in Vancouver for the opening match of the 2010 Winter Olympics it marked a hat-trick of appearances at the highest level for the Stonehaven curler. She made her debut in the Japanese city of Nagano in 1998 and was also part of the team for the 2006 games in Turin – but 2010 represented her best chance of securing a medal to go with the set she has from the sport's other majors.

Lockhart took up curling three decades ago and her CV makes for impressive reading, with seven Scottish Championship titles sitting alongside European silver from 2008 and an amazing run of World Championship success which saw her skipper the side to gold in 2002 as well as pick up a silver in the 1985 event and bronze in 2007. In 2007 she also collected her first silver in the Euros and there is no sign of the Aberdeenshire ace calling time on her incredible run.

The experience of the Winter Olympics was a mixed one for Lockhart, as the team suffered a semi-final defeat against eventual champions Canada in 1998 and did not reach the last four in Italy eight years later.

Olympic gold would be the icing on the cake for Lockhart; the only prize that could possibly trump the victory she savoured in the Worlds in 2002

City of Aberdeen Sports Personality of the Year winner Jackie Lockhart with her prize in 2007 (Picture by Colin Rennie).

The Scottish seniors curling team of Carolyn Morris (front) and, from left, Trudie Milne, Pat Lockhart and Linda Lesperance (Picture by Colin Rennie).

in Bismarck, North Dakota. On that glorious night she led her rink of Anne Laird, Katriona Fairweather and Sheila Swan to a dramatic 6–5 victory over Sweden to be crowned queen of the ice.

It sparked wild celebrations for her teammates in the US and among family and friends back in the north-east. Lockhart, born in Stonehaven but playing out of Aberdeen, had delivered the title hot on the heels of Rhona Martin's Olympic gold effort and Scotland were on top of the curling world. Lockhart had been runner-up in the Junior World Championship back in 1985, but made up for that disappointment in grand style.

The triumphant team was treated to a champagne reception when they touched down at Edinburgh airport, having been greeted by the patriotic sight and sound of a lone piper playing *Scotland the Brave*. She had defeated Martin in the Scottish Championship to qualify for the Worlds and winning in America was the realisation of an ambition she had been working towards from the moment she let go of her first stone.

Not surprisingly she was named Aberdeenshire's Sports Personality of the Year in 2002 and was treated to a civic reception by the local authority. It was a long way forward from her first experience of the game, when she was drafted into her mother's team as a late replacement as a 14-year-old who thought she was heading out on a shopping trip.

The reluctant curler was quickly engrossed by the tactical nuances of the winter sport and, playing under her maiden name of Jackie Steele, won the Scottish Junior Championship in 1982 at Kinross. From there she progressed steadily into the senior game and became established as one of the country's brightest young players.

Lockhart is far from the only star turn at the tiny Laurencekirk Curling Club and one of her fellow members at the Mearns outfit leapt ahead of her when it came to determining the first intake of members of the Aberdeen city sporting hall of fame. Lockhart, not having been born in Aberdeen, did not qualify for an immediate entry on the roll of honour, but her club-mate Linda Lesperance did and was installed in the hall of fame in 2006.

Lesperance was part of the Carolyn Morris rink which claimed the Scottish Senior Women's Curling Championship at Greenacres in 2003, joined by Jackie Lockhart's mother-in-law Pat Lockhart in the Laurencekirk Curling Club team as well as Trudie Milne.

Jackie Lockhart in action during the European Curling Championships in Aberdeen in 2009 (Picture by Raymond Besant).

The victory qualified the group for the Senior World Championships in Winnipeg and the quartet went on to win silver in Canada, losing 7–4 in the Final against the hosts. Along the way Scotland's women had defeated Switzerland, New Zealand, Italy, the US and Denmark. They also did the double against England, beating them in the group stages and the semi-finals to set up a showdown with a Canadian side who had beaten Scotland 6–5 in the group games.

Lesperance and the rest of the Morris rink won the Scottish senior prize again in 2005 to set up another attempt at the World Championship crown – and this time there was no fall at the final hurdle. Morris, Lockhart, Lesperance and Jeanette Johnston rose to the challenge in front of home supporters at the Lagoon Centre in Paisley and came back from behind to defeat Japan. The quartet were coached by Trudie Milne on their run to the trophy, with the influential player ruled out of the competition by a broken ankle.

With Milne back in the fray in place of Johnston, the well-oiled machine won the Scottish senior prize again in 2006 and made it a hat-trick in 2007 when they faced former teammate Jeanette Johnston and her Gogar Park rink in the Final.

The prospects of Lesperance, Lockhart and the other prolific north-east competitors were enhanced in 2005 when the £2.75 million Curl Aberdeen facility opened in Summerhill. With experienced player Tom Brewster installed as manager and ice maker, the rink ended the uncertainty which had surrounded curling in the city since the closure of the Stoneywood rink in 1996. In a nod towards the increasing popularity of the sport following the high-profile success on the world stage, the group of 650 curling club members donated and raised £500,000 between them to ensure the project got off the ground.

The curling event in Vancouver was one of the big draws for spectators, bringing a celebrity crowd, including summer Olympic legend Carl Lewis, to highlight the growing popularity of the sport. The Canadians provided a venue fit for the event and the raucous support became a feature of the competition – with the noise inside the compact arena building the tension and creating an atmosphere to remember.

Britain, led by 19-year-old skip Eve Muirhead, got off to the perfect start when they defeated reigning world champions China in the opening round robin match. Defeat against Sweden in the next fixture brought Lockhart and her teammates back to earth, and it proved to be a frustrating campaign. Victory against Russia and then Germany was followed by five consecutive defeats as medal hopes evaporated. There was domestic success soon afterwards though, with Muirhead's team, minus the injured Lockhart, claiming the Scottish Women's Championship after returning from Canada empty-handed.

While Vancouver proved to be an anti-climax, the big question is whether Lockhart will return for another crack at Olympic glory. As a star of the world stage, she already has the honours and accolades to mark a fantastic career, but could be tempted back to complete the set.

Anne Robb

While most teenagers were dreaming of finding a new Atari games console under the tree, 16-year-old Anne Robb had far loftier ambitions on her Christmas wish list in 1975. In fact the Aberdonian ski racer got her present early, with a call from the British Olympic Association on 22 December to inform her that she had won a place in the team for the winter Olympics the following year. The ambition of a lifetime had been fulfilled before her school days were out, although Robb still had plenty of adventures to embark upon as a world-class alpine exponent who travelled the world in pursuit of excellence.

The 1976 Olympics in Austria promoted Robb from rising junior talent to the status of an international star, mixing with the very best on the planet in the high-octane mix of the racing fraternity. In Innsbruck the rookie was blooded by British selectors

Anne Robb in Olympic uniform ahead of the 1980 Winter Olympics.

in the women's slalom, with good work in the event undone when the teenager missed a gate during a crucial run and was pushed out of the competition by default. For a newcomer to the greatest sporting stage of all, it was a learning point to savour and created memories to lock away in the bank for future reference.

The 1976 festival had been planned for Denver in the US, but funding issues saw the bidding process thrown open once again. Whistler and Salt Lake City emerged as contenders before the International Olympic Committee, in the face of further financial concerns from the potential hosts, opted for the safer option offered by Austria. Innsbruck had hosted the games in 1964 and the infrastructure remained in place. It ensured a short hop rather than a long haul for the Robb family, who followed their daughter to the Continent to cheer her on.

The Austrian excursion required the type of sacrifice which became typical for the speedy youngster. She left her home in the city's west end on Hogmanay in 1975 to join the British team for Europa Cup races in Poland, Czechoslovakia and Switzerland before the move to the Olympic base for the games in February 1976. When she returned to the Granite City as the calendar turned to March, it was the first time she had been at home that year. Separated from her family and friends for extended periods, Robb had to show grit and a steely drive both on and off the piste.

The foreign trips to far-flung resorts had become a habit for the technically strong and fearless skier from the day she bagged her first major title, winning the East of Scotland Junior Slalom Championship at Glenshee as a 13-year-old in 1973. The meet had attracted the cream of British youth talent, with racers from England and Wales joining the strong core of Scottish contenders. Robb, a pupil at Albyn school, jetted out to Austria later that year to compete in the British Junior Championships. She travelled as Aberdeen Ski Club's champion and won bronze in the UK event at Alpbach against far older rivals, sending a shot across the bows of the more established members of the scene. Another third place finish in the giant slalom, combined with her earlier result, led to third place overall and a satisfying overseas sortie for the flying Aberdonian.

She came from a family of ski enthusiasts, first taking to the slopes as an eight-year-old alongside her parents and elder brothers. Glenshee and Cairngorm were her favourite tracks, and she represented both Aberdeen and the Scottish Ski Club before joining the Scotland ski team. She also captained the Albyn team to the British schools title in 1973. The following year Robb's status as the country's fastest girl was confirmed when she swept to victory in the Schools Championship before adding the Scottish junior title to her collection just weeks later.

With the unpredictable Scottish winters not helping her bid to progress, the installation of an artificial slope at Aberdeen University's sports complex at the Bridge of Don proved to be a training lifeline for the budding racer, and the time spent on the steep plastic run proved valuable in pushing her on to Olympic qualification for the 1976 games.

Her campaign began in grand style just weeks into 1975 when Robb triumphed in the British Junior Giant Slalom Championship, earning silver overall. As a place on the British plane bound for Innsbruck became ever more likely, Robb took a sabbatical from her school studies to devote her attention to skiing full-time. The decision proved astute as she clinched the Olympic selection she craved and went on to sample the unique atmosphere of the games. It proved to be a turning point for Robb, as she launched full on into the women's sport and upon her return from Austria won the Scottish Women's Championship in familiar surroundings at Cairngorm and in 1977 was runner-up in the British women's competition at Val d'Isère.

The familiar friend of the Scottish title prize returned to Robb's mantelpiece in 1978, the year in which she made her debut in the World Championship at Garnish in Germany and also entered the World Cup fray. By then she was dividing her time between home in Aberdeen, the British Alpine team's land training base in Aldershot and the on-piste camp at the Hinter Tux glacier in Austria as the build-up to the 1980 Olympics at Lake Placid began in earnest.

Robb, who was a regular in the top 30 of World Cup and Europa Cup events on the Continent, beating the odds against strong competition from the Alpine nations, was assured of a place in the squad for the US spectacle. The dawn of the new decade brought a break with Olympic tradition – for the first time artificial snow was in use.

The British team warmed up for Lake Placid with a pre-games training camp at Hunter Mountain to acclimatise for the challenge facing them in New York State. Robb and her teammates represented the elite of winter sports in Britain, but they did not live in the lap of luxury while in America, with the athletes' accommodation in the Olympic village destined to be turned into a prison on completion of the event.

Liechtenstein ace Hanni Wenzel dominated the women's racing at Lake Placid, with the British contingent failing to break into the top 10 and Robb returning home with

Anne Robb in action in 1977.

Olympic ski racer Anne Robb.

another Olympic experience under her belt. Within three months of returning from the games the Aberdonian made the surprise announcement that she would not return for an Olympic hat-trick, deciding to step down from top level competition at the tender age of 20. She had finished 27th in a field of 55 in the slalom in the US and 21st in a field of 80 for the giant slalom and felt she had reached her peak.

While continuing to race domestically, the ambitious Aberdonian branched out into life as a ski coach and businesswoman when she launched the Anne Robb Sports Studio on St Swithin Street. The new dual role did not dent her competitive instinct, with Robb winning the British slalom title in 1981 and the following year taking the British Skier of the Year prize, based on style and technique, in London on an artificial course.

As the decade rolled on, business took priority for the switched-on skier. Anne Robb became Anne Boyle in 1989 when she married Mike Boyle at a ceremony at Craigiebuckler Church and, although the racing days were behind her, the Olympian maintained her link to the sport as an official at local and national level.

In more recent years the Olympic torch has been carried in the north-east by two male skiers, with Torphins racer Roger Cruickshank realising his dream in 2006 when he competed in the Turing games and recorded matching 37th place finishes in both the downhill and the Super G events. Cruickshank, a pilot in the RAF based at Leuchars, was born in the Netherlands but grew up on Deeside and learnt his sporting trade on the same slopes graced by Robb in her youth.

Banchory snowboarder Ben Kilner joined the select band when he claimed a place at the 2010 games in Vancouver.

COMMONWEALTH GAMES

Peter Nicol

To climb to the head of the world rankings in any sport is an achievement. To maintain that level of success for five whole years is quite simply an astonishing demonstration of endeavour and brilliance – two qualities squash star Peter Nicol had in abundance during his stranglehold on the sport during more than a decade as one of the planet's most successful athletes.

For 60 months during his heyday he sat at number one on the official list, leading a group of excellent competitors from all corners of the planet and rarely faltering in the face of cut-throat competition in one of the fastest moving events known to man. Speed of thought as well as fleetness of foot are vital and on both fronts he was ahead of the pack.

Nicol, born in Inverurie but a man who flew the flag for Aberdeen and Aberdeenshire in fine style, is one of the honorary Aberdonians to merit inclusion as a true Granite Legend. Born on Donside in 1973, Nicol was a talented all-rounder in his youth. His father Pat, a physical education teacher by profession, was himself an accomplished performer in several sports and that rubbed off on his young son as he began to shine as a football player and with a racquet in his hand.

Nicol, who trained with Aberdeen Football Club as a teenager, had a choice to make as a teenager and chose wisely, with the benefit of glorious hindsight. He opted to embark on a career in squash and although the rewards for a man who became a

Peter Nicol shows off his Commonwealth Games gold medal at the opening of his new squash centre in Elrick in 1998.

Peter Nicol's single-minded pursuit of his dreams made him one of the most decorated sportsmen of his generation (Picture by Colin Rennie).

global icon in the sport may not have matched those of his football equivalents, the glorious memories are worth far more.

At the age of 17 he left the home comforts of Aberdeenshire behind and moved to Harrogate to embark on his new life as a full-time sportsman, continuing the migration south two years later when he switched to London to work with respected coach Neil Harvey. He has always maintained that his Aberdeenshire roots, and the traditional work ethic associated with his home patch, were a major factor in everything he achieved.

Nicol worked tirelessly to establish himself in one of the most physically demanding sports on the planet. His training schedule in those early days would see him rise at 7am and often he would spend seven hours training in the gym, on the road and on court. With age he eased off on that gruelling programme, but the core fitness derived from his pursuit of physical perfection set him apart from any other player of his generation.

The key turning point was in January 1998 when he was installed as the world number one. Pakistan phenomenon Jansher Khan had held top spot in the rankings for a full decade, but was dethroned by the Scottish star – there was a new king of the court.

To confirm his status as the best on the planet, later in 1998 Nicol defeated Khan in the British Open Final to prise Pakistan's grip from the sport's most prestigious piece of silverware and become the first Brit to get his hands on it for a quarter of a century.

The Scot had played his first pro match in 1992, the year in which he won his first PSA tour title, and within two years was inside the top five in the world. In 1998 he hit the number-one spot for the first time and spent 60 months at the head of the list – the first Brit ever to occupy pole position. Once he had that honour in his grasp it took an almighty battle to wrest it back from him.

He reinforced his position as top dog by striding to the Commonwealth Games Final in Kuala Lumpur in 1998 and defeating fierce Canadian rival Jonathon Power in an epic Final in Malaysia. In addition to his singles gold, there was also victory in the doubles and Nicol clinched a further two gold medals in Manchester four years later when he played in the men's doubles and mixed doubles finals.

He was fit, fast and tactically astute. With his ability to chase down what looked like lost causes and turn defence into attack with a flick of his wrist, at the height of his form there was not a player on the earth who could live with Aberdeenshire's finest.

In 1999, in the shadow of the pyramids, Nicol ticked another box on his list of ambitions when he won the World Open title in Egypt. It was a momentous achievement, defeating home favourite Ahmed Barad in front of a partisan African crowd. That year, in recognition of his services to the sport, he was awarded an MBE. Closer to home he had been given the freedom of Inverurie as the gravity of his achievements in the sport resonated throughout the country.

In 2001, having qualified to play for England through his residency in the country, Nicol stunned the sporting world by turning his back on Scotland, after winning 66 caps, and enlisting for service with the Auld Enemy. It was a pragmatic move, with the court star opting to switch allegiance in order to gain access to the far greater support network open to English players as opposed to those representing Scotland.

It sparked heated debate and ostracised the player to an extent, but he had not climbed to the top of the tree without the ability to make tough decisions and had developed a thick enough skin to deal with the flak sent in his direction. Joining the England set-up provided him with fully-funded coaches and physios, releasing him from the burden of finding tens of thousands of pounds to employ specialists to travel with him. The whole issue highlighted glaring deficiencies in the help provided for sportsmen outside of the mainstream in Scotland.

Any criticism was tempered by the success he enjoyed with his new team, helping England to the European Championship title in 2001 in Nottingham to introduce himself to a new set of fans in the best of circumstances and then claiming the World Team Championship four years later. There was nothing new about his colleagues though, as he had spent his entire professional career based south of the border and travelled the world with the country's clutch of elite performers.

In truth it was Scotland which enjoyed Nicol's greatest years, as he rose from a teenage hopeful to become the greatest squash player Britain has ever produced. By the time he was playing under the flag of St George he already had one eye on the future.

Nicol the squash player has evolved to become Nicol the businessman. During his playing days he launched the Peter Nicol Squash and Fitness Centre in Elrick and the enterprise has gone from strength to strength. Following his retirement from playing in 2006, on the back of more than 50 professional title wins, he was also enlisted by equipment manufacturer Prince to help develop the players in their stable and in 2008 that relationship was strengthened further when Peter Nicol Squash took over the handling of all Prince player contracts as well as embarking on an online retail expansion for the firm. Event management is another facet of the shrewd former player's commercial portfolio.

Nicol has also worked quietly on a number of charity projects, lending his time willingly to support various projects. He was recently presented with a special award in recognition of his selfless work by the charity SportsAid.

In 2009 he and partner Jessica left London life behind to return to Nicol's roots, setting up home at Tough in the Donside countryside to enable him to devote more time and energy to his burgeoning club at Elrick. Nicol, whose father Pat has been an enthusiastic coach to the club's successful youth section, has also expanded his coaching commitments as the next generation of court stars are fostered by a family steeped in squash excellence. His sister Julie Ross rose to become a Scottish international and has also been part of the Nicol coaching dynasty at Elrick.

Now back on home soil, the Peter Nicol Squash and Fitness Centre is at the centre of the former world champion's attention and he has set his sights on unearthing the next gem from the mine of talent in the area. The aim is to find a player capable of playing professionally and it is viewed as a realistic goal by the club owner and his team. However, it is surely unlikely that they will discover a star capable of replicating Nicol's achievements.

Sheena Sharp and Neil Stirton

The Commonwealth Games in 2006 proved to be a good time to be an Aberdonian sports fan. For those willing to beat the time difference and track the exploits of the north-east's medal hopefuls, the images filtering back from Australia painted a fine picture of the Granite City's sporting pedigree.

The Melbourne rifle range was where most of the celebrations could be found as Huntly sharp shooter Sheena Sharp and Aberdeen marksman Neil Stirton did their country proud with brilliant performances to earn podium places.

Sharp led the way with two gold medals, one in the individual event and the other in the prone pairs. Her younger teammate Stirton did his best to keep pace and returned from the competition with a silver medal for his efforts, also coming in the prone pairs. The success sparked celebration at the Bon Accord Small Bore Rifle Club in Aberdeen, the outfit which both shooters represent on the international stage.

Sheena Sharp at the Denwood Shooting Range in Aberdeen.

Bon Accord, formed in 1912 to serve Aberdeen's aspiring target shooters, is based at the Denwood range at Countesswells and has emerged as one of the country's leading centres. At the 2006 Commonwealths alone it provided five members of the Scottish team, with Sharp and Stirton joined in the squad by clubmates Emma Cole-Hamilton, Heather Rudd and Shona Marshall. Sharp's joy at the Commonwealths in 2002 led to a surge in interest in the sport and the huge publicity surrounding her gold rush four years later, in addition to Stirton's visit to the podium, brought another spike in numbers at the city club.

For Sharp the double victory was the highlight of a career in shooting which has provided a wealth of opportunity and a succession of prizes both at home and abroad. Sharp, born in Torphins, has represented her Aberdeen club as well as Huntly Rifle Club, in her home town, in every corner of the world and has produced a long list of records and achievements.

Only three Scottish shooters have ever won individual gold at the Commonwealths, putting her in elite company. Sharp was a late starter to international competition, launching her career in 2001, but within a year she was a Commonwealth Games medal-winner after claiming silver in the 2002 pairs.

Since then she has put her name to eight of a possible nine Scottish record scores, and on her way to gold in Australia she set perfect 100-point totals to underline her credentials as the most accurate woman on the planet.

Sharp's hopes of confirming that status were dashed when her specialist discipline, the 50m prone, was removed from the programme for the 2008 Olympics in Beijing – but her performance two years previously in Melbourne told its own story.

She is certainly untouchable in Scottish terms, having been crowned women's national 50m prone champion four times at last count and winning the British title, and the Earl Roberts trophy which accompanies it, at Bisley in 2008. That UK triumph pitted her against the best men in the land, with Sharp becoming only the second woman ever to win the overall British prize.

The Aberdeenshire office manager first picked up a rifle as an 11-year-old, having been inspired by her father and brother's participation, but did not take up the sport seriously until her late 30s. By then her brother, Bill, had won the Scottish Championship. Before then she had been a keen golfer, serving as women's vice captain at Huntly Golf Club, but her revived passion for shooting curtailed her involvement and the rifle range rather than the driving range became her second home.

Sharp won her first Scotland women's cap in 1997 and has gone on to represent her country more than 70 times, as well as starring for Britain following her debut in 2001. World Championship and European Championship experience is also part of her CV, as well as a bronze medal at the prestigious Nordic Championships in 2005.

Crowned Aberdeenshire Sports Personality of the Year and Aberdeen city's Sportswoman of the Year on the back of her Commonwealth Games heroics in 2006, Sharp has since expanded her repertoire to take on fresh challenges in the three-positions and air rifle disciplines. Shooting experts believe those new events could bring even more success for the north-east's most famous sporting grandmother.

While Sharp was a late starter at the top level, Stirton arrived in Australia at the opposite end of the age range. He was just 25 when he lined up in the pairs final and

Neil Stirton with his Commonwealth Games medal.

overcame an eye problem to help Scotland to silver, partnering Martin Sinclair. Prior to the games the Aberdonian had lost focus in his right eye and had been equipped with a contact lens designed to combat it. On the eve of the Final he opted to ditch the lens, fearing it would jeopardize his chances, and it proved to be a good call as he and Sinclair set a new record in the 50m event – the first time the country had won a medal in the prone shooting competition for 20 years.

Stirton's adventure had begun as a 15-year-old, when he won his first international cap as part of Scotland's junior team. He made his first senior appearance for his country in 1999 and made his British debut two years later. These were heady heights for a boy who had picked up a rifle for the first time as an 11-year-old after finding Aberdeen's target club in the Yellow Pages.

Coached by Adam Gordon at Bon Accord, he made great strides and claimed the British and Scottish junior prone records before going on to win the 2004 Scottish Long Range Championship and the Commonwealth Shooting Federation pairs competition in the same year. He won silver at the CSF Championship in 2005 to go into the Commonwealth Games in 2006 as one of the clear favourites for a medal.

Stirton, a former Aberdeen Grammar School pupil and a graduate of Aberdeen University, combined his sporting passion with a full-time career as a business analyst before concentrating all of his efforts on shooting in the run towards the 2008 Olympics.

Despite smashing the British record to take silver at the World Cup in Munich early in 2008, he scored 599 and missed the world record by a single point. It meant he rocketed from 87th to sixth in the world rankings in the process, but it was too late to earn a place on the team for Beijing. The British Olympic Association pushed for a wildcard place for their shooting star, but their efforts were fruitless.

The major question is what the future holds for the two Commonwealth heroes, with

The Bon Accord Rifle Club members who represented Scotland in Melbourne are, from left: Emma Cole-Hamilton, Sheena Sharp, Neil Stirton, Heather Rudd.

London 2012 around the corner and the Commonwealths in Glasgow looming for 2014. Stirton, who in recent times has branched out to try his hand at the three-positions discipline, has his sights firmly set on both and has embarked on a rigorous training schedule to keep him ahead of his rivals. He believes working in the gym on strength and stamina could hold the key to further success and he is going flat out to prove the point.

Sharp, who was inducted to the Scottish Small Bore Rifle Association hall of fame in 2007, remains open-minded about her plans and has hinted that she could retire from competition before the Scottish games to concentrate on her developing interest in coaching.

The next generation of north-east shooters could well be the ones to fly the flag, with Robert Gordon University student Emma Cole-Hamilton among the great hopes. Born in Northern Ireland but brought up in Aberdeenshire, she is the daughter of fellow Bon Accord member and Commonwealth Games veteran Jim Cole-Hamilton. He competed in the games in 2002. Emma Cole-Hamilton has won the Scottish Women's Air Rifle Championship four times, to add to the list of junior titles she has claimed, and was also crowned Scottish Prone Champion in 2007 and the national 3x20 winner in 2006 and 2007.

Aberdonian Jon Hammond, now living and training in America as a rifle coach, is the other ace in the pack for the region. A two-time Scottish long range champion and winner of the 50m 3x40m title in 2003, he is another aiming to ensure a bright future for the sport in the north-east corner.

With the success of Melbourne still fresh in the memories of the crowds who greeted all of the Commonwealth medal-winners upon their return to the Granite City in 2006, there will be no shortage of support for Aberdeen's finest when they next take to the international ranges.

Ian Bruce

The Commonwealth Games in Auckland in 1990 proved to be a dream debut for Banchory bowler Ian Bruce. An established competitor on British soil, the venture to the southern hemisphere represented a trip into the unknown for a player who had never sampled foreign greens. He responded in style, winning gold at his first attempt as part of Scotland's fours team.

Bruce, playing out of Kincardine O'Neil on Deeside and representing Northern Bowling Club in Aberdeen, was one of the success stories of the New

Commonwealth Games gold medal winner Ian Bruce
is congratulated by wife Diana.

Ian Bruce in action in 1992.

Zealand games and helped preserve the country's place at the top of his sport's pecking order as part of a talented group who were sent to fly the flag.

It was the culmination of almost three decades of practice for Bruce, who aimed to play every day at the height of his success to perfect his technique. He had first picked up a bowl as a 10-year-old and was 38 when he boarded the plane for the Commonwealths, amassing a raft of experience in the years in between. Most importantly, he had retained the enthusiasm for the game that he had as a youngster starting out in bowls, and that was to be a key factor in his unruffled approach.

At local level there were few competitions that Bruce did not win. As part of the Bon Accord Bowling Association set-up, he claimed the singles title as well as the pairs, triples and fours prizes. Add into the mix the association's Champion of Champions Trophy, and the picture begins to form of a man on top of his game.

The success in the north-east events opened doors to bigger stages and Bruce hit top gear in his 30s. His talents were picked up on by Scotland selectors in 1984, when he was handed his debut at Larne, and that proved to be the springboard to personal success as his confidence and big match ability grew year on year.

Together with trusted ally Bruce Nicol he won the Scottish Indoor Pairs Championship in 1985 to push the duo further into the spotlight at national level. The glare was about to get far brighter for the modest north-east team as they set about pushing onwards and upwards, having been paired together by the Aberdeen Indoor Bowling Club.

In 1986 the Scottish champs ventured south to Bournemouth for the world pairs contest, among 32 of the best in the business gathered at the English venue to test themselves in a high-pressure environment. They breezed through their opening group games undefeated to tee up a semi-final against home hopefuls Bob Fairburn and Bob Stephenson. On their run to the last four they defeated Australian pair Kenny Williams and Don Williams, Irish champions Sammy Allen and Jim Baker as well as English contenders John Bell and John Ottaway. That set up the semi-final tie, when the rub of the green was with their opponents and the match ended in a 3–1 reverse. Red-hot favourites David Bryant and Tony Allcock went on to win the title.

The near miss in the doubles was followed within a year by a similar experience in the World Singles Championship. Bruce clinched his place in the 1987 competition at

Coatbridge when he came through Scottish qualifying, with the country's finest players bidding for just two places. National singles champion Hugh Duff took one of the spots and Bruce grabbed the other by defeating Scotland teammate David McGill in a tense play-off.

The worlds were held early in 1987 and Bruce blew away the New Year cobwebs with brisk progress, coming through the first round against Phil Skoglund, New Zealand's greatest-ever lawn bowler, before edging out Israel's Cecil Bransky to book a quarter-final berth. Bransky, born in South Africa, was another tough opponent, but nobody in the draw held any fears for the ambitious man from the north.

Irish star David Corkill, winner of the prestigious Super Bowl title, was the player standing between Banchory's finest and the semi-finals. In front of a packed Central Belt audience and the television cameras, the north-east bowler retained his customary calm and won a new band of supporters with superb tactical play and a subtle approach on a Coatbridge carpet not suited to aggressive play.

The legendary Tony Alcock, who went on to win his second consecutive world title, ended Bruce's run – but his biggest bowling prize up to that point, a cheque for £3,000 as a semi-finalist, helped cushion the blow of exiting the tournament. As an assistant bank manager with the Royal Bank of Scotland, the prize money was assured of safe keeping.

By the time he was confirmed in the 1990 Commonwealth Games squad, Bruce was established in the Scotland team for home nations competitions, going on to win 30 caps before retiring from the top level in 1996, and was ready to hit top form on the sun-soaked greens of Pakuranga. The motto of the Auckland games in 1990 was 'This is the Moment', and it turned out to be true for the visitor from Deeside.

Playing with Denis Love, George Adrain and skip Willie Wood in the fours team, the north-east stalwart had a decisive role to play in a dramatic Commonwealth Final against Northern Ireland. He clinically ditched the jack on the penultimate end to secure a coveted gold medal with a 19–14 victory. It later transpired that the father of two had delivered the key shot using borrowed bowls. The fast-running greens of New Zealand had taken the medal-winner by surprise and he made the snap decision to leave his trusty Henselite set in the locker room and make use of Drakespride bowls lent to him by Adrain. It was a shrewd choice, with the late switch in equipment helping to cope with the glass-like greens and testing cambers at the New Zealand venue. The surface made the challenge even greater, but it was the tartan contingent who mastered the conditions and emerged with the badges to prove it.

It had been a memorable team effort from the bowlers, who were part of a Scottish push that brought five gold medals and placed the nation ninth from 55 competing countries when the final standings were tallied up. Australia, with a staggering 52 golds among their haul of 164 in total, led the way. Scotland, who returned with 22 medals, bagged the four other golds courtesy of light welterweight boxer Charlie Kane, shooting pair Ian Marsden and James Dunlop, judo player Loretta Cusack and Liz McColgan's sterling effort in the 10,000 metre race.

Bruce had been one of more than 2,000 competitors in New Zealand, savouring an opening ceremony reflecting the host country's Maori heritage and a closing event

Ian Bruce in familiar surroundings at the Deeside Indoor Sporting Club in Banchory.

graced by the Queen. The impressive Mount Smart Stadium, built into a former volcanic cone, provided the setting and the Kiwis presented a wonderful spectacle for the spectators who travelled for the event and the viewing public across the globe.

For Bruce it had been a memorable first venture into foreign competition and the welcome the banker received when he arrived back on home soil was also unforgettable, with wife Diana and sons Cameron and Roland joining more than 100 friends and family at a surprise celebration as they greeted the medal-winner at his High Street home.

A civic reception was hosted by Kincardine and Deeside District Council to recognise his achievement at the authority's headquarters in Stonehaven. Also honoured at the ceremony were triathletes Ginny Pollard, John O'Donovan and Andrew Johnston following their participation in the Auckland games. Bruce was also honoured at the Aberdeen sports awards and crowned Amateur Sportsman of the Year at the city's prize ceremony in the winter of 1990, to cap a hectic but enjoyable period. Early the following year he was named as Kincardine and Deeside's Sports Personality of the Year, to ensure the trophy cabinet remained well stocked.

In 1992 Bruce, whose brothers Ronnie and Willie were both prominent players in their own right, began to curtail his bowling commitments. Having stepped up from assistant to manager at his bank branch, there was no shortage of calls on his time, but the main reason for taking a step back was to concentrate on his other sporting passion – football. He coached with Banchory Boys' Club, where his young sons were both talented prospects. Football came to the fore, but it was as a champion bowler that Bruce won his place on north-east sport's roll of honour.

Barry Collie

When the British junior gymnastics squad are addressed by head coach Barry Collie they know their mentor speaks from experience. The enthusiastic Aberdonian has dedicated his life to the sport and has been entrusted with developing the next batch of potential champions to follow in his medal-winning footsteps.

While Britain counts down to the 2012 Olympics in London, Collie can be forgiven for allowing his attention to drift. The target he has been set by bosses at British Gymnastics is not the home spectacle, but rather the 2016 games in Rio de Janiero. He is already working closely with a group of children hand-picked with the Brazilian sporting carnival in mind and has begun guiding them on the path he hopes will lead them to international stardom, working from the national centre of excellence at Lilleshall.

The Scottish coach, now in his 30s, was appointed in October 2006 following the arrival on British shores of Eddie Van Hoof as the sport's technical director earlier that year. Collie was one of three national coaches enlisted to help transform GB fortunes. The exploits of world champion Beth Tweddle, who was awarded an MBE for her services to gymnastics in the 2010 New Year honours list, has raised the profile of the sport to peak levels. Gymnastics has been given fresh impetus as a result.

When Collie took his first tentative steps in the sport in the early 1980s, the opportunity for trips to Buckingham Palace and celebrity status were not on the agenda. Instead, his motivation was enjoyment and the chance to excel after showing obvious natural ability from a young age.

Collie spent his formative years in the Deeside village of Banchory. He was a skilful and speedy football player before devoting himself to gymnastics as the competition wins began to stack up. Having had his first coaching session as a six-year-old primary pupil, Collie continued to thrive throughout his school career as a member of the Beacon Boys Gymnastics Club at Bucksburn, and by the time he sat his Highers to round off his studies he was a Scottish record holder in the holding handstand and double leg circle disciplines.

He was also an experienced Scotland international by that point, travelling to the national training centre in Largs regularly for sessions with the national squad. Upon

Barry Collie in his role as a gymnastics coach.

leaving Hazlehead Academy, to where he had moved following a switch from Banchory to Kingswells, he was accepted by Stirling University, but rejected the offer in favour of becoming a full-time gymnast at Hinkley.

In his final year in youth gymnastics, Collie realised his first major ambition when he was crowned Scottish junior champion at Perth in 1997. He had to defeat British champion John Mutch to do it, but came through the test with flying colours to confirm his place as the country's top-ranked junior. The result moved him up to third in the Scotland senior standings and booked him his place in the Commonwealth Games squad for Malaysia the following year. By then he had begun his work with the Hinkley Gymnastics Club and the Scottish win set him on the road to regular competitions on the Continent.

Collie's success at the top level was fitting reward for coach Russell Morrison, who has dedicated more than three decades to coaching at the Beacon centre. Morrison began teaching trampoline before crossing over into artistic gymnastics and was the man who set Collie on the path to a career in the sport, which has seen the pupil progress to become a teacher in his own right. Collie has returned to the north-east with fellow internationals at regular intervals to pass on his knowledge to the next generation of Beacon competitors, with the club continuing to go from strength to strength. The popularity of gymnastics in Aberdeen is booming, with Beacon welcoming an influx of 30 talented new youngsters following summer trials in 2009 ready for the completion of a refurbishment of the centre. The Beacon centre, home to more than 50 sports clubs, has become part of the new Bucksburn community campus.

It was at the Beacon centre that the seeds were sown for Collie's dream of a career as a professional athlete, although ultimately he had to look outside the Granite City

Barry Collie on his way to bronze at the Commonwealth Games.

to fulfil his ambitions, a cause of frustration for coach Morrison, who had guided him to international level in Aberdeen.

Collie had considered quitting the sport as a teenager during his Beacon days as he grew disillusioned by the lack of support for Scottish gymnasts. A move to Hinckley in Leicestershire saved his career as he tapped into the English network and continued his development in the Midlands with the help of funding from the national lottery. Soon after the move south he made his Commonwealth Games debut at the Kuala Lumpur event in 1998. Collie was just 19 and soaked up the experience like a sponge, calling upon the events of that trip when the Commonwealths landed closer to home in Manchester four years later. Collie was joined in the 1998 squad by fellow Aberdonians John Mutch and Lindsay Warrack, who had already become the first woman from the city to represent Great Britain and won the Scottish Championship while representing the Beacon club.

Collie was also a member of team GB in 1998, earning his first cap during a trip to Denmark, when he went head to head with gymnasts from the host country and the Czech Republic. It was a reward for his impressive displays during a training camp in the Russian city of St Petersburg earlier in the year, overcoming freezing conditions and a gruelling schedule to pass the initiation test with flying colours. He impressed enough in Scandinavia to retain his place and went on to represent the squad at the 2001 World Championships in Belgium, as the only Scot to make the cut, and he also went to Hungary the following year.

It was in the 2002 Commonwealth Games that he rose to prominence, winning a bronze in the vault and earning a cherished medal to provide a lasting reward for the thousands of hours spent perfecting his technique as man and boy. Collie's triumph came on the day that Scotland teammate Steve Frew won gold in the rings final to complete a dramatic day in the gymnastics hall, with a familiar story beginning to emerge as Frew lamented the lack of funding and contemplated retiring due to his struggle to maintain his standards while working full-time as a fitness trainer.

Like Collie, Frew found the pull of competition too strong to resist and he held on to claim his place in the 2006 Commonwealth Games squad, by then a veteran of 32 and taking part in his fifth games. He has since been appointed to the Glasgow 2014 athletics commission, joining other sportsmen and women as Scotland prepares to host the Commonwealths.

A certain Beth Tweddle also won gold for England during the Manchester gathering, to highlight the growing pool of talent in the United Kingdom and the level of competition Scotland's medal-winners faced during the event.

Collie's podium place came courtesy of a tally of 9.225 points at the end of his final performance. England's Kanukai Jackson was just ahead on 9.281, while Canadian star Kyle Shewfelt claimed the gold with a score of 9.443. The atmosphere as Collie approached his moment of reckoning was spine-tingling, with a packed audience putting national divides to one side and giving all of the Brits their backing. Scotland was represented in the predominantly English crowd, with Collie's family there to cheer him on from the sidelines as a lifetime of hard work came to fruition as he climbed the steps to the podium.

By the time he became a Commonwealth medal-winner, Collie's training regime had stepped up from the nine hours a week spent as a part-time gymnast during his schooldays in the north-east to a full 36 hours per week programme in England. He also began to coach, tapping into his growing knowledge base.

He made the short hop to Manchester as Scotland's champion, having won the national title twice in consecutive years, and on the back of a bronze medal in the floor section of the prestigious Poetsi Cup in Romania. His reputation worldwide was growing, having made the transition from a competitor on the domestic scene in his home country to a seasoned contender with extensive experience at the World and European Championships.

Tony Dawson

When the Aberdeen Sports Council revealed the first 21 members of the city's sporting hall of fame in 2006 it was fitting that Tony Dawson was on the list of honoured sportsmen and women. The international badminton and tennis player earned his place as a veteran of the Commonwealth Games and winner of a series of domestic championships, but he has also had a major input to the wider sporting scene in his home city and was the founding chairman of the ASC in 1983.

The respected solicitor's administrative contribution cannot be underestimated and he was a driving force behind the creation of the impressive £1.2 million Westburn Indoor Tennis Centre in the 1990s, a legacy just as important as the one he left as a competitor. Pushing forward that project was just one of a number of schemes he has had a hand in, and the sports council he helped to create has provided support to a succession of talented Aberdonians over a quarter of a century.

Tony Dawson in action in 1972.

When it was founded by Dawson and Alastair Gracie in the 1980s the sports council encompassed 37 different activities and that number has grown steadily since then.

His experience ensures Dawson is a man in demand, having been enlisted by a raft of governing bodies in the role of a troubleshooter during periods of reorganisation. Boxing, golf and cricket are among the sports in Scotland to have called upon the Aberdonian's administrative and management skills.

He is a man who understands better than most what it takes to succeed in a diverse range of disciplines. Although badminton was his strongest suit, he was, and still is, a sports fanatic. Tennis was another passion, while squash completed his racquet sports set and marathon running, with 26 races completed, was another pastime to sit alongside his participation in the gruelling Highland Cross endurance event three times. With his father playing rugby and tennis as well as representing Scotland at curling, and his mother a local tennis champion, the competitive spirit was in his blood.

His love of all things sporting took the Aberdonian to the very top, with his participation in the 1978 Commonwealth Games the undoubted highlight. Dawson cherished his place in the Scottish team for the event in Edmonton, Canada, and was already an established international player by the time he boarded the plane for North America.

He travelled to Edmonton as the country's top-ranked badminton player, a position he had reached by virtue of total devotion to the game. In the build-up to the games he would train in Aberdeen during the week and make the 240-mile round trip to Grangemouth each weekend for six-hour team training sessions. On the competitive scene, Scotland's leading light thought nothing of hopping in his car to drive to Wales for ranking tournaments. When not behind the wheel on his way to training or matches, Dawson could be found running laps at Kings College or jogging the length of Aberdeen beach in his bid to maintain peak physical condition.

Although he returned from Canada without a medal for his efforts, the experience whetted his appetite for life at the sport's top table. At the peak of his powers, Dawson toyed with the idea of putting his burgeoning law career on hold to turn professional in badminton, but opted against the idea after weighing up his options. Despite breaking into the world's top 50, it was a gamble too big to take.

Instead he concentrated on continuing a fine amateur career, which brought recognition throughout the 1960s, 70s and 80s. It was as a pupil of Robert Gordon's

College and member of the Four Courts tennis club that he first hit the headlines as a rising star, winning the singles and doubles titles at the Highland Tennis Championships in the summer of 1968. By then he was already the Aberdeen schools Under-18 title holder and in badminton was the north-east junior champion and Northern Junior Open winner, as well as a Scottish schools international in the indoor game. He had been a rugby player and cricketer at school, but became interested in badminton when Gordon's teacher Ian Calder launched after-school classes and,

Tony Dawson displays his trophy haul in 1976.

Veteran tennis player Jimmy Wood's career dovetailed with that of Tony Dawson (Picture by Kami Thomson).

although tennis remained his favourite sport, it was with a shuttlecock rather than a ball that Dawson enjoyed most success.

In 1969 he won the Scottish Junior Badminton Championship in Edinburgh and was called-up to play in the national Under-18 team that year before stepping up to play for the Under-21s just 12 months later.

In November 1970, by then a law student at Aberdeen University, there was wider recognition when the Scottish challenger won the British Universities Badminton Championship at Crystal Palace in London. He became the first Scot to win the prize. It was the biggest win of his career up to that point and the precursor to success in the Scottish Under-21 Championship in 1971 and the Scottish Universities title in the following campaign, when he also successfully defended his national junior crown.

In between, he was busy carving out a reputation as a wily tennis player and was actually capped in that sport before he was in badminton. On court he was self-assured and energetic, with his compact frame providing brilliant mobility. Dawson was also outspoken, never afraid to go head to head with those in authority when he felt it necessary as a player from outside the Central Belt mainstream.

He went on to win badminton's North, South, West and East of Scotland Championships in 1976 and could not be ignored by Scotland selectors any longer. He earned his first cap in a match against Ireland that year, a welcome if belated honour for the man from the north.

He continued to pile up domestic honours throughout the decade, as well as establishing himself as the north-east's top-rating tennis player when he edged ahead of Jimmy Wood in the pecking order and went on to claim nine north-east singles titles in a row. He and Wood combined in 1988 to help Cults Tennis Club win the Scottish Cup, another considerable feather in the cap of a pair who were teammates and friends as well as rivals.

Wood is an Aberdeen sporting legend in his own right – still competing and chasing glory on the world stage past his 75th birthday. Wood, who has claimed 10 titles at the Wimbledon Veterans Championship in recent years, is a familiar figure on the global over-75s circuit and still regularly competes internationally. He has also

Tony Dawson has been a champion of sport in his home city.

become a respected coach to the city's next generation, passing on the skills and wisdom accumulated during decades at the top level.

The retired art teacher began playing the game at the Four Courts club, which accepted members by invitation only. Wood won the North-east Singles Championship a dozen times from 1957 onwards and has 20 doubles victories to his credit in the same competition. At national level he won the Scottish Singles Championship in 1962 and 1964 and the doubles with George Kelly in 1964, as well as helping Four Courts to the Scottish Cup in 1957 and 1962.

It was a case of right place at the wrong time for Wood, who was into his 30s before his success in the Scottish Championship. It was too late to contemplate a professional career, despite his renowned ability. When he won the Scottish Cup with Cults in 1988 he was 54 years old, but still going strong.

For Dawson, the 1988 success in tennis followed a decade after his badminton accomplishment. The lawyer's year in 1978 had been built towards the chance of a lifetime at the Commonwealth Games – by which time he was Scotland's number-one badminton player, fifth in the British rankings and 39th in the world standings.

Dawson, who also played at the European Championships, gained a total of 13 caps before stepping down from top-level competition. That allowed him time to develop his interest in squash, helping the Aberdeen Petroleum Club to promotion in successive seasons from Division Six to Division One of the north-east league.

In 1994, at the age of 42, the solicitor had to call time on competitive commitments due to a hip injury, benefitting from revolutionary McMinn hip replacements which have since been adopted as mainstream treatment, but did not let that dampen his enthusiasm for sport in his home city and he has retained his link as a keen supporter and adviser to various clubs, organisations and individuals in the north-east.

Professionally Dawson continues to make a significant mark in his home city and was elected president of the Society of Advocates in Aberdeen in 2009, a position his father Philip also held during his legal career. In the same year Dawson was also honoured by Aberdeen City Council when he was installed as a Burgess of the Guild of the City of Aberdeen alongside Open golf champion Paul Lawrie.

FOOTBALL

Denis Law

If one man defines the spirit of sport in the Granite City it must be Denis Law. A global icon, a superstar who soared to the pinnacle of football – but a man who never let the fame and fortune detract from the fact that, deep down, he is a humble lad from Aberdeen.

Denis Law receives an honorary degree at the University of Aberdeen afternoon ceremony at Marischal College 2005.

Law, the son of a trawlerman, is arguably the finest player ever to grace Scotland's playing fields. In fact, for most who witnessed him in full flight, with his shock of blonde hair marking him out from the crowd, there is simply no debate – the Law man is the greatest of them all.

He is one of the greatest sporting personalities to emerge from Scotland, a character who endeared himself to all he encountered and whose wonderful spirit and love of the game, which brought him celebrity status and rich rewards, warms the heart. Law's wide smile and easy-going nature became trademarks of one of the most instantly recognisable stars of the era, but on the field it was a different story. A fierce competitive edge made Law a feared opponent and a burning desire to succeed ensured he had success to match his ability.

A child of the 1950s, Law was a bespectacled member of the Aberdeen school select side when he first began to shine. He helped the city team to victory in the Scottish primary tournament while a pupil at Kittybrewster school. His school commitments were combined with juvenile league games for Aberdeen Lads' Club, another of the household names to have been produced by that respected outfit.

Progressing to Powis school as a teenager, he was one of a succession of Scots picked up by Huddersfield Town and signed as an amateur at the age of 15. After completing his studies he moved south to begin his apprenticeship in Yorkshire and in 1956 became the youngest player ever to represent the club when he made his debut at the age of 16. Accomplished displays that belied his tender years ensured a professional contract was quickly tabled, and Law kept progressing at an astonishing rate.

In October 1958, still only 18, he won his first Scotland cap in a 3–0 win against Wales in Cardiff. The rookie scored one and made two goals, a perfect introduction to the Tartan Army for a youngster who had never played to a Scottish audience as a club player. His natural ability was clear for all to see, with his obvious goal threat always in evidence and his off-the-ball movement impossible for defenders to live with.

The Aberdeen squad that won the Scottish Primary Schools' Cup in 1951. Back, from left: Duguid, Taylor, Sim, E. Fraser, Ogston, Douglas, C. Fraser. Front: Buchan, Smith, Burns, Dawson, Lornie, Brack, Law.

In March 1960 Law moved to Manchester City in a British record deal worth £55,000 to Huddersfield. When it became clear that the Leeds Road club were willing to cash in on their prize asset, a long line of clubs began to beat a path to their door. Arsenal, Manchester City and Chelsea nudged to the front of the queue and at the end of a frantic round of bidding it was the Maine Road outfit who emerged with the hottest property in the English game.

Law's exploits in Sky Blue included a six-goal haul in an FA Cup tie against Luton Town in 1961. The match was actually abandoned after 69 minutes due to a waterlogged pitch, but Law's sensational scoring streak was still an achievement which saw his name up in lights.

Allied to his deadly ability in front of goal was a fiercely competitive streak, with the wiry yet powerful forward earning a reputation as a tough tackler and a player not to be messed with. His full-blooded approach to the game landed him in hot water with the authorities more than once, but his aggressive edge was a major part of his game and the manager knew better than to try and temper that aspect of Law's character.

With bravery to match his combative instinct, Law was a technically brilliant player who had the rare quality of being able to do the dirty work when required. It was the complete package for an attacking player and Italian side Torino were quick to seize upon his unique abilities, snapping Law up in the summer of 1961 as part of an Italian raid on the British top flight.

Denis Law in Manchester United colours in 1971.

The Aberdonian followed Hibs striker Joe Baker to Turin, while Jimmy Greaves had been recruited by AC Milan just days earlier. It cost Torino £100,000 to clinch the Law deal, but he continued to produce truly world-class displays with club and country to justify the heavy investment.

Baker and Law became close friends during their foray into Serie A, but found it difficult to break down the wary Italians within the club's squad. Matters were made worse when, following a car crash involving their British duo, Law was dropped from the team despite escaping unscathed. Around 15,000 Torino fans boycotted the next game in protest at the decision to play without their talismanic forward, while those who did enter the ground chanted for Law to be restored to the team. The side fell 2–1 to Udinese, and in time for the next fixture there was a recall for Law.

At the end of a stormy first season in Italy, Law's continental adventure was brought to an end when Manchester United weighed in with a £115,000 offer for the fair-haired goal-getter. Old Trafford manager Matt Busby, after a patient pursuit, had finally got his man.

Although he had never graced Pittodrie, the match of Law's life did take place in Aberdeen, just months after signing for United. Denis Law, of Printfield Terrace, married Diana Thomson, of Great Western Road, at Holburn West Church in December 1962. The wedding party, greeted by crowds of wellwishers, continued on to a reception at the Northern Hotel. Among the 150 guests was Archie Beattie, the scout who first caught sight of Law's potential and helped propel him into the senior game.

With his star rising, Law also chose Aberdeen to launch his business interests. The first move of the newly formed Denis Law Enterprises Ltd in 1963 was to launch a car rental firm at Commercial Quay in the Granite City.

On the field, Busby installed Law as his Red Devils captain as he returned to thrilling English crowds after his European sojourn. With speed, vision and power to go with his skill on the ball there was not a player to touch him. He was an inspiration for United,

Denis Law for Manchester United.

helping the club to the FA Cup in 1963 and then the Championship in both 1965 and 1967. He also had a starring role in helping United to the 1968 European Cup Final, although he missed the showdown against Benfica through injury.

In 1970, after being troubled by knee injuries, he was transfer listed by general manager Busby. He earned a reprieve on that occasion, returning to full fitness and fine form in the red jersey and going on to earn a testimonial against Ajax.

At the age of 33, he rejoined Manchester City in the summer of 1973 after more than 300 League appearances for their rivals. He had rejected attempts by Hearts and Motherwell to lure him back to Scotland to see out his career, choosing to stay in his adopted city. While with City in 1973 he also made his first senior appearance at Pittodrie, captaining the Sky Blues in a friendly against the Dons. His only other experience of the ground had been a 1954 schools cup final when he lined up for Powis against Rosemount.

The move to Maine Road enabled Law to fulfil his last ambition in football – to represent Scotland at the World Cup Finals. Law, who skippered the national side for the first time under Tommy Docherty in 1972, made a total of 55 appearances in Dark Blue. Five of those were as captain, as the forward adapted to his position as a wise old head in the international squad.

The World Cup Finals of 1974 in Germany were the culmination of that service, selected by manager Willie Ormond for the pool game against Zaire in Dortmund and inspiring his teammates to a 2–0 victory. Peter Lorimer and Joe Jordan were the goalscorers that day, but Law already had 30 of his own at international level. His goals to games ratio makes him the most prolific striker Scotland has ever had.

The national team famously crashed out of the World Cup that summer despite emerging with an unbeaten record from the German finals. It was a cruel way to exit, but in hindsight fitting that Law was part of the most successful Scotland team ever.

Despite playing his entire club career south of the border he remained intensely patriotic and a true hero to the Tartan Army. Adored and admired in equal measure, no individual has done more to represent Aberdeen on the worldwide stage than Denis Law.

John Hewitt

It was the single greatest moment in the sporting history of the city of Aberdeen and he scored it. John Hewitt's goal against Real Madrid in the Final of the 1983 European Cup-Winners' Cup Final changed the landscape forever in the north-east of Scotland. The Dons were no longer a good Scottish side, they were a lauded European force who promoted not only the club, but also the region as a whole.

When the Gothenburg Greats marked the 25th anniversary of their achievement in 2008 with a programme of testimonial events, it brought the familiar faces back together once again. The passage of time has served only to highlight the brilliance of that renowned campaign and the unique blend of the team that came together to make its mark on the world of football. For a Scottish provincial club to topple some of the most feared names in the game was quite simply incredible.

John Hewitt with his medal collection (Picture by Chris Sumner).

Given that it was an Aberdonian who had progressed through the youth ranks who struck the knock-out blow, it was fitting that a portion of the testimonial proceeds were ploughed back into the development department at Pittodrie by the legends of 1983.

It was Hewitt's intervention in the 111th minute of the pulsating tie in Gothenburg that ensured the coveted continental prize returned to the Pittodrie trophy cabinet. There was perfect poetry in the outcome, with the only Aberdonian in the all-Scottish side grabbing the all-important winner in the famous 2–1 triumph.

There was a strong local flavour to Alex Ferguson's team, with former Hilton Academy pupil Hewitt leading the way, with King Street Boys Club youth product Neale Cooper and Newmachar's Neil Simpson all playing major roles. Both Simpson and Cooper were proud of their north-east upbringing, but neither was born in the city they consider home, with Cooper's birth certificate stamped with the Indian mark of Darjeeling and Scotland international Simpson, by birth at least, a Londoner.

John Hewitt in his 1980s prime against Hearts at Pittodrie.

John Hewitt celebrating scoring the winning goal in the European Cup-Winners' Cup in 1983.

Hewitt had a long and successful career in football but will forever be remembered for that night in Sweden when the mighty Madrid were humbled. The date was 11 May 1983 and the match was on a knife edge after Eric Black's sixth-minute goal had been cancelled out by Juanito's penalty for the Spaniards.

Then it happened. Peter Weir sent the Dons scampering down the left wing and fed Mark McGhee, who in turn wriggled through the Real backline to cross for Hewitt to dive and head home the most iconic goal in more than a century of football in Aberdeen.

The sight of the number 15, who had replaced Black in the second half of the match, raising his arms in celebration is etched on the memory of every Dons fan – whether old enough to have witnessed the great feat in 1983 or not. The goal has been replayed over and over again for those not of sufficient vintage to remember it first hand, with the viewing of the Ullevi Stadium action a rite of passage for every Pittodrie fan.

Hewitt's own rite of passage was making the journey from being an aspiring young footballer on Aberdeen's public parks to becoming a fully-fledged Dons player on the hallowed Pittodrie turf of his home-town club.

That occasion fell on 15 December 1979 when he ran out at Pittodrie to make his debut in a 2–0 victory against St Mirren, a fresh-faced 16-year-old eager to impress in the familiar red shirt. Ferguson's decision to blood the teenager so early was a mark of his faith in the attacking starlet, as well as a vindication of Hewitt's decision to pin his colours to Aberdeen's mast after being pursued by a string of teams on both sides of the border.

As he grew up in the Cornhill area of the city, the scouts had been alerted by his starring shows for Middlefield Boys Club and Hilton Academy. He fielded approaches from Celtic, Manchester United, Middlesbrough, Aston Villa, Sheffield United and St Mirren before finally pledging his future to Aberdeen in 1978 as his school days drew to a close.

Sheffield United had been among the most persistent of the chasing pack, taking the young attacker to Yorkshire for a succession of training stints when he was still in his early teens and impressing manager Jimmy Sirrell. He was capped for Scotland schoolboys during his emergence in the juvenile game and his prolific form ensured there was no shortage of options open before he committed to the offer from Aberdeen at the age of 15.

Within a year of joining the Dons he had stepped up from the schoolboy scene and been promoted to the Scotland international set-up by SFA youth coach Andy Roxburgh, joining fellow Pittodrie trainee Andy Dornan when he was called into his first squad for an eight-nation tournament in Monaco in the winter of 1979. Roxburgh raved about his new recruit's 'magnificent' control and goalscoring instinct, and was quick to tip the Aberdonian for stardom.

His progress was watched at close quarters by Alex Ferguson, the man who had been the manager at St Mirren when they joined the chase for Hewitt. Ferguson resurrected his interest when he took over at the Dons, getting his man at the second time of asking after failing to lure him to Love Street.

Hewitt, a former ball boy at Pittodrie, gently settled into his stride in the senior game. By the 1981–82 season he was firmly established as a first-team player, with his introduction eased by a hat-trick against Rangers that term. He collected his first medal in the 1982 Scottish Cup Final victory against the Ibrox men and went on to amass an impressive array of silverware with the club as well as being capped at Under-21 level by Scotland.

His honours continued with another Scottish Cup badge in 1983 and a matching one three years later. He won Premier Division titles in 1984 and 1985 as well as the League Cup in 1985. In addition to the European Cup-Winners' Cup in 1983 he also played in the European Super Cup later that year to complete a collection which makes him one of the most decorated Aberdonians ever to grace the game.

He was used as a striker and a winger during his service to the club that gave him his break and had a habit of scoring in vital games. The winning goal in the European Final was the most obvious occasion, but the Dons would not have been in that showpiece tie had it not been for Hewitt's intervention in the quarter-final against Bayern Munich. In that game he again played the super sub role to perfection, appearing in time to knock home the winning goal in the 3–2 victory against the Germans in front of a thronging home crowd on what has gone down in history as the greatest night the stadium has ever hosted.

The first leg had ended without a goal and when Ferguson's team fell behind twice in the Scottish return it looked like a lost cause. Neil Simpson equalised first, Alex McLeish levelled the scores at 2–2 and then Hewitt took centre stage to wrap up the vital win. It was another job well done on the big stage.

The European heroics fell in the middle of the Granite City star's time with the club. After joining as an S-form signing in 1978, Hewitt remained with Aberdeen for more than a decade until moving to Celtic under Billy McNeill in 1989 following more than 350 games and 90 goals for the Dons. He had grown frustrated at the lack of opportunities in the central role he craved, having been utilised increasingly as a left-winger by Ian Porterfield and then Alex Smith.

The change in management had unsettled Hewitt, a player proud to have been one of Fergie's furies during the glory years, but he did not take the decision to leave lightly. During his time with the Reds he had been the subject of waves of interest from clubs on both sides of the border. Newcastle United, Norwich City, Charlton Athletic, Queen's Park Rangers, Bradford, Middlesbrough and Leicester City all made approaches at one stage or another as Hewitt's pace and killer instinct drew admiring glances from far and wide. When the Hoops weighed in with a £400,000 offer, Hewitt finally decided it was time for a fresh challenge. Celtic Park manager McNeill had initially made a move for the Dons striker two years previously, and was relieved to finally get his man.

While at Parkhead he played on loan in England with Middlesbrough before joining St Mirren after three years with the Parkhead side. Spells under former teammates Joe Harper at Deveronvale and Neale Cooper at Ross County, as well as a stint as manager of Irish side Dundalk, followed before a move to Cove Rangers' coaching staff under fellow Gothenburg great Doug Rougvie in the late 1990s. Hewitt retired from the game to concentrate on carving out a successful career in the north-east recruitment industry, maintaining his competitive spirit through his involvement in the local golf scene.

Stewart McKimmie

When Stewart McKimmie held aloft the League Cup at Hampden on 26 November 1995 he could not have imagined that he would be the last Aberdeen captain to get his hands on a major trophy for over a quarter of a century. More than that, he was a local boy made good and a rarity in the history of the Dons as an Aberdonian who rose to become a trophy-winning skipper of the Pittodrie side. Only Martin Buchan had previously held that distinction.

The first player chosen to lead out the Reds in the post-war years was Frank Dunlop, a Glaswegian recruited from junior side Benburb and the man who held aloft Aberdeen's first piece of silverware when he claimed the Southern League Cup in 1946 and the Scottish Cup the following term. He was replaced as skipper by Davie Shaw, a Lanarkshire native who had arrived in the north-east via Hibernian. In 1954 it was the turn of Jimmy Mitchell to lead the Dons, with Mitchell becoming another of the Glasgow contingent to have held the club's highest honour.

The list continued through the 1950s and 60s with Coalburn's finest Archie Glen, Jimmy Hogg from the Central Belt and Cowdenbeath-born George Kinell. Country boy Ally Shewan became the nearest to an Aberdonian captain when the defender, from Cuminestown near Turriff, was promoted before being succeeded by another import in the shape of Harry Melrose. Danish star Jens Petersen then took over before Martin Buchan took on the captaincy to fly the flag for the Granite City.

Between Buchan's move to Manchester United in 1972 and McKimmie's appointment as captain more than 20 years later there was a Dundonian captain in Steve Murray, two Edinburgh boys in the shape of Jim Hermiston and Willie Young and then the Glaswegian duo of Willie Miller and Alex McLeish.

To upset the odds and not only make the breakthrough with his home-town club, but also to lead them was a significant achievement – and to cap his tenure as captain with silverware was a dream come true for McKimmie. It was a fitting reward for first-team service spanning almost 14 years. During that time he was a dependable, loyal

Stewart McKimmie with the Scottish Cup at Hampden Park in 1984 after the 2–1 win over Celtic.

and committed performer who went on to win Scotland honours in recognition of his displays in the red of his home-town club.

Yet McKimmie had to travel the road and the miles to Dundee to get his senior career off and running. As a Kincorth Academy pupil he had rarely missed an Aberdeen home game as a fan, but had to limit his trips to Pittodrie when his playing commitments as a rising star of the juvenile game began to take priority. While playing at Under-16 level for Deeside A, the respected boys' team which fed into the Banks o' Dee junior set-up, he was spotted by Dundee and signed for the Dens Park club in 1980.

He was joining a club on the up, with the Dark Blues winning promotion from the First Division to the top flight in 1980–81 when they finished runners-up to Hibs. The Tayside outfit, with McKimmie establishing himself as one of the country's most promising young defenders, and Don Mackay at the helm as manager, consolidated their place in the Premier Division upon their return to that level and then in the 1982–83 campaign began to knock on the door of the top half of the table as the renaissance continued. Naturally other teams took note and the outstanding performers were cherry-picked.

McKimmie's defensive displays at full-back attracted the attention of Dons manager Alex Ferguson, who spent £90,000 to sign the 21-year-old in December 1983. The youngster had been under the impression that the scouts from Pittodrie had been watching teammates Tosh McKinlay and Iain Ferguson – but got a pleasant surprise when he was offered the move he had been hoping for since joining the Red Army on the terraces in the 1970s.

Stuart Kennedy's sickening injury during the run to Gothenburg the previous season had left Ferguson short of options and in McKimmie he was sure he had found the man to fill the considerable void created by Kennedy's absence. The youngster

Captain Stewart McKimmie celebrates League Cup success in 1995 with Roy Aitken, Duncan Shearer and Billy Dodds.

lived up to expectations and slotted into the distinguished Aberdeen team of the 1980s with ease. His club manager paid tribute to his two-footed ability, pace over the ground and slick passing as well as hailing the young defender's aerial talents. Within a year there was Scotland Under-21 recognition when he was selected by Walter Smith to join Willie Falconer, Eric Black and Bryan Gunn in the squad.

In 1985 McKimmie progressed from the young Scots to the full international squad, selected by Alex Ferguson to join the Dark Blues' pool for a friendly against East Germany at Hampden. It demonstrated Ferguson's faith in the versatile star, who was utilised in midfield as well as defence by the Dons in those early days.

It was not until 1989 that he made his first appearance for the national team, having spent four years on the fringes. The Aberdonian's debut was in a 2–0 defeat against England at Hampden, but there were far happier times ahead as he went on to win 40 caps over seven years. There was one goal during that tour of duty: the legendary screamer from distance against Argentina in 1990 to clinch a memorable 1–0 victory against the South American superstars. It was the first time the visitors had been beaten since they had lifted the World Cup four years earlier and it was a famous victory for the humble Scots, not least because it was won by a goal fit to clinch victory in any game. McKimmie was besieged by the media in the aftermath, missing out on the opportunity to swap shirts with the Argentine idols because of the clamour for interviews. It was all the sweeter for the match-winning hero as he was a late addition to the squad, filling in for the injured Richard Gough.

The Hampden showdown was a warm-up match ahead of the World Cup Finals in Italy, the tournament in which McKimmie sampled major championships for the first time. The defender was used by Andy Roxburgh in the matches against Brazil and Costa Rica and took his tournament tally to three when he appeared in the European Championship Finals of both 1992 and 1996 under Roxburgh and then Craig Brown. Kincorth Academy's most famous former pupil was living in exclusive company and did not look out of place as he became his home city's most established international performer during a successful Scotland career.

By the time he turned out at Euro '96 against England and the Netherlands, McKimmie was in the veteran bracket. The Auld Enemy showdown, in which Paul Gascoigne's stunning goal helped the hosts to a 2–0 victory, was to be his final appearance for Scotland and his Aberdeen days were also winding down.

There had been many highs as a Dons player, starting with his contribution to the European Super Cup win against Hamburg in 1983. From that point on the champagne continued to flow as the new recruit collected Championship-winners' medals in 1984 and 1985 before adding a League Cup and Scottish Cup double in the 1985–86 season. The domestic Cup double was repeated in 1989–90 before the League Cup win in 1995 against Dundee.

He had been appointed as permanent captain in 1994 as successor to Alex McLeish, having also been transformed from a full-back to sweeper during the same period. Leading the Dons was nothing knew to the confident defender, who had first deputised for McLeish and Willie Miller in the late 1980s. He had all the qualities required, with passion for the cause mated to a stubborn will to win and a refusal to hide even when the going got tough.

McKimmie, whose son Lewis has played at Highland League and junior level in the north-east to keep the family's link to the game alive, was released in March 1997 after making more than 550 appearances for Aberdeen. He went on to join Dundee United and spent a season and a half at Tannadice before calling time on his playing career as the Millennium loomed and establishing a career in the media as a newspaper columnist and radio pundit through his work with the *Evening Express* and Northsound. Having also worked as part of BBC television's team of analysts, McKimmie combined his column with the city's evening paper with a place as part of their match-day reporting team and has slotted as comfortably into that role as he did to that of player, captain and trophy winner with the Dons.

Stewart McKimmie in action.

Martin Buchan

Robert Gordon's College recently unveiled an impressive roll of honour at the school's Countesswells sports complex. The glittering list of international stars included great names from the world of rugby, swimming and a string of other disciplines, but football also featured on the proud chart of the city institutions rich heritage. Gordon's has traditionally promoted the oval ball game, but the occasional exception to the rugby-playing rule has broken through. In the 1960s John Sooberg would sneak off to play for Banks O'Dee and he was snapped up by Leicester City, going on to become a Foxes legend. In recent times Scott Morrison won Under-21 honours with Scotland while playing for Aberdeen between 2003 and 2005, but the man who stands head and shoulders above all former football playing former pupils of

Eddie Turnbull with skipper Martin Buchan.

the college is the legendary figure of Martin Buchan.

The Cummings Park School pupil's academic ability as a primary-school child earned him a place at Robert Gordon's and he quickly had to adapt to life in an environment where football was not on the sporting curriculum. The streetwise youngster soon realised he would have to buck the trend if he wanted to further his football ambitions and he body-swerved the regular rugby sessions in a bid to steer clear of injury and ensure he was fighting fit for the training sessions he had embarked upon at Aberdeen Football Club.

He first linked up with the Dons as a 12-year-old, joining manager Tommy Pearson's training sessions for budding young players on the car park opposite the Pittodrie main stand and getting a taste for life with the club he had grown up supporting. Even at that young age there was a groundswell of opinion within the club that Buchan had the ability to go all the way, with Teddy Scott among those to take the starlet under his wing.

The aspiring player's competitive instincts were honed with Banks o' Dee A, an outfit which had become a key feeder club for the city's professional side, and Buchan was snapped up formally by the Reds at the age of 15 as a youth signing.

The conscientious scholar found himself with a decision to make. He harboured ambitions of attending university, with architecture among the careers under consideration, but the offer of a full-time contract with his home-town club, at the age of 17 in 1966, was tempting. Buchan decided to take up Eddie Turnbull's offer (Turnbull had succeeded Pearson by then), but set himself a deadline. Had he not made it big by the age of 21 he vowed to turn his back on the game at the top level and begin his university studies. In the end the textbooks remained firmly locked away as Buchan went on to take the football world by storm, going on to captain his club and country as well as earning a big-money move to the English game with Manchester United.

Buchan was still just 17 when he made his debut for the Dons in a 1–1 draw against Dunfermline at East End Park. He emerged as one of Turnbull's key allies, an intelligent central-defender who could read the game well. Having captained the Scotland Under-23 team early in 1970, he enjoyed rapid promotion at Pittodrie and was appointed skipper of the Dons in February that year.

His first game in the role was far from a roaring success, with the team jeered from the pitch after struggling to overcome Clydebank 2–1 in a Scottish Cup tie. Jeers soon turned to cheers as, with the inspirational Buchan at its heart, the side stormed through to the Final of the competition and upset the apple cart by beating hot

Dons skipper Martin Buchan holds aloft the Drybrough Cup at Pittodrie in 1971.

favourites Celtic in the Hampden showdown of 1970. The Hoops, in the midst of their nine-in-a-row domination, were runaway favourites for the prize, but Jock Stein's side had not bargained on a Dons squad who were finely tuned by Turnbull and a match for any side on their day.

Buchan got his hands on the cherished old trophy and brought it back to the north-east for the first time since 1947 to ensure a place was etched in Aberdeen folklore. His place in the Granite City's sporting annals was guaranteed just weeks later when he became the first of its sporting sons to be named Scotland's Player of the Year by the Scottish Football Writers' Association. He also became the youngest winner of the prize and it appeared Buchan had the world at his feet.

In October 1971 he won the first of 34 Scotland caps in a 2–1 win against Portugal at Hampden, handed his big break by Tommy Docherty as a late substitute in the European Championship qualifier. A month later he made his first start in Dark Blue, fittingly celebrating the occasion at Pittodrie as Docherty and the Tartan Army headed north for the visit of Belgium. Buchan's big night ended with a 1–0 win.

Not surprisingly, an orderly queue of big clubs was beginning to form as they prepared to talk terms with the Aberdeen board. Buchan led his club side on a title challenge in the 1970–71 season, running eventual champions Celtic close, but after that disappointment decided it was time to find out whether the grass was greener on the south side of the border.

Martin Buchan in action for Aberdeen.

It took until 1972 for Buchan to get his wish, with Manchester United's club record £125,000 offer accepted by new manager Jimmy Bonthrone and his directors. Leeds United and Liverpool had also made moves to land the classy stopper, but he had his heart set on Old Trafford.

Red Devils manager Frank O'Farrell tripled Buchan's wages – but the move was about more than money for the Aberdonian. He set out on the road south intent on challenging himself against the best in the game, although the journey was not without turbulence.

Soon after moving to Manchester his new club dispensed with O'Farrell and introduced Tommy Docherty as manager. Buchan suffered the pain of relegation and the joy of promotion, going on to captain United. He won a place in the hearts of the club's loyal support when he led them to the FA Cup in 1977 with a 2–1 victory over fierce rivals Liverpool. Lifting the trophy at Wembley in front of more than 100,000 supporters was a sweet moment for the skilful and composed Scot, who had taken over from his hero Bobby Charlton as skipper of the team.

By the time he lifted the cup in England, Buchan was already an experienced World Cup campaigner. He is one of the elite club of stars in Dark Blue to have competed in two Finals, turning out in Germany in 1974 and in Argentina in 1978. The two tournaments saw the national team suffer contrasting fortunes, but Buchan emerged from both with credit. It is his part in the 1974 campaign, as part of the most successful Scotland team ever to play on the biggest stage of all, that shines most brightly on his CV.

Buchan was one of the gallant team members who guided Willie Ormond's side to an unbeaten run in the pool phase, only to miss out agonisingly on a place in the knock-out stage of the competition. No Scottish team since then has emerged unbeaten from the Finals and Buchan had a major part to play as he lined up alongside legends including Billy Bremner, Kenny Dalglish and Joe Jordan in the supremely gifted international side.

Buchan sat out the 2–0 win against Zaire in the opening fixture, but was brought in for the second match of the group as Ormond pitted his wits against the mighty Brazil. The Manchester United player did not disappoint, shutting out the South Americans in a 0–0 draw and keeping his place for the final pool game against Yugoslavia. The 1–1 draw against the Europeans was creditable, but not enough to keep the plucky Scots in the World Cup.

Ormond's team was characterised by its solidity and dependable nature. The Ally MacLeod side that Buchan found himself in for the World Cup Finals four years later was far less predictable and even the steadying influence of their Aberdonian defensive stalwart was not enough to prevent the hopes of a nation unravelling in spectacular fashion, with the now infamous defeat against Peru and draw against Iran not countered by the morale-boosting 3–2 victory against the Netherlands. It was too little too late.

Buchan, who had the honour of captaining his country in 1–1 draws against Romania in 1975 and Austria in 1977, played three more games for Scotland after the disappointment in Argentina but, with his 30th birthday looming, his career at that level was drawing to a close.

With United he played on until 1983, when he joined Oldham Athletic. He also sampled management with Burnley before embarking on a career in the sportswear industry with Puma before accepting an invitation to join the staff of the Professional Footballers' Association in Manchester. Buchan's connection with his home town was revived in the 1990s when his son Jamie starred as a youngster for the Dons, the first stop on a career which took him to Dundee United and Partick Thistle before returning to the north-east with Peterhead, Montrose and Cove Rangers.

David Smith

Martin Buchan was the first Aberdonian to be crowned as the nation's player of the year by the Scottish Football Writers' Association when he took to the stage to collect the coveted award in 1971. Twelve months later it was the turn of David Smith to take possession of the prize from the country's sports journalists and add his name to a who's who of the national game. Smith became the second player from the Granite City to be recognised in as many years. More significantly he remains, to date, the last from his home town to scale those heights.

More than 35 years have passed since the former Hilton Academy pupil was presented with the award

Dave Smith in Aberdeen colours in 1966.

by Labour's Harold Wilson at a glittering ceremony in Glasgow, yet his achievement has not been repeated by the generations who have followed him on the path from north-east youth football to fame on the international stage. The drought since Smith's success in 1972 serves to put his achievement, and that of his one-time Aberdeen teammate Buchan, into perspective and highlights the quality the city was producing during that era.

The Football Writers' Award was inaugurated in 1965 and has been voted on annually by the Scottish members of the association ever since, with more than 100 journalists on the list at any given time. Billy McNeill of Celtic was the first name on the roll of honour and luminaries added since then include Rangers legend John Greig, Hibs star Pat Stanton, Gordon Strachan of the Dons, Paul Sturrock during Dundee United's glory days and more recently Brian Laudrup, Henrik Larsson and Paul Lambert.

Pittodrie players to have been honoured since Buchan's win in 1971 and Strachan's in 1980 are Willie Miller in 1984 and defensive partner Alex McLeish five years later, but Smith was not on the Dons' books when he was rewarded for his starring role in the Scottish top flight. By 1972 he was a Rangers player, having learnt his trade with Aberdeen before moving to Ibrox.

Smith came from excellent football stock. Elder brother Hugh entered the senior game with Forfar before going on to represent Morton while Doug, the middle of what would become a trio of professional players in the Smith household, made his name with Dundee United. David, the baby of the family, followed tradition by excelling with a ball at his feet and progressed through school and juvenile football to join Aberdeen Lads' Club in the junior game. With Denis Law among the Lads' Club former players, he was in an excellent environment to learn the game.

The club, which did not restrict itself solely to football, was founded in 1924. Its proud aim was to promote the moral, social and physical wellbeing of youngsters across the city. The set-up, with a base at the Gallowgate in those early years, was a social hub as much as a sporting base and fostered a spirit which translated to success in various pursuits for A.L.C. Smith represented the club as a talented young table-tennis player as well as a footballer.

Aberdeen recruited the 17-year-old in 1961 and within a year he was in the top team, making his first appearance in January 1962 in a 1–1 draw at Pittodrie against St Johnstone as a left-half, deputising for stalwart Doug Fraser. By the start of the

Dave Smith accepts the Scottish Football Writers' Association Player of the Year Trophy from Labour's Harold Wilson in 1972.

1962–63 season he had been promoted to the starting 11 on a permanent basis and for the next four years was a fixture in the side under Tommy Pearson and Eddie Turnbull.

He entered a side struggling in the bottom half of the First Division table and desperately trying to rediscover the form which had made the Dons champions less than a decade earlier. The introduction of youngsters such as Smith, Charlie Cooke and Martin Buchan offered encouragement that success could return to the Pittodrie menu, but it took time to build for the future.

In four seasons as part of the first team, team honours eluded Smith and his teammates. Instead he had to be content with personal achievements, which included Scotland Under-23 caps and, in May 1966, a call-up to the full international side.

Smith was named by manager John Prentice in the team to face the Netherlands at Hampden in a challenge match, becoming the first Dons star to pull on the Dark Blue jersey since George Mulhall a full six and a half years earlier.

The fresh-faced Aberdonian was just 22 years old and was joining a Scotland side packed with household names. John Greig captained the team, Pat Stanton was at its heart and Willie Henderson and Willie Johnston provided attacking impetus. Smith slotted in without a hitch and his promotion to the Scotland team only added to the interest which was growing from elsewhere.

Everton expressed an interest as big teams began to close in, but it was Rangers who led the way. An offer in the region of £40,000 was lodged in the summer of 1966, and when the player made it clear he saw his future at Ibrox there was no option but for the Pittodrie board to cash in their chips and sell another of their assets. The cash injection was welcome for the Dons, even if the loss of one of their shining stars was not.

Smith was recruited by Gers manager Scot Symon and headed south in search of success at home and abroad. At the end of his first season he came within an ace of succeeding – appearing for the Light Blues in the 1966–67 European Cup-Winners' Cup Final against Bayern Munich, when the Germans took advantage of the Nuremburg venue to win a fiercely contested match 1–0.

It took five years, but the Aberdonian did eventually lay the ghost to rest. In 1972 Smith was part of the legendary Rangers team which defeated Moscow Dynamo 3–2 in the European Cup-Winners' Cup Final in Barcelona to claim the club's first, and so far only, continental prize. It was his

Dave Smith runs out for Rangers in 1973.

performance in the Final of the competition and in the ties leading to Spain, including his captain's role in the semi-final triumph against Bayern Munich, which persuaded the Scottish Football Writers' Association to crown the classy sweeper as their Player of the Year that season.

Smith clocked up more than 300 appearances for Rangers over the course of eight years on the staff, leaving in 1974 to accept a role as player-coach with Arbroath as the Angus club battled to retain top-flight status. He went on to sample football overseas with the Arcadia Shepherds and South Africa and in the glamorous North American Soccer League with the Los Angeles Aztecs in the 1970s, playing alongside George Best in the Aztecs side during the boom period for soccer in the United States.

Former Rangers teammate Alex Ferguson attempted to take Smith back to Scotland with St Mirren and there was interest from fledgling French side Paris Saint Germain – but it was the lure of management with Berwick Rangers which took him back across the Atlantic to stay. He took charge of the struggling Borderers in 1976 and by 1979 had transformed their fortunes, leading them to the Second Division Championship in style. It was the first time the Wee Rangers had won a title since joining the Scottish League set-up in the 1950s, and Smith's part was as a player as well as manager, earning him the division's Player of the Year award and, many years later, remembered fondly when the Berwick supporters recognised him as the club's Player of the Millennium.

Smith remained in charge of Berwick for four years and, after brief spells with Meadowbank and Hamilton, was tempted back to the north-east by Huntly, who installed him as player-manager. He also managed in the Highland League with Peterhead and coached in the juvenile leagues with Banchory St Ternan.

Smith, who retired from his role as a pub owner in 2008, was one of a number of veteran Scotland players to be awarded their international caps retrospectively after a campaign by the son of former winger Stewart Imlach succeeded in 2006. Smith's appearance during his Aberdeen days was matched by one while with Rangers, again facing the Netherlands when he played his second game in 1968. That match ended in a 0–0 draw.

Smith suffered a broken leg on two occasions while with Rangers, hindering his international prospects, but he battled back on each occasion and played on into his 40s when he returned to action with Aberdeen Lads' Club in the 1980s to end his career where it had started: on the parks of his home city.

Ron Yeats

When Ron Yeats finally called time on his decade of distinguished service to the Liverpool team of the 1960s he was paid a glowing tribute by the late, great Bill Shankly. The Anfield manager said: 'No player in the history of the Liverpool club has given greater service. Ron has been the cornerstone of our team. In fact, he proved the very foundation for our tremendous success and I cannot pay him too great a tribute.'

That brief but fulsome endorsement from Shankly, one of the most respected judges of a football player the game has ever known, says more about the Aberdonian defender than a million words from a mere mortal could. To have made an impression such as that on Shankly marks Yeats out as a very special talent.

Yet the stopper very nearly never made it as a footballer at all. He was a standout player at Hilton Academy on the north side of his home town and a major influence on his Aberdeen Lads' Club Thistle juvenile team, winning Scotland honours at schoolboy level. As a teenager he was quickly promoted to the Lads' Club junior team, combining his football with his work as a slaughterman in Aberdeen. A string of senior clubs began to show interest but, when trials with Forfar, Falkirk and Bury failed to earn him his big break, it looked as though the obvious potential of the imposing defender would go unfulfilled.

Just when it looked as though the chances of playing senior football were fading, Dundee United pitched up in the Granite City with an offer he simply could not refuse. It was time for Yeats to step up to the Scottish Football League and set about proving himself on the national stage. Yeats signed in December 1957 and joined as a part-time player, still plying his trade in the abattoir and often finishing a gruelling shift at work at 3am on the morning of a big match.

United at that time were a team building for the future, playing in the Second Division alongside the likes of local rivals Montrose, Forfar and Brechin. They were still in the shadow of city rivals Dundee. That was all about to change, as in 1960, with Yeats installed as their inspirational captain, the Taysiders won promotion to the top flight as runners-up to Second Division champions St Johnstone, and the following season they finished just inside the top half of the First Division to confirm their arrival at the Scottish game's top table.

During his time at Tannadice Yeats was called-up for National Service, and it turned out to be a turning point in his life and his career. Yeats, who had made his mark as a left-half as a youngster, established himself as the first choice centre-half for the British Army team and that brought him wider recognition.

Middlesbrough and Manchester United both expressed an interest in a player who had propelled himself to the fringes of the Scotland international team, but it was Liverpool who came up with a £30,000 offer in July 1961 to secure the deal. It was a hefty fee, but turned out to be worth every single penny.

In a nod towards the high standards in his native city, Yeats was replaced in the Dundee United side by another Aberdonian and yet another product of the Aberdeen Lads' Club. Doug Smith, brother of future Aberdeen and Rangers star David Smith, had been on the books at Tannadice at the same time as his friend, having signed in 1959, but it was the switch to Liverpool which opened the door for Smith to establish himself. He did it in style, going on to captain his team with distinction and playing in the first team through until his retirement in 1976 before rejoining as a director and eventually succeeding Jim McLean as chairman. He also rose to become a high-ranking official with the Scottish Football Association. Smith, now retired and still living in Dundee, was regarded as one of the Scottish game's gentlemen, never booked in almost two decades of action as a central-defender at the top level, as well as being one of the best uncapped players ever to grace the game.

Ron Yeats in action for Liverpool.

Smith had big boots to fill as he slotted into the spot vacated by his Liverpool-bound colleague. Bill Shankly was less than two years into his Reds revolution when he recruited Yeats, a powerful 6ft 2in pivot who at more than 14 stone had a lean and mean physique which made him stand out from the crowd. He joined a Liverpool side that was bidding to escape the Second Division, having narrowly missed out on promotion in the 1960–61 campaign when Ipswich and Sheffield United pipped them to the post.

Within months of settling on Merseyside, Yeats was honoured with the captaincy by Shankly. With their new Scottish skipper at the helm, the Anfield side powered their way to the Second Division Championship in 1961–62 with an eight-point margin over second-placed Leyton Orient.

It was the start of a love affair between Yeats, the club and its devoted followers. He was instrumental in wakening the sleeping giant from its slumber and in April 1964 the operation was complete when the defender got his hands on the First Division trophy. The dream had come true. Liverpool were where Shankly always believed they belonged, at the very peak of the English game.

Yeats was 26 and coming into his prime, as recognised by Scotland manager Ian McColl as he handed the Anglo his international debut just six months after his title triumph south of the border. He was called into the team to face Wales in Cardiff and handed the number-five shirt – slotting in between John Greig and Jim Baxter on the team sheet.

The boy from the Silver City had certainly arrived in exalted company, but there was a certain home comfort in the team for the British International Championship

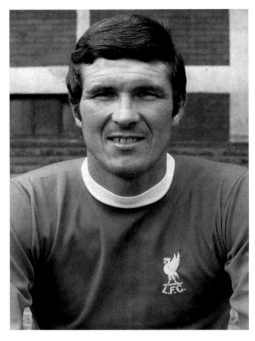

Ron Yeats in Liverpool colours.

tie against the Welsh. Captain of the Dark Blues that day was Denis Law, a fellow Aberdeen Lads' Club former player to keep Yeats company in the Scotland camp. The match ended in a 3–2 defeat and turned out to be one of two caps won by the Aberdonian, with the second coming against Italy in a World Cup qualifier in Naples in 1965 under Jock Stein. That match ended 3–0 in favour of the home side.

The challenges at international level were not matched in the club game as Yeats and his Liverpool teammates continued to establish themselves as a dominant force throughout the 1960s. In May 1965, a year after getting his hands on the League prize, Yeats climbed the steps at Wembley to hold aloft the FA Cup after a thrilling 2–1 extra-time win over Billy Bremner's Leeds United outfit.

The following season it was Liverpool's name etched on the First Division trophy once again as the honours piled up for the club and its increasingly popular captain. He grew in confidence and stature through his exploits with the hugely successful Shankly side. The 1965–66 season also brought Yeats close to the continental prize he craved, with his team beaten finalists in the European Cup-Winners' Cup Final at Hampden Park as Borussia Dortmund carved out a 2–1 victory to lift the trophy.

All good things must come to an end, however, and in December 1971, just a month after his 34th birthday, the Anfield years came to a close. Tranmere Rovers seized upon the opportunity to add Yeats to their staff as a player, captain and assistant to manager. His steadying influence helped Rovers stay in the Third Division and by the start of the 1972–73 season Yeats had been appointed manager of the club. He opted to continue playing for one more campaign and helped guide the side to mid-table respectability, consolidating their place in the division the following campaign. Relegation in the 1974–75 season brought his tenure to an end, although Yeats did leave the legacy of several emerging young players and a £74,000 kitty formed from his success in selling on some of the gems he had unearthed during three years in charge.

Yeats, who had a brief spell in charge of Barrow and also operated a haulage business in the north-west of England, sampled football in the United States with Los Angeles Skyhawks and Santa Barbara Condors in the second half of the decade. He captained the LA side to the American Soccer League Championship in 1976, a competition which fed into the main North American Soccer League and attracted good crowds. Yeats and his side played in front of 9,000 spectators when they clinched the title.

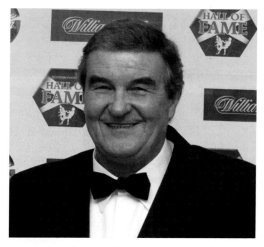

Ron Yeats as he looks now.

When Yeats returned to home soil he found his reputation for spotting talent had not gone unnoticed. In 1986 he was brought back to Anfield as Liverpool's chief scout, serving 20 years in that post until his retirement in 2006. He is still on Merseyside and in 2009 was among the first intake of residents to be named official Honorary Scousers by the city's Lord Mayor in a ceremony which also featured fellow former footballer Jan Molby. Revered and remembered in Liverpool as a true great, Yeats has also won a firm place on the Granite City's roll of honour with a truly momentous career at the very highest level.

Graham Leggat

Legendary winger Graham Leggat may live more than 3,000 miles from his home city, but the Scottish exile will always be remembered as one of Aberdeen's most cherished sporting sons. Leggat was one of the first Dons superstars, as the game evolved in the 1950s and 60s and its players savoured new levels of fame and adulation.

Leggat had all the attributes of a pin-up, with a suave sophistication to go with his silky skills. While the attention heaped upon the rising star added its own pressure, the wide man continued to produce scintillating performances week in and week out to go down in history as one of the greatest ever to pull on the famous red shirt.

Leggat emigrated to Canada in 1971 and has remained in North America ever since, but he will never forget his roots. As part of the squad of 1954–55, the year in which Aberdeen Football Club was crowned as the champion of Scottish football for the first time in more than half a century of competitive football, he is assured of immortality. He played 151 games and scored 92 goals while on the Pittodrie books, an impressive return for a winger, but his greatest contribution was sheer entertainment. From the day he made his debut as a 19-year-old in 1953, turning out against Stirling Albion, he proved to be a crowd pleaser.

He was part of the Banks o' Dee youth stable during a period in which the junior side fostered a succession of prospective Aberdeen players. He was slightly built and did not appear well suited to the hurly-burly of the Scottish game, but he proved that brain rather than brawn was the most important ingredient. He read the game like an open book, ghosting into optimum positions, and had a sweet striking technique which led to his potency in front of goal and ability to supply killer crosses.

Graham Leggat scores for the Dons against Airdrie in 1956.

Born in 1934, Leggat began his football education while on the roll at Woodside school. He continued to progress during his secondary days at Central School as he helped his classmates to the Aberdeen Secondary Schools' Shield. The development gathered pace when he began representing Torry former pupils in the city's burgeoning post-war juvenile leagues, gracing public parks with the same natural ability he displayed as a professional and impressing Scotland Youth selectors enough to gain a cap at that level.

In 1951 Leggat, who was also a talented golfer with a single-figure handicap during his days as a professional footballer, was signed on full-time forms by Aberdeen after completing his apprenticeship with Banks o' Dee, and it took just two years for him to push through the Pittodrie ranks and into the first team. The promising young player soon became a fully-fledged star.

After jumping to the head of the queue he never looked back, becoming a mainstay for manager Dave Halliday while still a teenager. Halliday had a reputation for spotting and rearing youth players and his golden touch remained strong when it came to Leggat.

The rookie scored his first Dons hat-trick during his maiden campaign, going on to bag another four sparkling trebles in the space of just five years. The goalscoring feats did not stop at three though, with a five-goal blast against Airdrie in 1957 proving his best-ever haul.

One of his most important strikes came in the 1955–56 League Cup Final at Hampden, when Leggat chipped in with the winner in the 2–1 victory against St Mirren to claim a winners' medal to sit alongside his League badge from the previous season. It appeared that the bigger the stage, the more the Aberdonian flanker relished the occasion.

After winning Scotland Under-23 honours during his formative years with the Dons, Leggat was capped for the first time by the full national team in 1956. Again he rose to the challenge, marking the occasion with a goal in a 1–1 draw against England at Hampden. More than 132,000 fans were crammed into the Glasgow ground to watch the spectacle, but the new boy was not fazed in the slightest and when he exchanged passes with John Hewie, on the hour mark, before deftly lofting a shot over England goalkeeper Reg Matthews, it looked as though the Tartan Army would go home celebrating the birth of a new match-winning hero. Instead the Auld Enemy hit back with a heartbreaking last-minute equaliser courtesy of Johnny Hayes, a man who would become Leggat's close friend in later years.

Leggat appeared a further 17 times in Dark Blue with another seven goals being chalked against his name. His career with his country took in the 1958 World Cup Finals in Sweden, as Leggat flew the flag for Aberdeen on the biggest stage of all. He was part of the team skippered by goalkeeper Tommy Younger when the tournament opened in Vasteras against Yugoslavia, with Jimmy Murray's equaliser giving the Scots a 1–1 draw to set the ball rolling.

He retained his place for the following game, but the match did not go to plan as Paraguay ran out 3–2 winners to dampen the hopes of progress. A 2–1 defeat against France in the final group game, by which time Leggat had dropped out of the starting 11, ensured the dream was over.

The winger from the Granite City continued to play for the national team for a further two years, having moved south of the border in 1958 when he switched from Aberdeen to Fulham. He had submitted a transfer request in April that year and, despite competition from Luton, it was the Londoners who won the day with a £16,000 offer. He helped the Craven Cottage side to promotion to the top flight, introducing himself to a new football public with a goal in each of his first seven games, and was a revelation as he paired up with England skipper Johnny Hayes.

During his time in the capital city he claimed an impressive record as he notched the fastest hat-trick in English League history, grabbing three in the opening three minutes of a 10–1 triumph against Ipswich Town on Boxing Day in 1963. His total haul in that game was four goals. With 134 goals in 277 games, he proved to be a

Graham Leggat fires in a shot against Queen's Park in 1956.

valuable attacking weapon – but it was his wizardry on the right flank which made him stand out from the crowd.

For eight years with Fulham he was a big favourite with the Cottagers fans, but all good things come to an end. In 1966 Leggat moved on to Birmingham in the Second Division and after two years with the Midlands side he joined Rotherham for a season. In 1969 he retired from playing and combined a coaching role at Aston Villa with a salesman's job. It looked as though his football career was drawing to a natural conclusion, but a new lease of life was soon to have Leggat back on the familiar right-wing beat.

In 1971 he was appointed player-coach by the Toronto Metros in the thriving North American Soccer League. The US competition had been established in 1968 and ran on until 1984, attracting a string of star names including Pelé and Franz Beckenbauer. Leggat was one of the early pioneers, leading his Metros side in a mini-division featuring Canadian rivals Montreal Olympique as well as American opponents New York Cosmos and Rochester Lancers.

The man who grew up on the earthy junior grounds of Aberdeen found himself catapulted into the surroundings of the compact Varsity Stadium, a ground which would play its part in the 1976 Olympics. The Metros were new to the glamorous NASL set-up when Leggat was lured across the Atlantic and he played his part in establishing them in the all-star surroundings, with his Toronto side finishing third in the northern territory section in their debut season.

Leggat spent a single year with the Metros, but can lay claim to playing his part in the city's football development, building a team from scratch by combing the English reserve leagues for young talent. His team merged with Toronto Croatia in 1975 and four years later became Toronto Blizzard, one of the best-known names in the American game.

After briefly gracing America's fields, he leapt to the other side of the fence by becoming a sports broadcaster. He covered the Olympics and World Cup for CBC before being snapped up by the Sports Network to head up their football coverage. Leggat, with his expertise and natural ability in front of the camera and microphone, became a star all over again in his new profession and did not retire until after he had played a starring role in the coverage of the Euro 2000 tournament. Inducted to Canada's soccer hall of fame in 2001, Leggat remains an enthusiastic follower of the beautiful game and a distant follower of his home-town team's fortunes.

David Robertson

Flying full-back David Robertson has gone down in history as the most successful Aberdonian ever to play in the Scottish domestic league. He won six League Championship medals as part of the Rangers nine-in-a-row squad during the 1990s and a string of cup successes to ensure he left the country with a bulging case of medals when he emigrated to the United States to pursue a career in coaching in 2007.

Born in October 1968, he first signed for Aberdeen as a 13-year-old and won the Scottish Youth Cup twice with the club. He had initially been recruited as a left-winger, a position he played to perfection with Harlaw Academy and Deeside Boys Club. It was while with Aberdeen during a pre-season tournament in Keith that the transformation from attacker to defender began. As part of a squad of youngsters being mentored by reserve coaches Teddy Scott and John McMaster, injury problems forced the duo

David Robertson in action.

to turn to Robertson to fill a void on the left side of their defence. Already powerfully built and with incredible speed over the ground, he had the natural attributes required for a modern full-back but he did not take to the position immediately.

Robertson reverted to playing on the wing for his school and juvenile side and was capped at Under-16 level by Scotland as a flanker. Over time he was moulded by Scott and the Dons coaching team to become a consummate defender. He was blooded by the Dons at first-team level in August 1986 in a 2–0 home victory against Hamilton. His pace, tenacity and capable left foot ensured he had a long-term future in the side and soon he had pinned down the number-three jersey as his own.

Robertson spent five years on the books at Pittodrie as a first-team player, making 176 appearances for his home-town club and chipping in with three goals. The left-back position has always been a difficult one to fill and in the mid-1980s, as the overlapping full-back became more commonplace and the physical demands placed on the man in that berth increased as the attacking part of the job became more prominent, it became an even harder task to find the ideal candidate. Robertson solved the headache for the Dons and patrolled the beat for five years. Since then the Pittodrie club has tried many options to find a replacement but, more than two decades on, the search for a player of the same high calibre as the Aberdonian continues.

Having been signed from Deeside by Alex Ferguson, Robertson was fast-tracked into the first team by the legendary Dons boss. Ferguson soon departed for Manchester United, but it did not halt Robertson's progress and he continued to develop under Ian Porterfield and Alex Smith. That brought him a Scotland B cap at the age of just 18, as well as Under-21 honours in Dark Blue, bringing him to the attention of Britain's biggest clubs.

After winning a League Cup and Scottish Cup double in the 1989–90 season, when Rangers and Celtic were defeated in the respective Finals, he went on to play a key role in the dramatic challenge for the 1990–91 League title. The Dons lost out to Rangers in that famous race, prompting their young left-back to look to Glasgow for the Championship medal he craved. In the summer of 1991 he left the club he had supported as a schoolboy and accepted the invitation to join Rangers in a £950,000 deal.

David Robertson shows the Dons fans the Cup after their Scottish Cup victory in 1990.

David Robertson in action for Rangers.

He was still only 22 and found himself in an unfamiliar city, at an unfamiliar club and in a dressing room full of big personalities. None of that altered Robertson's approach to the game and his exemplary attitude ensured he became a stalwart of the nine-in-a-row team. With Rangers he won six consecutive League Championships, the Scottish Cup three times and collected a League Cup-winners' medal on three occasions.

The team assembled by Walter Smith, on the foundations built by Graeme Souness, was the most successful domestic side ever to call Ibrox home. When Robertson was recruited a hat-trick of titles had been bagged, but the long haul of nine in a row was still stretching out ahead of the Light Blues. The left-back helped them pip Hearts to the League in his first campaign, then Aberdeen in the next two before Motherwell and then, in the final two years of the run, Celtic were consigned to the runners'-up spot. Chairman David Murray spent big to guarantee success, with Paul Gascoigne and Brian Laudrup among the multi-million pound men, but there was always a place for Robertson in the cosmopolitan line up.

Like so many before and since, Robertson found his international chances enhanced when he moved onto the big platform provided by Old Firm football. Within a year of his change into Light Blue at club level he had won a Dark Blue shirt as a full international player. Scotland coach Andy Roxburgh threw him the number-three jersey for a friendly against Northern Ireland at Hampden early in 1992, playing on the opposite side of the back four from former Pittodrie teammate Stewart McKimmie. An Ally McCoist goal gave the hosts a 1–0 victory.

Robertson's competitive debut did not come for another 18 months, with an appearance in the World Cup qualifier against Switzerland at Pittodrie, with fellow home-town boy McKimmie again alongside him on the team sheet. The duo helped

Roxburgh's side to a 1–1 draw, with John Collins on target, but ultimately the bid for qualification for the Finals in America failed.

Craig Brown was promoted by the SFA to rebuild the national squad and Robertson did not feature in his plans. Brown capped the left-back once, in a 1–0 defeat against the Netherlands at Hampden in the spring of 1994, but favoured a succession of full-backs in the years which followed. The dependable Celtic skipper Tom Boyd was Brown's first choice, with Rob McKinnon and Tosh McKinlay brought in as deputies to leave Robertson well down the pecking order. The Scotland situation was the only frustration for Robertson in a gilt-edged career.

Robertson decided to head for new pastures in 1997, lured to the high-profile English top flight by Leeds United. He was 28 and viewed as a key player by Elland Road manager George Graham, who had clinched a bargain £500,000 transfer for the speedy defender. The all-conquering Gers team he had been part of was beginning to disband as the Dick Advocaat era loomed in Glasgow, and there were options for the Aberdonian to consider as he weighed up his next move. After consistently playing in the Champions League he had won admirers on the Continent, with Torino and Valencia among the clubs expressing an interest, but England was the destination of choice. Leeds had finished just a point outside of the top half of the table and had ambitions of regaining a foothold in the upper tier, but Robertson's part in that effort proved small. A cruciate ligament injury put paid to his hopes of continuing his rich run of form after moving to England and after just 31 appearances for the Yorkshire side he retired from the game in 2000.

The man from the Granite City began to concentrate on life outside of the game which had been his career since he signed for Aberdeen as a schoolboy. He established a computer business in England but soon the lure of home became too strong to resist and he returned to Aberdeenshire with his family, settling near Drumoak.

In 2002 he was tempted back to football when Montrose manager John Sheran invited the experienced former international to assist as part of his coaching staff at the Third Division club. It put a new spring in Robertson's step and he decided he was fit enough to make a playing comeback with the Angus side, slotting into the team as though he had never been away from the game. It was a temporary return to duties on the field, however, as in 2003 he was appointed manager of Elgin City and retired from playing once and for all to concentrate on that role.

David Robertson's career took him from Aberdeen to Glasgow and Leeds, and now to the US.

He teamed up with respected Aberdeen-based youth coach Kenny Black at the Moray side. Black, who had worked with north-east youngsters on behalf of Dundee United and Celtic in the past, was enlisted to assist Robertson as he attempted to rebuild struggling Elgin. Eventually Black, a successful businessman with interests in the decorating and pre-school childcare sectors, mounted a bid to buy City. His ambitious plans failed and it led to the pair being edged out of Borough Briggs.

Black turned his attention to Montrose and became owner of the Links Park side in 2006. He inherited Eddie Wolecki as manager, but as the side struggled he appointed Robertson as joint boss, before eventually the former Dons man took charge in his own right.

After parting company with the Links Park side in 2007 following a poor run of form, Robertson opted for a change in direction. Having rejected the opportunity to move abroad during his playing days, the former defender joined American youth development club Sereno in a coaching role. In 2009 he was promoted to the position of director of Sereno's boys division, having impressed with his knowledge and enthusiasm after his move to the States.

Eoin Jess

In 2009 the emergence of the talented young crop of Aberdeen starlets led by Fraser Fyvie, Peter Pawlett and Michael Paton sparked heated debate among Dons supporters. Were the new kids on the block the best to roll off the Pittodrie conveyor belt in modern times, or were they simply pretenders to a throne still occupied by a king from a previous coronation? The arguments raged to and fro, but time after time the discussion swung back to one man: Eoin Jess. The former Scotland star remains, in the opinion of the vast majority of fans in his native city, the finest youth product of his generation.

Jess retired in 2007, but the memories linger long in the minds of those who worshipped him from the Pittodrie stands during a career which touched the 1980s, peaked in the 1990s and edged into the post-Millennium years. He was a Cup-winner with the Dons and also an integral member of Scotland's squad for the bulk of his career, winning 18 caps along the way, to ensure his place among the legends of the Granite City.

What sets Jess apart is that he is a country boy at heart. Although born in Aberdeen, he grew up in the fishing village of Portsoy. Being removed from the thriving inner-city football scene did not hamper the silky skilled

Eoin Jess, pictured in 2001, became an Aberdeen icon.

Eoin Jess strikes for the Dons, with Celtic 'keeper Pat Bonner helpless, in 1991.

youngster's progress. He did not hail from a football family, but developed a passion for the sport as a player with his primary school and then Banff Academy, helping his secondary side to win the North of Scotland Cup at Under-13 level.

With no juvenile club or League in the Banffshire area at that time, Jess entered the man's world of the Buckie and District Welfare League with Portsoy FC in his early teens. Despite his youth, he learned to live with the rough-and-tumble approach of his older and bigger opponents. Rangers picked up on the teenager's talent and hosted Jess at a series of training sessions slotted around his school commitments. A registration mix-up when Jess turned 17 delayed the attempt to sign him to the Ibrox squad and the episode frustrated the north-east hopeful, leading him to eventually reject the offer to move to Glasgow.

At that point George Adams, then Aberdeen's youth supremo, stepped in and took Jess to Pittodrie on a week's trial. He shone during that time and Adams, together with wise old owl Teddy Scott, persuaded manager Ian Porterfield to add the local lad to his staff.

Jess was taken under Scott's wing in those days and was also mentored by Porterfield's assistant Jimmy Mullen, before the management duo were replaced by Alex Smith. It was Smith who gave the new recruit his big break, handing him his debut in May 1989 in a 0–0 draw against Motherwell in the League at Pittodrie. Within months the 18-year-old had become a winner, included in the Dons team to face Rangers in the 1989–90 League Cup Final. Paul Mason's double clinched a 2–1 victory after extra-time and the celebrations began for the rookie.

He was still feeling his way into the senior game at that stage, but in the 1990–91 campaign the boy from Banffshire came into his own. Along with Dutch star Hans

Gillhaus he tormented Premier Division defences and finished tied on 15 goals with his strike partner at the top of the Dons scoring chart. That tally included all four goals in a 4–1 demolition of Dunfermline at East End Park and a hat-trick in a thrilling 3–2 win against Dundee United at Pittodrie.

His impressive form led to recognition from his fellow professionals, with the Scottish Professional Footballers' Association awarding him the coveted Young Player of the Year award in 1991. He collected the prize again in 1993 as his stock continued to rise.

He rose to prominence alongside fellow Aberdonian hot-shot Scott Booth. Booth, who made more than 200 appearances for the Dons, made his debut in 1990 and went on to earn 22 caps in a career which took him from Pittodrie to Borussia Dortmund, Utrecht, Twente Enschede and back to Aberdeen in 2003. The former Oldmachar Academy pupil, from the Bridge of Don, was another glowing endorsement for the club's youth system.

There were tough times for the duo though, with Jess and Booth left deflated by the sacking of manager Smith in February 1992. Jess rates the veteran coach as the man who had the biggest influence on his career and remained in regular contact with him throughout his playing days for advice and encouragement.

After the sad departure of Smith from the Granite City, the show had to go on. For Jess the year ended on a high note when he won his first international cap.

The big occasion fell at Ibrox as Scotland entertained Italy in a World Cup qualifier, and it was Andy Roxburgh who saw the potential in the 21-year-old Reds star. Jess made his debut from the bench in November 1992, replacing Gordon Durie after 71 minutes, and helped the home side hold on for a 0–0 draw against the superstars from the Continent. His first start in Dark Blue was against Malta three months later, donning the number-11 shirt for the 3–0 victory in which an Ally McCoist double and a strike from Pat Nevin clinched the win.

The bid to earn a place in the 1994 World Cup Finals in America failed, but the campaign had established Jess as a fully-fledged Scotland player. Roxburgh's successor Craig Brown continued to involve the promising youngster and he was part of the squad that won a place in the European Championship Finals in England in 1996, with Jess grabbing the first of his two Scotland goals during the qualifying campaign when he netted in a 5–0 victory against San Marino at Scotland. His other goal in the colours of his country was in 1999 at Celtic Park, when his contribution was not enough to prevent the national team slipping to a 2–1 defeat against the Czech Republic in the Euro 2000 qualifiers.

By then he had experienced the thrill of playing in a major international tournament as part of the pool for the Euro '96 adventure. Jess faced stiff competition for an attacking berth, but enjoyed a brief opportunity to sample life on the big stage when he came on as a late substitute in the 2–0 reverse against England at Wembley. He turned out at Euro '96 as a Coventry City player, having made the move from Aberdeen to the Midlands in February that year. He had begun the 1995–96 season by helping steer the Dons to the League Cup with a 2–0 victory against Dundee in the Final.

Eoin Jess celebrates scoring against Rangers in 1998.

To reach the Hampden showdown, the club had defeated Rangers 2–1 at the national stadium in the semi-final. Billy Dodds scored both goals, but it was not the most endearing moment for the travelling Red Army – that was masterminded by Jess, who teased Gers counterpart Paul Gascoigne with an impromptu keepy-up routine which had the Dons fans in raptures and the Rangers support baying for blood. It was an audacious moment in the attacker's career, typical of the creativity he was capable of when confidence was high. Jess, at home in midfield or up front, was as happy playing provider as he was tucking away the many goals he scored, and his quick thinking and subtle touches were admired by clubs across Britain.

Months after the League Cup success, Jess was on his way to the promised land of English football when the Sky Blues succeeded in a £1.75 million raid. Former Dons hero Gordon Strachan was the Highfield Road assistant manager at the time and the Scotland legend helped persuade Jess that his future lay south of the border. Manager Ron Atkinson still relied on Strachan as a player as well as a coach, pairing him with Jess in the top flight. It was the lure of working alongside the Gothenburg Great at the heart of the Coventry team that persuaded the Aberdeen star to reject advances from Newcastle and Blackburn Rovers. He spent 18 months at Highfield Road, playing 44 games, before returning to Aberdeen in July 1997 in a £650,000 move.

Roy Aitken was the manager who sold him to the English side and also the man who brought him back to his spiritual home. Jess went on to work under Alex Miller, Paul Hegarty and Ebbe Skovdahl as the once-successful Dons struggled to recapture the form they had enjoyed during his first spell in the red jersey.

He was sent out on loan to Bradford City for the second half of the 2000–01 season and in the summer of 2001 joined the club on a permanent basis when his contract with Aberdeen expired. It presented him with another crack at the English game, this time at Championship level, and he was a regular for the Bantams in his first full campaign. He joined Nottingham Forest in time for the 2002–03 season and spent three years with the club before two years with Northampton Town brought his playing career to a close. He helped Northampton to promotion from League Two under former Scotland teammate Colin Calderwood in his first season with the club.

Jess, who suffered a health scare in 2009 when he suffered a stroke and also required heart surgery, began working on his coaching qualifications after leaving Northampton and currently serves as a youth coach with Nottingham Forest.

Harry Yorston

The Yorston family has gone down in Aberdeen football folklore. In the 1920s and 1930s the name became established through Benny Yorston's amazing exploits for the Dons, and in the 1940s and 1950s it was revived in glorious fashion when Harry Yorston burst onto the big stage with the Pittodrie club. The pair were second cousins, related on the side of Harry's father. Both were extraordinary goalscorers and clearly the knack of hitting the back of the net was imbedded in the Yorston genes. Their home-town club became the major beneficiary of the family's rich talent and two generations of supporters were treated to a sharp-shooting bonanza.

Benny Yorston.

Both super strikers can boast their own particular claims to fame, but it was Harry who gained the most tangible reward for his efforts on the turf. As part of Aberdeen's historic 1954–55 Championship-winning team, the first side from the city to be crowned as Scotland's finest, he just edges the claim to Yorston family bragging rights.

Harry had first made his mark when he scored on his debut late in 1947, with his maiden goal against Third Lanark followed in the 1948–49 season by a haul of six goals in six matches. As an 18-year-old who was new to senior football, it was an introduction which suggested the new boy had a bright future ahead of him. His potential had first been spotted as a youngster growing up in Aberdeen's east end, learning his football skills on the cobbled streets around Pittodrie. He grew up on Park Road, just a hop and skip away from the city's football stadium, and played juvenile

Harry Yorston (right) is congratulated by George Hamilton during the 1953 Cup Final against Rangers.

football for St Clements in the local leagues. The Dons scouts were quick to pick up on young Yorston's natural ability.

After recruiting Yorston in 1946, as football attempted to get back to normal at the end of World War Two, the club had to be patient. The teenager had national service to complete before he could even contemplate a career as a footballer. It was during a return home on leave that he made his debut against Third Lanark at Cathkin Park, scoring after just five minutes to settle the nerves. The goal could not prevent the Reds from falling to a 3–2 defeat, but it at least gave their youngster a taste of what life would be like in the First Division.

Within a year his spell in the army had come to an end and Yorston was able to devote his full attention to establishing himself in a team that was fast developing a reputation for attacking flair and flowing passing football. He slotted into a five-man forward line as the inside-right. His opposite number, working the inside-left channel, was Bob Wishart, while Graham Leggat and Jack Hather were on either wing and centre-forward Paddy Buckley marauded through the middle. The goals came quite literally from left, right and centre as manager Dave Halliday's team set about making their mark in style.

Yorston could score goals as well as provide them and in his first full season in the starting 11, the 1949–50 campaign, he topped the club's scoring chart with an impressive finishing total of 17 goals. He was still a young man, but he was fast gaining experience and proving a handful for far more experienced opponents up and down the land.

The Aberdonian experienced the shattering disappointment of losing both the 1953 and 1954 Scottish Cup Finals – but the good times were just about to roll for the home-town boy and his colleagues. The 1954–55 season would prove to be the finest of his career and ensure his legacy amounted to far more than simply marks on the goalscoring sheet.

The historic title-winning journey began at Pittodrie on 11 September 1954 when the season opened against Stirling Albion. The Dons won 5–0 to signal their intentions for the months ahead and Yorston was the man who capped the impressive victory with the last goal of the game. Throughout the League run he scored a total of 12 goals in 28 matches as the country's biggest prize was brought back to the north-east for the first time.

Yorston was already a Scotland international when he got his hands on the League trophy, having made his debut in Dark Blue earlier in the season. The appearance came in Wales on 16 October 1954 in a national team packed with household names. Rangers captain George Young was skipper on the day, Tommy Docherty wore the number-four shirt and Aberdonian midfielder Doug Cowie was at the heart of the side. Ibrox winger Willie Waddell, a future Gers manager, was part of the attacking operation and Dons talisman Buckley spearheaded the forward line. In front of more than 60,000 fanatical fans at Ninian Park in Cardiff, it was Buckley who popped up with a diving header in the closing stages of the game to win the British International Championship tie for the Scots and give his Aberdeen teammate Yorston a winning start as an international player. Surprisingly the game turned out to be the end for Yorston at that level, with the solitary cap his only reward despite his incredible record for his club.

Yorston made 277 appearances for Aberdeen and scored 141 times to end with a ratio better than a goal in every second game. For any striker that would be an achievement to be proud of. In addition to the League-winner's medal in 1955, the forward also won a League Cup prize in the 1955–56 season when St Mirren were beaten at Hampden. He was 26 when he collected that badge and should have had his best years ahead of him. Instead the Cup triumph proved to be his last taste of success as a shock change in direction was just around the corner.

Harry Yorston (right) fires in a shot against East Fife at Pittodrie in 1951.

On 8 June 1957, the day before his 28th birthday, the prolific striker announced his decision to retire from football and take up a position as a porter at the city's fish market. He was following in his father's footsteps in a profession which offered a weekly wage marginally better than his Pittodrie pay packet provided. He had to make the move before the market's age restriction of 30 for new starts barred him from the profession for life, and he never regretted the decision.

In the end financial security came from a different and less predictable source, with the canny Aberdonian turning a 25p pools stake into a £170,000 prize in 1972. He continued to work as a driver in the city even after that win and wound his way back to Pittodrie four years later to work under Ally MacLeod on developing the club's youth system, having also scouted for Manchester United and played briefly in the Highland League with Lossiemouth after leaving the Dons.

Yorston, who died in 1992 at the age of 62, was a headline-maker throughout his life – both in and out of football. Just like the football skills that appeared hereditary, the ability to generate publicity also seemed to be a Yorston speciality. His cousin Benny blazed the trail as far as media interest was concerned. Born in Nigg in 1905, the senior member of the Yorston playing dynasty boasted a return of 125 goals in just 156 matches for the Dons. It makes him statistically the finest marksman ever to wear the shirt, earning him a single cap to match that of the family's future star Harry.

Benny, who led the scoring chart at the club in each of his four full seasons on the books, enjoyed his finest run in the 1929–30 programme, during which he banged home 38 goals in 38 League matches and a further eight in four Scottish Cup ties. It was a record-breaking haul for a single campaign and one yet to be matched.

Benny died in his adopted home city of London in 1977, taking with him the answer to the great Dons mystery of the 1930s. The striker, a product of the

Sunnybank boys club who progressed to the top flight via Mugiemoss and Richmond juniors and then Montrose, was famously one of five Pittodrie stars shown the door in the wake of match-fixing allegations. The grounds for the rumours were never made public, but the concerned management and directors chose to leave nothing to chance and took swift action to ensure the club's reputation would not be tarnished. Yorston was given the chance to bounce back when he joined Sunderland in a £2,000 deal in 1932, and he also served Middlesbrough before moving to London to develop property interests.

Both Benny and Harry left their mark on football in the Granite City, each becoming a legend in their own special way and providing hours of entertainment for the Dons faithful on either side of the war. They were two men who emerged from humble beginnings to reach the very top of their profession and proved that their local club did not need to look far to find players with the ability to put the country's best defences to the sword. Goalscoring was quite simply in their blood.

Shaun Maloney

If ever there was a case of 'the one that got away' then surely that 'one' is Shaun Maloney. Although born in Malaysia, the acclaimed Celtic attacker was raised in the leafy suburbs of Aberdeen, but was spirited away from the Granite City by the Hoops as a teenager before his home-city club could get a look in.

With the cut-throat competition for the best young players growing with every passing season, the loss of Maloney to a club from outside the area was not an isolated incident. The future Scotland star was part of a clutch of talented teenagers who were plucked from the Aberdeen and District Juvenile League on either side of the Millennium by a string of alert talent-spotters representing a variety of teams the length and breadth of the country.

One of the first notable exiles from that golden period was Gavin Rae, another Old Firm and Scotland star in the making. Rae, a pupil at Oldmachar Academy in the Bridge of Don and player for Glentanar Boys Club, was recruited by Dundee in 1996 and spent eight years at Dens Park before earning a move to Rangers. By then he had already won eight caps for his country and he went on to add to that collection while at Ibrox and then after joining Cardiff in 2007, with 14 appearances for Scotland to his credit by the end of the 2010 World Cup qualifying campaign. Rae was also called upon to captain the Light Blues during his time in Glasgow, another accolade for an accomplished midfielder.

Gavin Rae (right) celebrates with Darren Fletcher during Scotland v Lithuania at Hampden Park in 2003 (Picture by Gordon Lennox).

In the age division beneath Rae was another batch of Aberdeen's finest, featuring future national team players Russell Anderson and Barry Robson. While Anderson, who turned out for Dyce Boys Club alongside Caley Thistle stalwart-in-the-making Ross Tokely, was picked up by Aberdeen, there was no local move for Barry Robson.

Robson was arguably the pick of the Aberdonian crop during that rich harvest in the local leagues and he came back to haunt his home city's supporters when he made his debut for Celtic. He first pulled on the hoops in January 2008 and he did it at Pittodrie – scoring with his first touch for his new club as the Glasgow outfit cruised to a 5–1 victory against the Dons.

Robson, who had seven Scotland caps to his name by the end of the 2010 qualifiers, first came to the attention of senior clubs when he began to star for Colony Park Boys Club in his home town. The tall teenager had the physical presence to make an impact and, with his commanding midfield performances, was soon being courted locally and nationally. From Colony Park he went on to turn out for leading juvenile side Deeside and then moved on to Rangers as the Ibrox side stole a march on other admirers in the professional game.

Robson moved to Glasgow full-time with the Light Blues after completing his studies at Inverurie Academy and served a long apprenticeship with the Gers as he battled to make the breakthrough at a club who were spending heavily to ensure the run to nine Championships in a row continued. In the end the fiery youngster had to concede defeat and drop down to the First Division to ignite his career, being snapped up by Steve Paterson at Caley Thistle in 1997 and given his first run of first-team football.

Barry Robson (right) in action against former club Caley Thistle during his Celtic days (Picture by Gordon Lennox).

After a loan spell with Forfar to gain experience in 1999, Robson was a revelation upon his return to the far north. He repaid Paterson's faith in him with starring performances for the Caley Jags. With a cultured left foot and wicked dead-ball delivery, Robson was a valuable attacking weapon for the Inverness side and also had the close control and power to provide surging runs from deep.

After smashing through the 100 appearances mark, Robson was emerging as one of the Scottish Football League's hottest properties. When manager Paterson took charge of Aberdeen he hoped to lure Robson to Pittodrie with him, but it was Dundee United who won the race. A £50,000 transfer in the summer of 2003 finally gave Robson the top-flight stage he had targeted when he first signed for Rangers as a schoolboy, and at Tannadice he continued to build his all-round game, becoming a mainstay in the team during four and a half years on Tayside.

He was appointed captain of the Arabs during the 2006–07 season and was elevated to the fringes of the international squad when he was called-up to the Scotland B team. In 2007 he made his full debut for the national side against South Africa, rewarded for his fine club form by boss Alex McLeish. He was also used heavily by George Burley during the ill-fated World Cup qualifying campaign in 2008, by which point he had completed his £1.25 million switch to Celtic Park. Hoops manager Gordon Strachan swooped in the second half of the 2007–08 season and Robson proved valuable in the Parkhead side's march to the SPL title that campaign. He followed Strachan's path to Middlesbrough in 2010.

He and his former Aberdeen and District league opponents have continued to cross paths at regular intervals, with Maloney becoming his closest ally. Maloney, a former pupil at Cults Academy, was plucked from the Bridge of Don-based club Albion by Celtic in 1999 and made his debut for the Glasgow outfit in 2001. As a fan of the club, it was a dream move for the starry-eyed teenager.

His introduction to the SPL was far from quiet as he replaced Tommy Johnson during a 3–0 victory over Rangers at Ibrox. It was sink-or-swim time for a prime catch who had slipped through Aberdeen's net, and for those who had watched him progress through the juvenile leagues in the north-east there was no surprise when he effortlessly adapted to his new surroundings. He was walking with legends following his promotion to top-team duties, rubbing shoulders with Paul Lambert, Neil Lennon, Henrik Larsson and Lubo Moravcik. In that type of company the alert and silky-skilled young pretender to their thrones did not look out of place.

Scotland Under-21 caps soon followed and the new kid on the block went on to represent the young Scots 20 times, scoring six goals during his formative years. Maloney was a part of the Championship-winning squad in 2001–02 and the following season came on from the bench in the UEFA Cup Final against Porto, as Celtic suffered an agonising 3–2 extra-time defeat.

Another title triumph in 2003–04 helped the mercurial forward and his teammates over their anguish and the Cults former pupils won another SPL badge in 2005–06, the same season in which he made his Scotland debut in 2005 under Walter Smith. Maloney continued to be a mainstay under Alex McLeish and George Burley, with 17 caps under his belt by the end of the failed bid to qualify for the 2010 World Cup Finals.

Shaun Maloney leads a Scottish charge at Hampden in 2008 (Picture by Kenny Elrick).

The 2005–06 campaign proved to be a memorable one for many reasons as the versatile attacker, comfortable through the centre or as a winger, collected the Scottish Professional Footballers' Association Player of the Year and Young Player of the Year awards at the end of the term. He became the first player in the history of the ceremony ever to walk away with both titles, which are voted for by fellow professionals. It capped a season in which he had also scored in the 3–0 League Cup Final win against Dunfermline at Hampden to add to his growing reputation.

In January 2007 he was lured to Aston Villa by his former Parkhead mentor Martin O'Neill in a £1 million deal. He was followed just a few months later by fellow Aberdeen juvenile product Russell Anderson, who joined Sunderland for a similar fee in the summer of 2007. Both found themselves a long way from home and suffered similar disappointments as the promised land of the English glamour League failed to live up to expectations, in a football sense at least.

Anderson's career with the Black Cats was stalled by serious injury, while Maloney failed to settle in the Midlands and returned to Celtic at the start of the 2008–09 campaign, receiving a standing ovation when he made the first appearance of his second spell as a Hoops player.

The Celtic star will not celebrate his 30th birthday until January 2013, but with an impressive array of honours already accumulated he is already one of the Granite City's most successful footballers. With time on his side, Maloney looks certain to cement his place in Aberdeen's hall of fame.

RUGBY

Chris Cusiter

Every sport needs great rivalry to stir interest and in Chris Cusiter and Mike Blair the Scottish rugby public has a duel to whet the appetite. The difference with Cusiter and Blair is that they are teammates, fighting together for the Scotland cause while all the time battling for personal supremacy. Both could claim to be victims of circumstance, as world-class scrum-halves vying for a single place in the national team. Cusiter had the upper hand initially, with his sparkling displays earning Lions honours in 2005, but the Aberdonian drifted out of the team to make way for Blair during Frank Hadden's tenure as head coach.

Chris Cusiter has become Scottish rugby's leading light.

In November 2009 new chief Andy Robinson made his intentions clear when he named Cusiter and Blair as co-captains of his new-look Scotland team for the autumn internationals. The message was loud and clear – may the best man win. Robinson's inability to separate the pair is telling. Both have been deemed good enough to lead their nation, yet there is only room for one in the team. Robinson described the pair as 'two world-class players, two world-class people' when he announced his surprise decision to run with a joint captaincy.

For the opening match of the series against Fiji at Murrayfield it was Cusiter who got the nod ahead of his more established rival for the role, rewarded for his consistent start to the season at club level and his willingness to take responsibility and run with the ball even when under the most intense pressure. The pair quickly accepted the unusual decision to ask them to split responsibility, both for the scrum-half duties and the captaincy, and both pointed to their mutual respect for each other's ability as the key to the bold plan for the future. In time for the 2010 Six Nations campaign, Cusiter had won the right to lead the team.

To be appointed skipper was an honour fitting for a player of Cusiter's attitude, on and off the park. Through difficult times, when Blair had jumped to the head of the queue, he remained committed and focused on the Scotland cause. He refused to complain or panic, knuckled down and came back sharper and brighter ready to push his peer to the limit.

Having sampled life and rugby on the Continent, the Aberdeen-born star is an older and wiser player than the one who made his international breakthrough in 2004.

Then the livewire scrum-half was taking his first steps on a long path to establishing himself and now he is one of the role models in an increasingly youthful squad.

Cusiter first excelled at rugby as a pupil of Robert Gordon's College. The city-centre school continued its fine tradition of rearing top-class players when it pushed Cusiter through the youth system and he was still on the roll when he first wore Scotland colours.

In fact, it was a family affair when the Cusiters of Aberdeen became an international rugby clan in 1997. Chris and his elder brother Calum both earned their maiden Scotland call-ups on the same day, with the future international captain being named in the Scotland Schoolboys Under-15 side and Calum, a fellow pupil at Gordon's, picked for the Under-16 squad. The siblings took their inspiration from their father, Stan. He was a stand-off with Gordonians in his heyday, a talented player in his own right who won district honours with the north and midlands.

Both Cusiter brothers turned out at scrum-half and were being hotly tipped for success in the game after breezing through the international trials in Edinburgh. Cusiter had been a schoolboy football player with Mile End Primary School in Aberdeen, allied to a keen interest in tennis and golf, and did not sample competitive rugby until switching to Robert Gordon's as a 10-year-old, when he turned out against George Watson's in a P6 match. From that point on he never looked back. He went on to play at schoolboy and international level at every age from Under-15s up, playing in the Under-19 and Under-21 World Championships and the IRB World Junior Finals. In between he had turned out for the north district to further his experience of representative rugby.

The highlight of his apprenticeship with Scotland came on home territory when Scotland's Under-21 side travelled north to play Italy at Countesswells in the 2003

Chris Cusiter's name is added to the Robert Gordon's College international honours board in 2004 (Picture by Colin Rennie).

Chris Cusiter lifts the Calcutta Cup (Picture courtesy of Ian Jacobs Photography).

shadow six nations event. Cusiter stole the show in front of an appreciative Aberdeen audience, scoring a stunning solo try in a 41–11 win. His display was no flash in the pan, with the scrum-half featuring in every single one of the competition's games that season as he continued to learn the ropes against Europe's finest emerging talents. Cusiter always looked confident and comfortable in that elite company.

The path to stardom had taken him south, combining law studies at Edinburgh University with playing commitments for Watsonians and then Boroughmuir. He was part of the travelling group of fans following the Lions tour of Australia in 2001 – not even daring to dream that within years he would be on the other side of the fence, turning out in the red shirt of Britain and Ireland during the 2005 adventure Down Under.

In 2002, at the age of 20, Cusiter was called up for Scotland A honours. He made his first appearance at that level as a replacement in a victory against Romania and was soon fast-tracked through the ranks. The Aberdonian made his debut as a Dark Blue in 2004, having turned professional with the Borders Reivers the previous year, and quickly became established as the nation's hottest young rugby property.

By the age of 23 he had 15 caps in his locker and was knocking on the Lions door by the time the 2005 tour rolled round. Coach Sir Clive Woodward was swayed by Cusiter's ability to cope under pressure, a vital quality for any prospective player, and included him in his squad alongside compatriots Gordon Bulloch and Simon Taylor. The Scottish rookie did not play in the test matches against the All Blacks, but that disappointment was tempered by impressive displays in the midweek side and there was no doubt that the young Scot emerged with great credit from the tour. The experience was invaluable as the steep learning curve continued at club and international level.

In 2007 Cusiter's career reached a crossroads on two fronts, with his international journey taking him to the World Cup Finals in France and his club career following the same path when his Borders team was disbanded. The route he chose in the domestic game was a long-distance one, with Perpignan the destination. Cusiter quickly settled into French life, immersing himself in the culture of the his new home city and his adopted club, having readied himself with an Open University course in French early in his pro career.

With Scotland the autumn of 2007 saw Cusiter sample the glamour of the World Cup for the first time, entering a competition growing in profile with every passing tournament. Cusiter was a try-scorer in the quarter-final against Argentina in St Denis, but his side suffered a painful 19–13 defeat and he was left to concentrate on his new life in the country's club league.

Cusiter spent two years with Perpignan, making a big impact immediately after his move across the channel to the Catalan side, before being tempted back to Scotland by Glasgow in 2009. Having rebuffed approaches by the west coast side in favour of moving to the Continent just 24 months previously, he saw enough potential in Glasgow to agree to the move at the second time of asking.

At Firhill he has been handed a key role by coach Sean Lineen as a leader on and off the park, vice-captain to Alastair Kellock and one of the stars charged with raising the bar in Scottish professional rugby. He arrived back in Scotland to find a forward-thinking side geared for success, although under no illusions about the challenge ahead as Glasgow attempt to make a real impact in Europe.

Cusiter's sparkling form during his first six months back in Scotland led to him being named as captain of Scotland A for the Nations Cup in Romania in 2009, and he led by example with a try in the opener against Russia as a win in that game and victory against the French ensured the trophy was taken back to Murrayfield. Cusiter's rugby skills were not in question, but his ability as a leader was under the microscope in Bucharest. He passed the test with flying colours and won the right to take the armband for the senior internationals later in the year.

Cusiter, a play-making back with intelligence mated to true Scottish grit, has had to take some big hits during bruising encounters with the game's giants, but always comes back for more with the never-say-die spirit which has propelled him to the captaincy of the Scotland team.

Donny Innes

The affable Donny Innes is Aberdeen's original Calcutta Cup hero. Dr John Robert Stephen Innes, better known to a generation as Dr Donny, or by his initials JRS, was the proud captain of Scotland when the national side edged out England 6–3 in the 1948 Auld Enemy clash at Murrayfield and his name will forever be etched on the grand old trophy.

The distinctive prize has become a familiar friend in British rugby and its colourful origins make it all the more special. When the Calcutta Rugby Club disbanded in 1878, just five years after the Indian outfit's first game, the members decided to withdraw the £60 bank account balance and have the 270 silver rupee coins smelted down to provide the metal for the intricate creation.

With its three handles in the form of King Cobras and the Indian elephant sitting proudly on top of the trophy, there is no mistaking the origins of the distinctive design. The Calcutta Cup was donated to the Rugby Football Union in England and officials decided against introducing it as the reward for a club competition, instead awarding it to the winner of the match between Scotland and England in 1879 and subsequently whenever the two teams met.

Dr Donny Innes (centre) had a reputation as a fearsome tackler.

The only exceptions have been when the nations have clashed on World Cup duty and at the end of rare non-competitive celebration fixtures. It became the tradition for the winning captain and his losing counterpart to have their names engraved on the base of the cup, and that is how a humble young doctor from the Granite City came to have his moniker etched alongside his fellow giants of the international game.

Between the inaugural match in 1879 and the 130th anniversary in 2009, a total of 116 Calcutta Cup showdowns were staged. Fourteen ties ended in stalemate, but England hold the upper hand with 63 wins to the 39 recorded by the men in dark blue, to put the achievement of Innes and his teammates in context. When the Aberdonian got his hands on the cup in 1948 he prised the coveted piece of silverware back from England for the first time since 1938, with the English having won the last pre-war contest in 1939 and picked up where they left off when rivalries resumed in 1947. The 1947 match ended in a thumping 24–5 defeat for the Scots at Twickenham, but they regrouped under the esteemed leadership of the hugely respected Innes and bounced back with a hard fought 6–3 win. More than 70,000 were squeezed into Scottish headquarters to witness their home heroes fight back from 3–0 down at half-time to win with tries from Borders stalwart Charles Drummond and Ardrossan-born flanker William Young after the break. It was to be Young's final appearance for his country and he bowed out on a high note.

For Innes the triumph in Edinburgh was also the perfect swansong after an admirable adventure in rugby. He retired from the national side having skippered them in all five internationals in 1948, nine years after making his debut. The outbreak of World War Two interrupted his career, but the Aberdonian believes the disruption was a positive influence on his career. Having initially played for his country pre-war, when play resumed in peace time he was an old head with the experience which made him an ideal candidate for the captaincy. Despite losing six years while serving with the 52nd Lowland Division, the city doctor still represented Scotland on eight occasions.

He was one of the Aberdeen Grammar School former pupils to wear the national colours with pride, introduced to the game which made him a household name during a taster session at the school's Rubislaw playing field and getting a painful lesson in the nature of the sport. Innes was knocked to the ground and severely winded in virtually his first tackle – but dusted himself down and soon found he had a natural talent for the oval ball game.

Under the tutelage of games master Duncan McGregor, Innes developed into a wonderful all-round player, with a reputation as a fierce tackler despite his slight frame, while performing alongside eminent peers Dallas Allardice and Doug Smith. The Rubislaw turf was becoming a breeding ground for remarkable young players and Innes was one of the finest to pass through the school system, remaining as devoted to his sporting passions as he was to his studies in the school's classrooms.

Innes, whose father, grandfather and mother were all doctors in Aberdeen, followed family tradition by launching a career in the medical profession. He continued to combine his work towards qualifying as a GP with his exploits in the colours of his home city and his progress did not go unnoticed. During the final year of his university studies, captaining Aberdeen's varsity side, he was called-up by Scotland for his first cap. It brought delight to north-east rugby fans, who had not had one of their own in the national team since Aberdeen University forward R.S. Cumming in 1921. Innes received 70 telegrams of congratulations on the eve of his first match, a measure of the regard in which he was held in local rugby circles.

The big moment came against Wales in 1939, having initially been drafted in as a reserve but winning promotion to the starting line up when injury struck J.G.S. Forrest just 24 hours before the big match. Welsh journalists were impressed by the new recruit, claiming in reports that the young Aberdonian looked as though he could 'tackle a carthorse'. Reliable handling was another Innes trait, with his prowess in all departments not coming as a surprise to those who had watched him excel at both cricket and athletics as a schoolboy at Aberdeen Grammar School.

Scotland lost the game in Cardiff 11–3 and in his first year as an international the new boy also played in defeats against England, when the Auld Enemy won 9–6, and a 12–3 reverse away to Ireland despite his maiden try at the top level. When he crossed the line at Lansdowne Road for his one and only Scotland try, the national team was attempting to claw back a nine-point lead carved out by a side from the Emerald Isle which was in fine form.

It was after serving in the war that Innes could finally settle into life on and off the park. He took over his mother's medical practice in Rubislaw in 1946 and was also appointed captain of Aberdeen Grammar former pupils rugby team. The following year he was part of the national team that was defeated by tourists Australia at

Dr Donny Innes and Chris Cusiter accept their place in the Aberdeen Sporting Hall of Fame in 2006 (Picture by Kami Thomson).

Murrayfield. The pain of the 16–3 reverse was tempered by his personal pride at being awarded the Scotland captaincy, with Innes leading out his men for the first time when the Wallabies travelled north on a cold winter's day. His first win as skipper came in his next outing, the 1948 triumph against France in Edinburgh at the start of the Five Nations campaign, which brought the curtain down on his playing career at the very highest level.

The assured winger from the Silver City also featured for the Barbarians at the height of his powers and was there to roll out the welcome mat for his Baa-Baas when the world's most famous rugby select side arrived in Aberdeen in 2005 to play Scotland at Pittodrie. The visit of the team he once represented brought Innes back into the media spotlight and the dapper city doctor, by then in his late 80s, handled the attention in typically charming style.

The Barbarians experience was another feather in the cap of Innes, who was as devoted to his club commitments as he was to the more glamorous representative sides. After his international retirement in 1948 he also began to wind down his club commitments, playing on with the Grammar second string to lend his experience before moving into the administration side of the game and eventually taking on the presidency of his home club. The infectiously enthusiastic rugby man also served as a coach and referee, adding to his outstanding contribution to the sport at all levels during his lifetime.

His experience with Aberdeen Grammar former pupils stood Innes in good stead as he furthered his service to the game by becoming the Scottish Rugby Union's north district representative before working his way up to the SRU presidency in 1973 after a year in the vice-president's role.

Dr Donny Innes, pictured in 2006, has been an inspiration for generations of Aberdeen rugby players (Picture by Raymond Besant).

Innes, who spent 40 years doubling as the prison doctor at Craiginches, retired from his GP's surgery in 1987 but worked on as part of Shell's medical team in Aberdeen, finally taking a well-earned break from work in the early 1990s to spend more time on his other great sporting passion, golf. Innes, a member at Royal Aberdeen, and a regular on the Balgownie and Silverburn courses, may be more familiar with a club rather than a rugby ball in hand nowadays, but it is as a Murrayfield hero that he should forever be remembered.

Jason White

Jason White is a big man with a big heart and a huge talent for rugby. He became the rock that the Scottish national team was built on as an inspirational captain in the dark blue of his country and earned his place in the sport's hall of fame with his powerful and full-blooded displays against the finest in the world.

One game in particular epitomised what the former Cults Academy pupil brought to the table and fittingly it was one which mattered more than most. The 2006 Calcutta Cup match against England at Murrayfield presented a masterclass in forward play from White, all 6ft 5in and 16st 10lb of him. That afternoon, in front of 67,500 raucous Auld Enemy fans, he was untouchable as he asserted his authority in a way that delighted the home support. Any hope England had of bullying their hosts was blown away by the skipper, who provided a platform for a memorable 18–12 victory in which Chris Paterson's five penalties and a Dan Parks drop goal did the damage in the England half. Paterson's familiar accuracy with the boot was admirable,

Jason White has been a dominant force in club and international rugby for a decade (Picture by Kami Thomson).

but it was White who walked away with the Man of the Match trophy, as well as lifting the grand old Calcutta Cup and having his name engraved onto the base of the distinctive prize.

At the end of the campaign White also claimed Scottish rugby's Player of the Year award, voted for by sports writers, in recognition of his contribution that term. It was his first full season as captain, having been awarded the honour in the autumn of 2005, and the promotion had worked out perfectly.

In addition to the prize from the rugby press, White also collected the Players' Player of the Year trophy and completed a wonderful hat-trick when he was named Player of the Year in the star-studded English top flight. His move to the cut and thrust of the Premiership was a calculated risk, given the fierce competition south of the border, but he took to the high-pressure environment with ease.

While the mantra from Scottish headquarters related to the drive to encourage the country's stars to stay at home with the SRU-backed clubs, there was no way the Sale star could be overlooked and his appointment as skipper recognised just how important a figure he had become in the sport.

White was in full flow, turning 28 during the Six Nations campaign in 2006 and at the height of his physical powers. Cruelly, as the year drew to a close, the Scotland skipper was cut down in his prime when he caught his studs in the turf at Murrayfield during an Autumn Test against Romania and suffered sickening cruciate ligament damage.

With the World Cup just around the corner, it was a double blow to the country and the player. Reconstructive surgery at the hands of American specialist Bill Knowles set White back on the road to recovery, but it would be a slow and painful path as he battled back from the career-threatening injury, calling on all of his renowned strength of character during the rehabilitation process.

Spurred on by Sale teammate Charlie Hodgson, who was receiving treatment at the same clinic at the same time for a similar injury, he made his target – returning to the Scotland fold in the World Cup warm-up match against Ireland at Murrayfield. Showing no signs of rustiness, White led his troops to victory and went on to play a key role in the 2007 World Cup games. His captaincy lasted for 19 matches in all.

While White made it back in time for the tournament in 2007, continuing to star for club and country, the first half of 2006 will always be remembered as the headiest period in a top level career which took him from the mud and thunder of club rugby in Aberdeen to some of the world's biggest and best sporting venues.

Although born in Edinburgh, White will always credit his passion for rugby to his early days in the Granite City. He moved with his family to Peterculter as a schoolboy and attended Cults Academy. It was while a pupil at the suburban school that he was persuaded to give rugby a go, linking up with Aberdeen Wanderers to see if his obvious physical attributes would translate into promise with the oval ball. Rugby was not part of the sporting curriculum at Cults, but Wanderers provided a warm welcome to a young man who looked destined for big things from the moment he first strode onto the training pitch. Wanderers have since renamed their humble pavilion, on the fringe of Hazlehead Park in the city's west end, in honour of their most famous former player.

White was bitten by the rugby bug immediately and became a fully-fledged Wanderer, playing and training with the Groats Road club until his promise was picked up on by the sport's establishment and he was tempted to George Watson's College for the final year of his school studies, combining academic commitments with a place in the Watsonians team in Scotland's domestic top flight.

At representative level, the hard-hitting youngster was appointed vice-captain of the Scottish Schools team for a tour of South Africa in 1996 and captained the national Under-18 side the following year before progressing through the system with the Scotland Under-21s and A team before stepping up to the senior squad.

Described by legendary coach Jim Telfer as 'pound for pound the hardest tackler I have ever worked with', even as a teenager the boy from the north-east cut a fearsome figure on the field. Quietly spoken and mild-mannered off the pitch, White became a monstrous figure when he crossed the white line and produced courageous performances year in and year out. His fearless tackling became a trademark, but White is a player at ease in possession and his ability to run with the ball at pace made him a perfect modern international.

Jason White, with the Calcutta Cup for company, at the opening of the Aberdeen Wanderers' club house in 2006 (Picture by Kami Thomson).

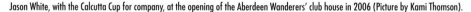

Jason White in action against France at Murrayfield (Picture courtesy of Ian Jacobs Photography).

He made his full Scotland debut in 2000 when he travelled with the touring party in New Zealand, featuring in both tests against the All Blacks and holding his own in esteemed company despite his lack of experience. The rookie flourished in his new surroundings and has now been part of the national team for more than a decade, ending the 2009 season with 77 caps to his credit and looking forward to building on that tally in 2010.

He may even add to the collection of four tries for Scotland, the first of which came against the USA in 2002. He also crossed the line against South Africa and twice against Italy in two separate matches.

Although the captaincy was passed to Mike Blair following the 2007 World Cup Finals and has subsequently been inherited by Chris Cusiter, White remains an inspirational figure within the Murrayfield dressing room. With the experience of the Lions tour of 2005 under his belt, nobody can question his credentials.

While the forward's service to Scotland has been exemplary, his club career has also been impressive. He began life in the professional game with Glasgow Warriors before switching to English Premiership giants Sale Sharks in 2003. The powerful Scot spent six seasons with the Sharks, winning the Premiership title in 2006 and going on to captain Sale after that triumph. He made more than a 100 appearances for the north-west side before opting for a change of scene and signing for French side Clermont Auvergne in 2009.

White, who turned 31 in April 2009, had a long-standing ambition to play club rugby in the French League and joined an ambitious side who play to 16,000 sell-out crowds at every home game as they challenge for honours at home and in the European game. The move to the Continent coincided with Andy Robinson's appointment as coach of the national team and the reinvigorated forward embarked on his Indian summer.

Although settling into the French way of life with his wife and young daughter, White's links to the north-east remain strong and he has developed partnerships with local firms, with one eye on his future beyond rugby as his playing days enter their final phase. Whether White chooses to remain involved in the game or seek fresh challenges in a new industry, his name will always be intrinsically linked with rugby in the Granite City as a Scotland legend, club star and perfect role model.

Douglas W.C. Smith

Douglas William Cumming Smith is one of the Granite City's finest rugby products. Born in Aberdeen in 1924, D.W.C. Smith has gone down in the sport's history books as man of steel and substance, a star of an era when rugby retained the purity of its amateur roots.

Smith was an all-round sportsman in his Aberdeen Grammar School days. Not surprisingly he captained the west end school's rugby team, but he was also skipper of the cricket side and a record-breaking athletics champion to boot. He boasted a 100 yards time of 10 seconds flat, a time never beaten before metric put paid to that particular distance, and set a truly immense best of 337ft 8in in the cricket ball throwing event. His throw was longer than the Pittodrie pitch and an achievement to be proud of at a time when the discipline formed a major part of athletics meets up and down the country.

Dr Doug Smith in his role as Lions manager in 1971.

Smith was a truly formidable competitor, maturing to take on a physique which suggested he could well have been hewn from the stone of his native city. Tipping the scales at 15 stone and measuring in excess of 6ft, there was no mistaking the powerful figure. He had brain to match his brawn and his success was as much about technique as it was strength.

He came into his element on his home turf at Rubislaw, home to Grammar's rugby team since 1914. The club itself was founded in 1893 and in well over a century of play there have been few individuals who have represented the Aberdeen school as well as

D.W.C. Smith. The famous name and those of his similarly well decorated peers will always be linked with Grammar as a standard for all pupils and former pupils to aim for.

Prowess on track and field did not lead Smith to neglect his studies and in 1941 he was accepted by Aberdeen University, graduating with a degree in medicine six years later. His student days allowed him to further his sporting passions, representing Scottish universities at rugby and athletics as he continued to show incredible promise. Shot, discus and long jump were among his strongest sports, but he also maintained his sprint prowess and could cover ground with the confidence of a thoroughbred race horse. During the war years he even turned out for Aberdeen Football Club as an amateur player, adding a further string to his bow as one of the most versatile and complete sportsmen the city has ever seen.

He had caught the eye of the Dons while playing junior football for Banks o' Dee, with a cup final performance tempting his home-town team as well as Motherwell and East Fife to make efforts to lure him to the professional game. He declined the invitation but did wear the shirt of Aberdeen as an unpaid player – turning down manager David Halliday's invitation to turn out against Rangers at Ibrox in favour of representing his university at rugby against St Andrews.

Smith, who had fostered a keen military interest during his university studies, left his post at Aberdeen Royal Infirmary in 1950 to move south. He combined his passion for medicine and the armed forces by serving with the Royal Army Medical Corps, lending his considerable talents with the oval ball to both the army teams and to London Scottish, as captain, for more than a decade. For a man fiercely passionate about his home country's sporting health, playing for the exiles at Richmond proved to be a home from home.

Dr Doug Smith (right) is presented with a gift from North District SRU representative Bill Connon at the Douglas Hotel in Aberdeen in 1972 to mark his Lions achievements.

As well as a loyal club servant he was a winger of international class, winning his first Scotland cap in 1949 and going on to be picked eight times by his country over the next four years. His first year of top-class rugby saw Smith thrust into action against Ireland, England, Wales and France. His debut was in Colombes against the French in January that year, playing in an 8–0 victory to open his account in style in front of a crowd of 28,000. He played in the ties against Ireland, Wales and the French the following year and also turned out against the Irish in 1953 to round off his experiences with the national team.

Smith's skills reached a wider audience thanks to his exploits in dark blue and in 1950 he was awarded the greatest honour of all when he was named in the British Lions squad to tour New Zealand and Australia, the same year in which he began life as a GP at Grays in Essex. A broken arm kept him sidelined for the first half of the adventure, but he recovered in time to score three tries and a conversion during the trip, helping the tourists to 22 wins in 29 outings. He made his Lions test debut in the opening match against Australia in Brisbane and was part of the team which won 19–6.

The Lions had started with a draw and three defeats against New Zealand, but bounced back in style against the Wallabies. It was the first time the team had worn the now-famous red jersey and in D.W.C. Smith they had a player who did it justice. In addition to the test match he played against a Manawatu Horowhenua select, winning 13–8, and then in a 30-point whitewash against another Kiwi composite side before rising to the occasion against New South Wales Country in Canberra with two tries and a conversion in a 47–3 win. In the final warm-up match he contributed another try, in a 22–6 victory against New South Wales Waratahs, before stepping up in the big match against the Aussies at the Brisbane Cricket Ground. It was an impeccable tour of duty for Smith, who never faltered when called upon over the summer of 1950.

Twenty-two years later the Aberdonian's services to his beloved sport were recognised at Buckingham Palace when he collected an OBE in reward for a lifetime's devotion to the game, by which time he had played a key role in another adventure with Britain's finest.

In 1971 he managed the Lions during their epic 26-match tour of Australia and New Zealand, just one of his accomplishments after hanging up his boots. His team showed flair and courage as they stormed to a series victory, winning two and drawing one of the four main games. On arrival at Auckland airport, in typically confident and charming fashion, Smith had announced to the waiting press pack that his side would record exactly that record in the four tests and he was proved 100 per cent correct.

Smith's prediction was born out of supreme confidence in the side he guided, teaming up with coach Carwyn James for the tour. Smith's role was wide and varied, doubling as team doctor and physiotherapist as well as media spin doctor when required. He filled every role ably and has been noted as perhaps the finest Lions manager ever to fill the role. With a bold personality to match his appearance, Smith commanded respect from his charges and won the immediate support of the star-studded squad. They responded with some wonderful rugby.

The 1971 expedition was the first and to date the only time a British side had won a test against the Kiwis and the first time the All Blacks had lost a home series since the South Africans triumphed in 1937. It remains one of the finest Lions tours of all time and the presence of Smith as figurehead was a vital cog in the machine. The 1971 squad was dominated by Welshmen, following the Wales grand slam in the Five Nations that season, but with the likes of Alastair Biggar, Chris Rea, Frank Laidlaw, Ian McLauchlan, Gordon Brown and Roger Arneil in the travelling party there was no shortage of Scottish company for the tour boss.

He also had many friends among the English contingent, having been heavily involved in the game south of the border since his move early in the 1950s. After retiring from playing in 1957 he continued to support London Scottish in a variety of administrative roles as well as helping the Scottish Rugby Union chart the way forward, becoming a junior vice-president of the SRU in 1984 and stepping up to become president two years later, with fellow Aberdonian Bill Connon as his senior vice-president. He followed in the footsteps of the city's two former presidents, Robert Ledingham, in the early 1960s, and Donny Innes, in the 1970s. Charlie Ritchie, a Peterhead-born fellow Grammarian, was another north-east official who rose to the top of the SRU tree.

Smith, who had grown up at his family home on Ashgrove Road West and went on to marry London model Kay Druery in 1951 in a high-profile ceremony, died in 1998 at the age of 73. He will forever be remembered as one of the silver city's most loved and most talented sports stars.

Stuart Grimes

With 71 Scotland caps to his credit and the national team captaincy on his CV, Stuart Grimes ranks among Aberdeen's most experienced rugby stars. While the great names of the past such as D.W.C. Smith and J.R.S. Innes represented the halcyon days of the amateur game, Grimes epitomises the vibrancy of the professional era.

The Aberdonian lock had the power and guile to assure himself of a starring role for his country over the course of eight years on either side of the Millennium, as an athletic performer with admirable ball-handling skills. Another product of Robert Gordon's College, Grimes turned professional at the end of 1996 after a rapid rise to prominence.

Stuart Grimes in 2005 (Picture by Kevin Emslie).

He honed his skills as a school player on the Gordon's playing fields at Countesswells, making the daily commute from the family home in the Mearns between 1988 and 1992 when his family settled back on home soil after his father's travels in the oil industry ceased.

Grimes was a late starter in terms of competitive rugby and first began to make a real name for himself as a Watsonians player and Edinburgh University student. He represented Scotland in the Student World Cup in South Africa in 1995 as he worked towards a degree in accountancy and economics. He was called into the Caledonia select side on the back of that. His displays for Caledonia in the Heineken Cup led to Under-21 international honours and a Scotland A cap against South Africa in 1996 in Hawick, where a starring display sent Grimes on the path to the professional game with Glasgow.

His 6ft 5in frame, coupled with the mobility required for the modern game, ensured Grimes had the stature to command respect and, by the end of 1997, as a 23-year-old, he had been blooded at full international level as a replacement in a 37–8 defeat against Australia at Murrayfield. Grimes had been drafted into the squad following Andy Reid's withdrawal, and an injury to Iain Smith just 35 minutes into the game completed the swift rise through the ranks for Grimes, who got his chance earlier than expected against the Wallabies. He was far from the biggest second-row player ever to grace Murrayfield, but he made up for that with his fitness and reading of the game.

Within two years he was celebrating a key role in the revered Five Nations tournament triumph of 1999. Grimes, paired with Scott Murray, was integral to Jim Telfer's plan for his team and the blueprint worked to perfection as the rank outsiders came from nowhere to earn the coveted prize. Gregor Townsend stole the headlines with a try in each of the five rounds of the Championship, but the contribution of every member of the side was immense. The highlight for Grimes was crossing the line to score against Ireland at Murrayfield in the penultimate match of the campaign, helping his side to a 30–13 win which set up a title decider against France in Paris. A 36–22 win at the Stade de France ensured the last-ever Five Nations title, before the competition expanded to six teams in 2000, went back to Murrayfield with Telfer's side.

It was an emphatic end to what had been a tumultuous campaign, with the brave Scottish side locked on six points with England at the final whistle, but winning courtesy of their superior points difference. France had been hoping to make it three consecutive victories, but had not bargained on the plucky and well-drilled Scots making such a huge impact on the competition. The 1999 Five Nations campaign ranks as the crowning glory in a glittering career for Grimes, but there were still memorable occasions to follow.

In 2002 he was selected as captain for the tour of Canada and the United States to add another highlight to a growing list of accolades in the game on his way to a 71-cap haul, putting him among an exclusive batch of players to have made more than a half century of appearances in dark blue.

Three years later the childhood Dons fan got his wish for Pittodrie stardom, albeit with ball in hand rather than at his feet. Grimes, who grew up living at Fetteresson

Castle near Stonehaven and was tagged with the nickname 'Lord' by his teammates in later life, used to cheer on Aberdeen Football Club as a schoolboy and followed in the boot steps of his former heroes when he ran out to represent Scotland at Pittodrie when the Barbarians visited the north-east in 2005. With his family and friends in the crowd, Grimes ensured the visitors did not have a happy trip as they were beaten 38–7.

By then he had featured in two World Cup Finals. The first, in 1999, was hosted by Wales, but used a combination of stadiums throughout Britain, Ireland and France. Scotland took their place in the expanded new-look tournament. The Dark Blues were one of 20 teams to qualify for the last phase of the competition and landed in a testing pool alongside South Africa, Spain and Uruguay.

After falling to a 46–29 defeat against the Springboks at Murrayfield, the Dark Blues bounced back with victory in their remaining pool games to qualify for the quarter-finals. Awaiting Grimes and company in the last eight were New Zealand: a classic David versus Goliath encounter. Goliath triumphed, with the Kiwis edging to a 30–18 win.

Grimes was back in the World Cup fold four years later in Australia. It turned out to be England's year, but not before Grimes and his teammates made an admirable attempt at creating their own piece of history. After coming through a group featuring France, Japan and the USA, it was the Aussie hosts who crushed Scottish hopes in the quarter-finals with a 33–16 win. Grimes returned home with a souvenir from the trip, with memories of a World Cup to savour after crossing the line against Japan with his country's second try in a 12–6 opening match win.

Success was not limited to international rugby for Grimes. After moving from Glasgow to the Newcastle Falcons in 1999, the Aberdonian won the domestic cup with

Stuart Grimes (centre) carved out a long and distinguished career at club and international level.

the English outfit in 2001 and 2004 during a seven-year association which brought 139 appearances in Falcons colours. That included a century of games in the physically demanding Premiership, where he emerged as one of the most consistent and reliable players in the English game. He had already sampled League Championship success with Watsonians in 1998 before his move into the professional game, but the standard in England took the Aberdeenshire native to a whole new level. With his Scottish club he sampled the highest high in the domestic game when he and his teammates travelled to the Greenyards to defeat Melrose and lift the big prize. It was a huge achievement for the Edinburgh side, but in the big-money surroundings south of the border the ante was upped considerably.

Grimes was one of the many international stars attracted to Newcastle in the aftermath of the city football club's then chairman Sir John Hall's takeover in 1995, when the club dropped the Gosforth tag from its name and was reborn as part of Hall's masterplan for an all-encompassing sports club covering football, rugby and other disciplines. The transformation included a change of colours to bring in the black and white so synonymous with football in Newcastle.

New Zealander Inga Tuigamala, Scotland stars Gary Armstrong and Doddie Weir and England duo Rob Andrew and Tony Underwood were among the early recruits, while the likes of Grimes and Jonny Wilkinson were part of the ongoing drive for quality even after Hall was replaced as chairman by Dave Thompson in 1999. Grimes, with his dedication to the cause, was quickly accepted by Falcons fans and the cup success against Harlequins in 2001 and Sale three years later cemented the relationship.

The Granite City rock played out his career with Borders, spending two years with the Scottish club side after joining in the summer of 2006, and Italian club Petrarca Padova. The move to Petrarca fulfilled his ambition to play abroad and follow in the footsteps of the likes of former Scotland teammate Gregor Townsend. He led his inexperienced Italian colleagues to the semi-finals of their domestic championship, losing out to eventual title-winners Calvisano in 2008.

That summer Grimes returned to Newcastle as assistant coach. Under director of rugby Steve Bates, he has been detailed to specialise in the club's line-out capabilities. Bates, a long-time mentor who had worked with the Aberdonian during his playing days at Newcastle and the Borders, was quick to unite him with fellow Scot Alan Tait on the backroom staff.

After sampling life in Italy the Aberdonian had planned to move away from rugby and carve out a new career as a surveyor, a qualification he gained during his first stint in Newcastle, but the lure of a return to the big time was too strong to resist. As the playing chapter closed a new one in coaching began and the Stuart Grimes success story looks certain to roll on for years to come.

Bert Bruce

When Bert Bruce was described in an international rugby programme as an Aberdeen Grammar former player it brought a growl of indignation. For a fiercely proud

Gordonian, the writer's slip was no laughing matter. As a player and official, Bruce flew the flag for his club with great aplomb in a spirited career. He gained a reputation as one of the hardest scrummagers ever to emerge from the Granite City and holds a special place in the north-east corner's rugby heritage.

He was capped four times by Scotland in 1947 and 1948, making his debut against Australia before playing against Ireland, Wales and France. He played on both sides of the front row and in the back row during those games, the mark of a versatile and committed player who was comfortable anywhere on the field. What shone through above all else was his instinct for the game and his determination to do well.

In 2008 Bruce's memory was brought to a whole new audience when items of memorabilia from his career were donated by his family to Scottish Rugby Union's collection at Murrayfield. The SRU closed its official museum in 1993 and moved its hoard into storage during the revamp of the Edinburgh ground but, after a gap of 15 years, it has begun the process of preparing its intriguing treasure trove for public display once again. Items include international caps dating back to the 1870s, photographs from the same era up to the present day and match programmes from as early as 1905. All are being painstakingly catalogued and will be displayed in a dedicated museum at Murrayfield, including the tokens from Bruce's own career as a nod towards the post-war years.

The SRU took delivery of his Scotland cap, national team jersey and a France kit he had exchanged with scrum-half Bergougnan at the end of his match against the continental side in Edinburgh. It was a time when Scotland players received one home strip and one away kit to last them their entire career – Bruce took the gamble that he would not need his white change outfit and swapped it with his French counterpart.

When Bruce tackled the French he was up against a side who had only recently rejoined the Five Nations after an enforced absence. France had initially been introduced to the competition in 1910, but were banned in 1931 after being found guilty of paying players. The idea of professional rugby union was being fiercely resisted, and would be for well over half a century. At the end of the war there was

Bert Bruce in Scotland colours
(Picture courtesy of the SRU library).

peace among the rugby nations, with France allowed back in and Britain's finest being given a chance to test their mettle against the continental stars from across the Channel.

The modest Bruce, who died in 2001 at the age of 78 after a career as a bank manager and hotelier, had kept the cherished items from his French encounter and other internationals stowed away in a box in his attic. He was bashful about his achievements in the game he loved so dearly, but had every reason to shout from the rooftops about his pedigree at the top level.

His special relationship with Murrayfield began with his international debut in 1947. More than 50,000 were packed into the Edinburgh ground as Bruce ran out in Scotland colours for the first time. He could not prevent the Scots from falling to a 16–7 defeat, but it was an experience to savour nonetheless.

Bruce came back for more the following year and sampled the winning feeling at Scottish rugby headquarters when he and his teammates came through a thrilling encounter against the French in January 1948 to win 9–8. His other two appearances were in a 14–0 defeat against Wales in Cardiff and a 6–0 reverse against the Irish at Lansdowne Road.

Five Nations rugby in Bruce's era was wide open. In his first season as an international player the honours were shared between Wales and England, while in his second it was Ireland who claimed the prize, completing a Grand Slam to reinforce their superiority. Scotland were the odd team out throughout the 1940s and 1950s, not winning the crown until they finished tied with the Welsh in 1964. They did not win outright until 1984, but Bruce and his peers battled hard against the more established rugby-playing nations.

After retiring from playing Bruce went on to become president of Gordonians between 1974 and 1976 as well as a tour manager with the city side, who dominated the north-east rugby scene throughout that era. He led the club through a transitional period, as in 1974 the membership policy changed to an open-door approach rather than the previous stipulation that players must be former pupils of Robert Gordon's College.

Gordonians, founded in 1904, moved with the times during that fast-paced era. The club had slowly and steadily evolved, but by the mid-1970s found itself in the middle of a changing landscape in the Scottish domestic scene. The original closed membership system had allowed Bruce in the 1940s and Ian McCrae in the 1960s and 1970s to flourish and win international honours, but the new open-door policy introduced many more skilled and talented players who became proud to be part of the Gordonians family in the decades since the brave decision to change the constitution.

The period coincided with the introduction of the National League set-up in the Scottish game, a system in which the Counteswells outfit flourished. The city side won promotion from the Third Division in 1973–74 and completed the climb to the First Division in 1979–80.

Bruce had been in at the start of that journey in a official capacity, but his reach extended beyond the confines of his familiar club home. He served as secretary and selector for the north district as he put his great experience and expertise to good use to mould the best of the north's talent into a respected and talented squad. He knew the area, and particularly his home city, well. Bruce had begun his sporting life as an enthusiastic primary school football player, educated at Woodside before earning a bursary to study at Robert Gordon's College in 1934 and beginning the transformation from round to oval ball.

He was named as his new school's Otaki Shield winner in 1940, an award presented to the head boy at the end of their final year in school. The scholarship brought with it an extended trip to New Zealand and had been introduced to commemorate a World War One sea battle in which former Gordon's pupil Captain Archibald Bisset Smith played a heroic role, saving the lives of crew members from the SS *Otaki* following an attack by a German raider. Bisset Smith went down with the vessel, but was awarded the Victoria Cross posthumously and his family in turn donated the Otaki Shield to his former school.

The New Zealand Shipping Company initially offered free passage to the winner for their trip to the land of the Kiwis, although in later years the New Zealand government has stepped in to offer financial support for the scheme. Bruce never had the chance to savour the hospitality of the New Zealand people as World War Two interrupted, leading him to serve with the Royal Irish Rifles and then the Cameronians.

When he eventually sampled island life it was far closer to home, with the Aberdonian founding Stornoway Rugby Club while living on the isle of Lewis in the 1950s through his work with the TSB Bank. When he arrived in the western outpost

Bert Bruce, second from left in the back row, pictured with his Scotland teammates prior to their match against France in 1948 (Picture courtesy of Yerbury Photography).

he was frustrated to find his beloved rugby did not feature on the sporting spectrum and, together with fellow oval ball enthusiast John Morrison, who had developed his passion for the game in South Africa, set about educating the locals.

Stornoway Rugby Club was formed, playing against visiting teams from Royal Navy ships in the early days, and more than half a century since it is still going strong in the Scottish regional league system. Bruce helped his new club to a 16–0 victory over HMS *Cook*'s ship team on 1 November 1952 and from that triumphant start the outfit has grown and grown, now featuring a burgeoning youth system and fostering a love for the sport on the island. The part the club's founding fathers had to play has never been forgotten.

Bert Bruce has gone down in history as the first Gordonians player ever to represent Scotland, but he left his mark far and wide in the game, as his Western Isles sojourn shows. When he died in 2001, in excess of 400 mourners gathered at Mannofield Church for the funeral. The great and good of Scottish rugby were among those who paid their respects to a much-admired figure who had left an indelible mark on the game which made him one of Aberdeen's sporting heroes.

Ian McCrae

On a winter afternoon in a corner of Paris, a small piece of rugby trivia was claimed as Aberdeen's own. When Ian McCrae ran on in Scotland colours to face the French he became the first ever replacement in Five Nations rugby and ensured he had a slice of the famous tournament's heritage to call his own. In the man's game there had traditionally been no place for the substitutes favoured by other, more sensitive, pursuits, but the landscape changed in 1968 when the Lions introduced Mike Gibson in place of the injured Barry John during a test match against South Africa in Pretoria. From that point on the wounded soldiers no longer had to battle on regardless of the extent of their injuries and a new option was open to the previously hamstrung coaches.

Scotland took note, and just months later took the new concept into the Five Nations when they thrust McCrae into action in the opening match of the competition on 11 January 1969, helping them on their way to a 6–3 victory at the Stade Olympique in the suburb of Colombes. Gordon Connell, of Lions fame, was the man who made way and it proved an inspired change as the player with the fresh legs pounced on a loose ball to set up Jim Telfer for the winning try.

Little has changed in the decades since then, although in the build-up to the 2010 Six Nations the clamour for the introduction of unlimited rolling replacements began to intensify. Whatever happens in the future, McCrae's place in history remains secure.

The unique moment in France was just part of the McCrae story, a tale in which he was a reliable performer for his country over the course of a five-year career in dark blue. The former Robert Gordon's College pupil burst onto the scene in 1967 as a 25-year-old scrum-half with a solid track record as a club player in the domestic leagues, making his debut against England in the cauldron of Twickenham as part of a team featuring a string of household names. Teammates on the day included Lions stalwarts

Ian McCrae of Gordonians makes a dramatic pass during a match at Rubislaw in 1969.

Jim Telfer, Sandy Hinshelwood and Frank Laidlaw, but the rookie Aberdonian kept pace admirably with the stars around him. Right through to 1972, the Grammar star was in and around the Scotland team and his talents were broadcast to an audience across Britain as he continued the fine tradition of his home club's provision of committed players for the Murrayfield selectors down the decades.

Scotland had silenced the London crowd by moving into an 11–8 lead at half-time as McCrae settled into the international fold on his debut in 1967, but he soon discovered that in top-class rugby there is no such thing as an easy win. The hosts hit back and eventually claimed a 27–14 victory to dash the Granite City rock's hopes of a maiden win. He returned to the team in the following season's Five Nations Championship when Scotland faced Ireland at Lansdowne Road, but again the experience was tinged with disappointment as the Irish celebrated a 14–6 win.

McCrae's next involvement was to make history in France as the first replacement and, in a game of firsts, it brought him a flavour of success at that level. McCrae was promoted to the starting 15 for the 17–3 reverse against Wales at Murrayfield just weeks later. Those two appearances in 1969 proved to be McCrae's last for three seasons, with his reintroduction to the Scotland team coming in 1972, in time for a 20–9 triumph against France in Edinburgh in front of an enthusiastic 50,000 crowd. That January appearance proved to be the penultimate one for the man from the north-east, with his swansong coming in December of 1972 when New Zealand arrived on tour. McCrae regained the coveted number-nine shirt to face the All Blacks at Murrayfield but, despite Andy Irvine's efforts with the boot, it was the Kiwis who left the ground smiling after a 14–9 win.

This brought the curtain down on McCrae's service on the international stage, an adventure which capped his achievements on the club front with his Gordonians team. He had progressed to the club side from the Robert Gordon's College side, a team he captained in 1958 and 1959. The Aberdonian went on to spend decades with Gordonians, winning north and midland district honours during two decades at the height of his powers in the 1960s and 1970s as he became renowned as a scrum-half with seemingly endless reserves of energy and fantastic ability with the ball in hand.

Those qualities helped take the city side on a marvellous journey through the club game. When the Scottish National League was established in 1973 it gave hope to provincial sides such as the Seafield team, who dreamt of one day challenging the giants from the Borders. Gordonians steadily clawed their way through the ranks before arriving in style in the First Division, the top tier of the domestic game, in 1980. It brought the big guns north on a regular basis and they proved to be the halcyon days, bringing crowds flocking to the compact ground on the edge of the city.

McCrae was part of the team that ran out in front of an Aberdeen audience on 4 October 1980 for the most famous victory in the club's proud history, as the Green Machine of Hawick was humbled by the upstarts from the Silver City. A record crowd of 1,500 turned out to see Gordonians make their Division One debut at home and the result was emphatic, as they announced their arrival with a crushing 26–13 triumph against their highly-fancied visitors.

McCrae and his colleagues went on to finish in a respectable sixth place, becoming the most successful club side produced by Aberdeen up to that point. The achievements of that famed Gordonians side have yet to be matched, although Aberdeen Grammar former pupils did put the city back on the map in the post-Millennium years with their exploits in the top flight. Gordonians have since gone through a rebuilding exercise, dropping out of the national league for a period before regrouping and hitting the promotion trail once more, and the dream years of the late 1970s and early 1980s remain the inspiration for all involved in attempting to take the club back to the heights it once scaled.

Unearthing a player of McCrae's calibre is another challenge for the current regime. His peak years also brought McCrae to the attention of Barbarians selectors, turning out for the Baa-Baas on nine occasions, during an accomplished career as a player noted for his panache and style.

While it was rugby which made Ian McCrae a household name in Scottish sport, his passion was not restricted solely to the oval ball game. As a founder member of the Aberdeen Sports Council, the former Murrayfield hero proved he had his city's best interests at heart when he set about providing support and encouragement to competitors from all disciplines when he helped establish the organisation in 1985. It proved to be a busy year, with the scrum-half finding the time to skipper the Aberdeen Strollers team of golden oldies when the club entered its first veterans World Festival in London after coming out of retirement for the occasion.

Even after officially hanging up his boots, McCrae never lost his love of rugby and he played in the Bermuda Classic four times for Scotland. The classic, launched in 1972, brought together former international players from countries across the world to revive old rivalries in a friendly environment. In 1988 the tournament became the World Rugby Classic and it is an event which has captured the imagination of supporters across the globe.

While continuing to dabble with non-competitive rugby, McCrae developed other sporting commitments in his home city. His own tastes and talents were varied, with cricket among the other pursuits favoured by the all-round sportsman. McCrae became a regular for Stoneywood Cricket Club and is one of the select band of players to have scored a century for the side. In 1991 he also proved a leader off the field for Stoneywood, helping steer the club through its amalgamation with Dyce Cricket Club to form Stoneywood-Dyce. The new club has gone from strength to strength over the past two decades, producing a string of talented young players who have gone on to play at county level in England and for the Scottish national team at full and youth international level.

McCrae added the MacRobert Thistle Trophy, awarded by the National Playing Fields Association for his services to rugby, to his haul and joined an illustrious list of former players to have their name etched on the trophy. Others recognised by the NPFA include Andy Irvine, Nairn MacEwan and Finlay Calder. No stranger to living in esteemed company, it was a fitting reward for a lifetime devoted to the sport in which he became an international star.

CRICKET

Colin Smith

As 2009 drew to a close a celebration far more significant than the dawn of a new decade took place at Aberdeenshire Cricket Club. A select band of the sport's luminaries joined with the family and friends of Colin Smith to mark the end of a glorious era for the club, the player and the national team as he officially let the curtain fall on his Scotland career.

Colin Smith, Aberdeenshire and Scotland wicketkeeper and batsman prepares for the match with Namibia at Mannofield, Aberdeen (Picture by Jim Irvine).

After 181 caps, it was time to pass the gloves to the next generation.

Smith's contribution to the cause as first-choice wicketkeeper for a decade had been exemplary and he also proved a valuable asset with the bat in venues near and far, playing a major part in some of the most memorable chapters in Scottish cricket's story. The Aberdonian played in the 2007 World Cup as well as the World Twenty20 Championships of 2007 and 2009. In between were excursions to Africa, Asia, Europe, the Caribbean, North America and, more importantly, south of the border to play against English county cricket's finest as the Scottish Saltires established themselves as a competitive force. For an amateur sportsman, who, for the majority of his career, combined his playing commitments with work as a postman and latterly as an officer with Grampian Police, it was a huge challenge to go head to head with full-time professionals, but in Smith the country had a man capable of living in any company due to his doggedness and determination as much as it was to do with talent.

In his youth Smith had been a keen swimmer, competing with the highly successful Aberdeen ASC alongside the likes of the Cochran brothers, only turning his attentions seriously to cricket after illness curtailed his activity in the pool for 18 months. Although he had been a member of Aberdeenshire's youth set-up from the age of 11, it was as a 14-year-old that he turned his back on dreams of aquatic stardom and focused on his favoured outdoor pursuit. Swimming's loss proved to be cricket's gain as he set about making up for lost time by quickly progressing into the international reckoning at age group level while a pupil at Robert Gordon's College.

Smith went on to study building surveying at Robert Gordon University and then land economy at Aberdeen University before cutting short the latter degree to concentrate on cricket, dividing his time between the north-east and foreign shores for six seasons in his early 20s. Smith played for Whitfords Cricket Club in Western Australia, a club which has played host to a succession of Scottish players over the years, including former Aberdeenshire star Mike Smith. The club has also produced Aussie internationals such as the Hussey brothers and Marcus North. For a player who grew up idolising Australian star Ian Healy, it was dream come true to play in the southern hemisphere. Smith combined cricket commitments with the club, near Perth, with a role as groundsman, but would return during the Australian winter to turn out for Aberdeenshire. It ensured competitive cricket 11 months of the year and was another stage in a cricket education which had included representing Scotland at Under-15, Under-16 and Under-19 level.

As Smith excelled at club level, promotion to the senior international side appeared to be just around the corner, but the man from the Granite City had to be patient. He was 26 when the call finally came through in 1999, and he quickly established himself as an integral part of the Scotland set-up.

At club level, Smith was part of the Shire team that charged to victory in the inaugural Scottish National Cricket League in 1996 and helped them land the Scottish

Scotland's Colin Smith in action at Mannofield in 2008 (Picture by Jim Irvine).

Cup in the same season. Four years later, after earning international recognition, he was rewarded for his dedication to the cause when he was appointed captain at Mannofield. While the domestic scene was always close to Smith's heart, as the son of Shire stalwart Howard Smith, the experiences he savoured in the dark blue of his country were some of the most exhilarating of his long service to the sport.

He was part of the Scottish Saltires team when it made its debut in the Totesport League in 2003 – playing a starring role as he hit the winning runs when the side opened its account south of the border with a stunning win against Durham at Chester-le-Street in the opening fixture and followed it up with victories against Somerset at the Grange in Edinburgh and a draw against Middlesex in the next home fixture. They were heady days for a Saltires team brimming with confidence. Smith revelled in the assignments, although it proved to be a painful exercise on occasion – not least when he took a Dominic Cork bouncing delivery to the head in a match against Derbyshire and again from Chris Cairns against Nottinghamshire at Trent Bridge in that eventful maiden season on the county circuit – which also included a dramatic victory against county giants Lancashire on their Old Trafford stomping ground, a game in which Smith top scored with an invaluable 60 runs and took perhaps the best stumping of his career to dismiss Aussie Test player Stuart Law with a leg side take off the medium-fast Craig Wright. Sussex were also beaten at Hove.

There were lows to match the highs, with the crushing disappointment of missing out on a place at the 2003 World Cup in South Africa. Smith's individual performances in the qualifying tournament hosted by Canada made him the leading batsman and saw him described as 'Test class' by ICC president Dr Ali Bacher – but it was not enough to earn a World Cup place and led to the loss of Smith's status as a full-time pro player with Sport Scotland and a place on the dole queue. True to form, Smith picked himself up and dusted himself down to help drive the national team forward in the following years.

Colin Smith (left) faces Namibia in the Intercontinental Cup at Mannofield in 2006 (Picture by Kami Thomson).

In the winter of 2004 there was joy in the sunshine as Scotland won the inaugural ICC Intercontinental Cup at the Sharjah ground in the United Arab Emirates, defeating Canada in the Final. It sparked wonderful scenes of celebration and those were repeated in 2005 when the ICC Trophy in Ireland saw Smith and his colleagues sail to the Final and beat the hosts by 47 runs in Dublin.

The progress continued apace as qualification for the 2007 World Cup in the West Indies was secured. Smith was on the plane for the global festival, an achievement in itself since he had been on the brink of quitting top-class cricket four years earlier due to the difficulties in combining the sport with his work and family commitments.

Smith's form brought interest from Sussex and Warwickshire but his dream was to play professionally for Scotland, something made impossible by the lack of funds available to the governing body. He enrolled with the police in 2003 and was unsure how the new career would sit with his life as an globe-trotting sportsman. After completing his training, the force were very supportive and his burning ambition to sample the World Cup atmosphere flickered back into life.

Scotland were defeated by eventual winners Australia in their opening match and suffered reverses against South Africa and the Netherlands, a harsh introduction to the competition but a learning curve for all involved. For Smith the Caribbean trip brought personal satisfaction at least, with a sparkling half-century against the Aussies in St Kitts earning plaudits from the watching media corps. The stand of 51 included seven fours against an attack which ripped apart a string of opponents that summer on their way to winning back-to-back World Cups. The Aberdeenshire star became the first Scot to record a one-day half-century since Gavin Hamilton in 1999.

There was no time for Smith or his colleagues to reflect on the World Cup display, as the Twenty20 World Championship in South Africa in the winter of 2007 proved an understandable distraction, with enticing group fixtures against Pakistan and India on the cards. The first ended in defeat while the second was hit by rain, robbing the Scots of the chance to test their mettle against an Indian side which went on to lift the trophy.

The Twenty20 showpiece in 2009, in which South Africa and New Zealand got the better of Scotland, proved to be Smith's international swansong. With coach Pete Steindl building for the future, he bowed out to concentrate on his contribution to the Aberdeenshire cause. He had claimed a record 261 dismissals at the top level for the national team and scored 3,763 runs, including his personal best of 93 against Kenya during the run to the Intercontinental Cup title in 2004.

He was a major player for Shire in the glorious 2009 campaign, in which the Mannofield outfit claimed the SNCL Premier Division title in their first season after promotion back to the top flight. Smith, who was approaching his 37th birthday when the prize was won, was an old head in a youthful Shire squad. Victory in the Scottish Cup Final against Dunfermline ensured it was a double celebration, with Smith joined by Neil Macrae and Kevin Thomson in the group of survivors from the twin trophy success of 1996.

Since then Smith has become a husband to Karen, father to Khiya, an international cricketer of great repute, a time-served police officer, *Press and Journal* cricket columnist and inventor into the bargain. As director of equipment firm Ledgends, the innovative player has designed and created the Katchet device for fielding practice and his design has won glowing endorsements from coaches across the globe. In use by every international team, including the superstars of Australia, the invention ensures Smith's involvement in the game at the highest level lives on despite his retirement from playing.

Frank Robertson

Frank Robertson announced his arrival to international cricket in the finest possible style when he produced a stunning nine-wicket haul on his maiden appearance. It was the perfect debut and set the rookie on the road to a long career in Scotland colours, flying the flag for Aberdeenshire Cricket Club across the world during a decade playing at the highest level.

The date for Robertson's dramatic introduction to the global game was 22 June 1971 and the venue was Belfast. The Tartan tourists were tackling an Irish side enjoying their richest vein of form ever and that went on to finish the year undefeated in six matches.

He was a 27-year-old pace bowler with a wealth of experience in the club game when he got the nod to step forward and accept the challenge, taking the place of the retired Doug Barr in the squad. His predecessor had been a stalwart for years and was recognised as one of the finest ever to play for his country, so there were big shoes to fill. The new man was undaunted and began to carve out his own niche in the team.

He got off to a blistering start as the first three Irish batsmen fell victim to his talents inside the first five overs, at the cost of a miserly 10 runs. The man from the Granite City went on to record a match return of nine for 79. It was a truly incredible performance and a debut that will never be forgotten by Scottish cricket fans of the 1970s.

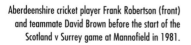

Aberdeenshire cricket player Frank Robertson (front) and teammate David Brown before the start of the Scotland v Surrey game at Mannofield in 1981.

It also took the name of Frank Robertson to a wider audience as the impressive figures were picked up on by *Wisden*, the cricket bible. The Scot's display in Belfast was noted in that year's edition as one of the greatest individual displays of the season and caused a major stir on the British scene.

The 1970s were transitional years for the game north of the border as the sport grew in popularity and began to move towards participation in mainstream competitions in England, with entry to the Benson & Hedges Cup and NatWest Trophy not coming until the following decade.

Robertson's own career ran until 1981, and he had a big role to play in paving the way towards a place at the top of the table as he played in the first five Benson & Hedges games in 1981, making 45 appearances for Scotland as the country attempted to gain a foothold. Although the first competitive fixture was played in 1865, it was not until 1994 that the nation joined the International Cricket Council as an associate member.

During Robertson's tour of duty the game was still developing but it did not hinder his opportunities. As well as playing on home soil against Pakistan, Australia, New Zealand, the West Indies, Sri Lanka and India he was included in travelling parties in destinations as far-flung as Thailand, Hong Kong, Malaysia and South Africa, as well as enjoying game time at legendary venues such as Lord's.

Those exotic ports of call were a far cry from the paths he trod while establishing himself as a player with great potential. He learnt the subtleties of the game as a pupil of Robert Gordon's College and went on to represent West St Clements in Grade Two of the Aberdeen Cricket Association set-up, braving the chilling North Sea winds at the links pitches after accepting an invitation from one of his teachers to join the

enthusiastic group of players at a club which had been part of the grades scene since the 1930s. The West St Clements name disappeared from the flourishing competition in 1971, by which time the man who would become their most decorated former pupil had already moved on.

He started life as a batsman of great repute, topping the grade 2 averages with a figure of 68.4 in one of his six seasons with the club. Robertson always considered himself an all-rounder and insisted that working with a bat in his grasp was always more fulfilling than bowling, with the obvious exception of his notable debut.

Frank Robertson demonstrates his skills in 1981.

Over time the Aberdonian's bowling ability came to the fore and, despite two first class 50s for Scotland, it was with the ball in hand that he became better known as an international player. His move towards Scotland honours began when he was tempted to step up from grades cricket to the Strathmore Union with Gordonians. In 1969 he was promoted to county level with Aberdeenshire and within two years of that move the call came from the national team's selectors.

It was while starring for Shire at Mannofield that bowling began to dominate Robertson's contribution to the team and it was in that role that he won elevation to the Scotland squad. He had arrived at Aberdeenshire, where his younger brother Peter also played his cricket, with a medium-paced delivery before having his action reshaped and his speed increased dramatically – adding what became trademark aggression to his armoury. Inspirational Shire captain and coach George Murray was among those to help Robertson on the path to success during a period in which the west end club produced a fine crop of cricketers. He had already shown flashes of that potential at local level and in one 1969 match for Gordonians he bagged nine wickets for eight runs against a shell-shocked Montrose outfit.

Robertson went on to make his mark with Aberdeenshire and in turn won selection for the Scottish counties select side. Vic Coutts, the former Buckie and Aberdeenshire bowler, was the proud president of the Scottish Counties Board as the player he had passed on his expertise to began to make a name for himself on a wider platform. The counties representation proved a stepping stone to the international scene, where he claimed some notable scalps.

The most famous casualty of Robertson's bowling was Australian favourite Greg Chappell. The Baggy Greens had travelled north to Perth to face Scotland in 1972 and thousands of eager supporters had turned out at North Inch to see the superstars of the Aussie game in the flesh.

In the end it was a player from far closer to home who stole the show, with Aberdeen's finest shocking the tourists when he claimed one of the early order through an lbw in the second over. Australia had just two runs on the board when Chappell strode forward to steady the nerves and put the Scottish upstarts in their place.

Facing just his second ball, Chappell could only watch in horror as a fiery Robertson delivery ripped his middle stump from the Perthshire soil and sent him trudging back to the pavilion. The Aussies recovered to win by six wickets, but it did not detract from the Aberdeenshire bowler's moment of glory. It was the only occasion on which the esteemed star from the southern hemisphere failed to score during that summer's tour of Britain, a campaign which included victory against England in the Auld Enemy's back yard.

Chappell was not the only big name to suffer at Robertson's hands, with Indian batsman Sunil Gavaskar and English duo Dennis Amiss and John Jameson also discovering to their cost that the man from the north could bowl a decent ball. Chappell, however, was very much the jewel in the crown. The Adelaide-born veteran is regarded as one of the greatest batsmen ever produced by his country, captaining the side in two separate spells and winning high praise for his reactions and style.

Robertson was his equal that day in Perth and it was an undoubted highlight. The Aberdeen-born player set records along the way, becoming Aberdeenshire's most-capped player when he smashed through George Youngson's long-standing record of 25 appearances for Scotland in 1979. Youngson, also a bowler of some repute, played between 1947 and 1955, but was relegated to second place on the all-time list at Mannofield when Robertson made his 26th appearance against Warwickshire at Edgbaston. His form led to the award as Scotland's Man of the Season in 1979 and a call-up to the county squad of professional side Worcester two years later.

A further 19 appearances followed before the final delivery of his international career in 1981, with Robertson continuing to represent his former club Gordonians with dedication in the years that followed and also indulging his passion for Aberdeen Football Club. Robertson was part of the Red Army as it marched on Gothenburg in 1983 to witness Alex Ferguson's team win the European Cup-Winners' Cup against Real Madrid. He could also spend time on his other hobbies, including golf and swimming, while devoting more time to life outside of sport. He was made an honorary member of the Aberdeen Sportsman's Club in 1982 and three years later became a founder member of the Aberdeen Sports Council.

In tandem with his cricket accomplishments he was forging a successful career as an architect and has risen to become a partner in respected Aberdeen firm Thomson Craig and Donald.

George Youngson

At close to 6ft 5in tall, Dr George Youngson was a fearsome sight for the batsmen he loomed large upon. The Aberdeenshire and Scotland bowler is regarded as one of the finest exponents of his discipline ever to take to the field in his home country and even today, almost half a century since his last appearance at county level, the Aberdonian's record stands up to the closest of scrutiny.

He had cut his teeth pre-war with Gordonians and was already a hero at the Seafield club after his late show in the Three Counties Cup Final against Strathmore at Brechin in 1939, when he scored two runs off the last ball of the game

George Youngson pictured in Aberdeenshire whites in 1960.

to clinch a single-run victory. The umpires had actually called time on the match prematurely and awarded the victory to Strathmore, before the scorekeepers realised an error had been made in calculating the number of deliveries in the final over and the teams were sent back out for the sixth and all-important ball. Under pressure, the youngster stepped up and delivered the match-winning blow.

Youngson, who was also a talented badminton player, had been added to the Gordonians squad in 1937 after leaving Robert Gordon's College and was regarded at that time as an opening batsman. At one stage he contemplated quitting the game altogether, but was talked round by club secretary John Bisset, who asked him to turn out for the reserve side in a grades fixture against Stoneywood. He did not bat that day, but Youngson did take five wickets for 20 runs with the ball in hand and from that point on his reputation as a bowler grew week on week.

He was instantly promoted to the Gordonians first team and eventually joined the list of players blooded by the club who went on to play for Scotland. Ronnie Chisholm and brothers Tom and Frank Findlay were among the other prominent names who made the grade at the highest level.

His career outside of sport took him on a mini-tour of Britain. After graduating he worked with ICI Explosives in the west of Scotland and Welwyn Garden City before a posting as a lecturer at Robert Gordon's Institute of Technology brought him home to the Granite City. He served at RGIT until his retirement, combining his prominent role at the institution, which has since become the Robert Gordon University, with his burgeoning sideline as a cricketer of worldwide repute.

Youngson's ability with bat and ball during his early days with the Gordonians team did not go unnoticed and he was soon given a bigger stage to perform on. When competitive cricket resumed in the aftermath of the war, Youngson began to hit his stride with Aberdeenshire. In the first season of the county game, in 1946, he finished second equal in the country's bowling average table. He was tied with Perthshire's English professional Bill Barber, an indication of the level to which Youngson was bowling.

The following year Youngson's good form was rewarded with his first international cap, and as the seasons rolled on he got better and better. In 1948 and for the next three years he topped the bowling average in the county game, with a figure as low as 6.61 in 1949.

The four post-war seasons in which Youngson flourished had coincided with Shire's dominance in Scottish cricket, clinching a quartet of County Championships in succession in what has been noted as the finest period in the rich history of the club. Founded in 1857, Aberdeenshire won its first county title in 1903, but the dominance of the 1940s was unparalleled. Indeed, after the 1949 triumph there was a 26-year wait for the trophy to be brought back to the west end of Aberdeen.

It is no coincidence that the glory years incorporated Youngson's personal progression. He was a tremendously technical player, with a mixed bag of tricks and a wonderful technique which ensured he used his height to great advantage as balls rained down on beleaguered batsmen from his elevated stance.

His first appearance for Scotland in 1947 hinted at what lay ahead as he began as he meant to continue, claiming six wickets for just 19 runs on his first appearance for

George Youngson in action for Aberdeenshire in 1962.

Scotland. The match was played in Cork against Ireland, but the luck was certainly with the visitors as they unearthed a gem of a new recruit in Youngson.

His swift rise to the national team, just a year after making his Aberdeenshire debut, was a ringing endorsement of his skills and in 1948 he was Shire's sole representative in the famous match against Australia at Mannofield as Sir Donald Bradman made his farewell appearance on British soil. Sir Donald responded with a century to thrill the north-east crowd crammed into the charming city ground, but they had their own star in Scotland colours that day. Records show that 20,000 filed into the confines to witness Bradman's swashbuckling style at first hand, a record that will never be broken since the modern-day capacity is set at 6,000 on health and safety grounds.

Youngson served for 11 years with the national side before deciding to retire from the international fold in 1958, turning down the opportunity to face New Zealand because he did not feel suited to the rigours of three-day internationals. He had won his 25th cap in 1955 but opted not to add a 26th when the Kiwis toured. He was already Aberdeenshire's record post-war cap holder, a figure not beaten until the emergence of Frank Robertson in the 1970s.

His concerns about his ability to perform for Scotland were not reflected in his county displays, with his 1958 campaign proving his best on record at county level as his average was cut to just 5.1. In the same season he also set a new counties record by taking nine for seven against Clackmannan at Mannofield. He had taken nine against Fifeshire at his home ground in 1953 and went on to repeat that feat in 1960 against West Lothian.

In 1956, in recognition of his decade of service to the county, Youngson was appointed captain of Aberdeenshire and he continued to be a mainstay for the Mannofield men. He held the coveted position through the 1957 centenary year, an eminent figurehead to lead the club in its celebrations. The highlight of the 100th anniversary programme was a visit from English county champions Surrey.

He served as skipper for three years in total and then the 1959 season saw Youngson become the first player in the history of Scottish county cricket to claim 500 wickets, reaching the milestone in a match against Perthshire. Unbeknown to the player, officials squirrelled the ball away and had it inscribed before presenting it as a memento of the remarkable accomplishment months later. Youngson was a modest man and gentle soul, despite his imposing physical stature, which made a cricket bat look like a toy in the grasp of his hands, but he did not have to shout about his contribution to the cause to be noticed. His actions spoke far louder than words.

The late 1950s were heady days for Shire, who had recruited Rohan Kanhai from British Guyana in 1958. Over three years the West Indian professional bagged more than 4,000 runs as he clocked up century after century. With Youngson doing the damage when the opposition were in to bat, there was a twin-pronged attack.

In 1962, as Youngson's 17th season with Aberdeenshire wound down, the affable scientist announced his decision to retire from the game and indulge more fully in his developing hobby as a keen angler. He had taken up the serene pastime during his cricket days and many noted that the patience required on the riverbank had added an extra edge to his game as he matured, an ideal quality to compensate for the slight loss of pace every bowler suffers as the years are racked up.

At championship level he bowled close to 2,600 overs, with almost 850 maidens, took more than 570 wickets and finished with an average of 9.4 runs per wicket. It had been a wonderful journey. His final appearance at Mannofield in a county fixture was against Fifeshire on 28 July, a sad day for cricket fans in the north-east as they waved farewell to one of their heroes.

Youngson died in hospital in Aberdeen in December 1982 at the age of 62, but lives on in the memory of Aberdeenshire members as a legendary former captain and international star.

Dallas Moir

For any budding Scottish cricketer growing up in the Granite City there are two major goals to aim for. One is to represent the country and the other is to earn a crack at the English county game – a double that Dallas Moir managed to achieve during the 1980s as he set about making a name for himself on both sides of Hadrian's Wall.

County contracts have proved harder to come by than Scotland caps for generations of north-east players, but Moir is one of the few to have succeeded in carving out a career in the promised land of England's domestic game. With competition for places on playing rosters fierce, it takes an extra-special talent to overcome geography and catch the eye of selectors while playing in the often-forgotten cricket lands of Scotland.

In recent years Stoneywood-Dyce youth product Kyle Coetzer has blazed a fresh trail, leaving Aberdeen Grammar School behind to join the youth academy at Durham

Dallas Moir during his Derbyshire days in 1982.

Dallas Moir and Jeremy Moir pictured in 2007.

and progressing to the first team with the English club. He made his breakthrough in the Durham team and helped them to the Friends Provident Trophy in 2007 to open his account as an honour-winning professional cricketer.

Coetzer, Aberdeen-born to a South African family, first came to Durham's attention when he played for Scotland A against their second string in the summer of 2001. Within months he had been tempted south to join their youth academy, becoming the seventh Scotsman to be recruited by Durham. He was already a member of the Scotland Under-17 squad, as an all-rounder who excelled with the bat, and continued to progress after concentrating full-time on the sport. He rose to captain the Under-19 side.

In 2003 Coetzer, whose brothers Shaun and Stuart are Stoneywood-Dyce stalwarts who have also been involved with the Scottish national set-up, was called up by his country as his career in England began to take off. The following year he became a senior pro with Durham and in August 2007 he enjoyed his best outing to date when he smashed 142 runs against Warwickshire at the Riverside in the County Championship to join a distinguished group of Scottish players to have scored centuries in the English game. That group includes former England captain Mike Denness, Brian Hardie, Willie Donald, Dougie Brown and Gavin Hamilton – as well as a certain Dallas Moir, the first Aberdonian ever to hit the magical mark in a county game.

Coetzer's confident adjustment to life in the competitive county scene is proof positive that talent will be spotted no matter how far removed from the traditional county hotbeds a player may be. For Moir that was also the case and it presented him with some memorable moments. Born in Malta as a twin in 1957, Moir is another of the honorary Aberdonians to qualify as a Granite Legend. He first began playing competitively as a pupil at Hazlehead primary school and continued to impress after switching to Aberdeen Grammar School.

He and twin brother Jeremy played side by side throughout their school days, playing for the school first XI as well as in the Grammar former pupils team in grades cricket by the age of 14. Both slotted in comfortably to the man's game, both went on to step up a level play for Aberdeenshire, at separate times, and both claimed a wicket on their Shire debuts. The twins went on to study accountancy and also shared sporting interests as keen golfers and basketball players for Aberdeen Thistle, although it was cricket that took precedence.

As the pair matured, Jeremy settled with Grammar former pupils and Dallas emerged as a slow left-arm bowler and right-handed batsman with Aberdeenshire. He won the Scottish Championship with Shire in 1977 and the following season, at the age of 21, was crowned as the country's Young Cricketer of the Year.

By then the 6ft 7in starlet, who stood out as much for his ability as his towering presence, had sampled representative cricket with the Scottish Colts against an English school select at Perth in 1975 and he went on to make the progression to the full Scotland side.

Moir was a key part of the squad for the national team's first venture into county cricket, playing in the Benson and Hedges Cup in 1980 and making a big impression on the teams he came up against. Worcestershire, Nottinghamshire and Derbyshire all made advances towards the up-and-coming young Scot.

The Aberdeenshire player sounded out some of the major influences on his career, including Scotland manager Brian Close, and plumped for the three-year contract tabled by Derbyshire. The mid-table Midlands outfit were seeking a replacement for veteran spinner David Steele as he began to wind down and the fact that Moir offered a rare left-arm delivery was an added bonus. His economical bowling had been a major feature of Scotland's foray into the B&H competition and he also starred against the West Indies at Forthill in 1980, taming even the most aggressive of the visiting batsmen and producing a knock of 19 with the bat.

Derby's plan was to ease Moir into life as a professional in the second string as he fell under the wing of their more experienced campaigners, including England vice-captain Geoff Miller. Moir followed in the footsteps of 1960s Aberdeenshire player David Stewart, who made the move to Worcestershire at his peak, and turned his back on a promising job as a computer operator to try his hand in pro cricket. Computing was an emerging field and one offering potential for the future, but any young sportsman offered the opportunity to mix with the very best in his game of choice would find it difficult to resist and Moir packed his bag to relocate and engross himself in life at the County Ground.

He made his top-team debut in his maiden season but came into his own in 1982, when he was promoted permanently and established himself as Derbyshire's leading bowler with 76 wickets. Experts tipped the young bowler from Aberdeen to become the first Scotsman to play for the English national side since Mike Denness.

Moir, whose brother Jeremy also went on to represent Scotland, had enjoyed tremendous personal success in his first full season as a county player, but it was not enough to convince him that his long-term future lay in England. He contemplated a return to Aberdeen at the end of the 1982 campaign, turning out for the Mannofield XI while back in the Granite City to consider his plans, and by the end of the year announced his decision to reject the offer of a two-year deal and turn his back on the paid game. It was a bold move, with the player citing a lack of security in the sports world as his primary reason. He had also struggled to adjust to the concept of playing cricket for cash rather than enjoyment and found the daily grind of practice had taken the shine off the game for him.

Derbyshire described the shock news of Moir's loss as a 'disaster' and set about attempting to persuade him to rethink the move. In the spring of 1983 the English side struck lucky, finally convincing Moir to return south with the offer of a two-year contract on improved terms.

In July 1984 the spin bowler savoured his finest moment and it was with bat rather than ball that he hogged the limelight, claiming a century against Warwickshire at Chesterfield just weeks after falling two runs short against Gloucestershire. Even the might of former England captain Bob Willis failed to trouble Moir, who calmly crashed three sixes off the deliveries of Willis on his way to 100 from 75 balls in the space of just 95 minutes. It was just a minute outside of the fastest century of the season. That season he was also second in the bowling stakes at Derby, behind West Indian star Michael Holding.

Every winter he would return to the north-east to await the start of the new season, keeping in shape with regular outings for the Grammar former pupils rugby club's third team, and report back for action as the covers came off around the county scene. The 1985 campaign proved to be his final experience of the English game as Moir returned to Aberdeen, surrendered his professional status and rejoined his friends at Aberdeenshire. For the first time in five years cricket became fun, rather than a job, and he could once again savour the guile of the Scottish domestic scene after enduring the pace-obsessed nature of the game in the south.

Moir, who continued to represent Scotland through to 1986, dropped out of the Shire side in 1987 due to the travel commitments involved and concentrated instead on life in the Aberdeen grades with Grammar former pupils. While Dallas was taking a step back, his twin Jerry was on the rise and represented Scotland until his retirement from the international game in 1992.

MOTORSPORT

David Gillanders

Blood, sweat and tears have been vital ingredients for many of sport's greatest triumphs, but for rally driver David Gillanders it was a combination of mud, guts and thunder that earned him a place in his sport's history books. The mud was on the surface of the road at Telford Park in Shropshire, he had the guts and determination to overhaul a substantial deficit to live his dream, and the thunder came courtesy of the finely-tuned V6 engine of his trusty Metro 6R4.

Mixed together they gave Gillanders the perfect result – the National Rally Championship prize. When the Aberdeen businessman, who built a multi-franchise garage group, won the 1987 title he became the first Scotsman to be crowned top dog in the prestigious UK-wide competition. The gravel and tarmac rally series had become established as a testing

David Gillanders during his peak years.

ground for leading manufacturers and Gillanders helped establish the distinctive Metro as a car to be reckoned with as well as underlining his own credentials as a fearless driver with the ability to squeeze the very last second out of the vehicle.

The talented north-east speedster went into the final round of the NRC season knowing he required victory to clinch the Championship he had been working towards all year. The programme concluded with the Audi Sport Rally in Telford, Shropshire, and the meticulous Gillanders left nothing to chance. On the eve of the event, in pitch darkness, he could be found pacing the final stage through Telford Park to get a feel for the challenge ahead. The mud under foot helped him make a vital decision, plumping for gravel tyres. He went into the final stage five seconds off the lead but by the end of it had dragged himself ahead, winning with a four-second victory and securing the points needed to lift the season's big trophy.

Gillanders, who teamed up with Welsh co-driver Ken Rees for his victorious campaign on the British scene, finished just a single point ahead of English challenger Terry Smith. It was a thrilling end to a memorable season for the man from the Granite City, the culmination of more than a decade of hard work and dedication.

David Gillanders (left) and co-driver Ken Rees celebrate victory in the British National Rally Championship in 1987.

As the son of a city garage owner, cars were in his blood. As soon as he got his driver's licence, Gillanders joined the competitive motorsport scene in and around his home city in tandem with a career in the same industry as his father. He was a leading hill climb competitor and also began rallying as a teenager, serving a long and thorough apprenticeship throughout the 1970s as he learnt his trade.

Gillanders started out in a reliable if unspectacular Volvo 140 before switching to a Ford RS2000 and then Ford RS1800 in the late 1970s. It was the introduction of the wild Metro 6R4 to the rally landscape in the 1980s that paved the way for Gillanders to fulfill his potential.

He first tested the Metro in 1986 and immediately found it to his liking. By the time the 1987 season opened he was settled in the driver's seat and ready to show the best in the business just how difficult he would be to match in a model that had overcome considerable teething problems during more than four years of development by Austin Rover, who were attempting to blend the qualities of the legendary four-wheel drive Audi Quattro with the nimbleness of the Renault 5 Turbo.

The compact Metro proved a trusty partner for Gillanders and the National Rally Championship win in 1987 was the highlight of the year and one of the peaks of his career, although the season could have been even better had it not been for a controversial sting in the tale. Following his success at UK level in the NRC, Gillanders turned his attention to the Scottish Rally Championship. He had already won the East of Scotland prize and wanted the national trophy to complete a hat-trick of coveted awards.

He entered the final event in the Trossachs as the series leader – but then disaster struck. Gillanders clipped a rock during the opening stage and ripped a front wheel from its axle. He and navigator Rees took time out to carry out a makeshift repair and limped through a succession of stages to the designated service stop. They overcame the difficulties to climb from 59th place, where they had languished after the accident, to 19th spot. It was enough to win the Scottish title by a single point from Murray Grierson – but his rival had other ideas.

A protest was lodged by Grierson on the basis that Gillanders had received illegal assistance to get his car back on track. The disgruntled challenger was backed up by eight witnesses – but all offered conflicting versions of events, ranging from claims

David Gillanders displays the Martin Challenge Trophy he won for claiming the National Rally Championship in 1987.

that the Aberdeen car had been fixed by a crew of mechanics in boilersuits out on the stage, to a tale that the repairs had been conducted hidden from view behind a petrol station. Despite the discrepancies in the accounts, stewards opted to uphold the complaint and Grierson was named as the 1987 Scottish champ. Grierson collected the prize again in 1993 and also went on to work closely with Colin McRae and his brother Alistair during the pair's World Rally Championship adventures.

It was a sickening blow for Gillanders at the end of a year in which he had established himself as one of the most talented rally drivers of his generation. He opted against an appeal, believing a long drawn-out wrangle would have harmed the sport he loved, but could lay claim to being the unofficial national winner having got the better of his rivals throughout the year.

The powerful and heavily backed works rally teams sat up and took notice of the rising privateer who had swept to prominence, but the respected city businessman continued as an independent driver throughout his career.

Gillanders moved with the times as technology developed in the notoriously expensive pursuit, swapping his trusty Metro for one of the new generation of Escort Cosworth models in the early 1990s. The aggressively sculpted Escort, with its huge rear wing, was as agile as it was fierce – the perfect weapon for an assault on the major titles. Having grown up competing in the raucous Escort-based RS2000 and RS1800 Fords of the 1970s, it was a case of going back to his roots for the Aberdonian.

Just as it had in the previous decade, the change of machine provided a fresh impetus and in 1994 Gillanders was just one victory away from a second National Rally Championship. On that occasion he was edged out by just 17 seconds as

David Gillanders is one of the Aberdeen drivers to have made it to the top in rallying.

Cumbrian ace Chris Mellors took the season's honours, but it demonstrated that Gillanders was still able to live with the best in the business. Just one point was the difference between first place and the runner's-up spot and Gillanders was understandably high on confidence.

In 1995 that belief translated into a storming performance in the Scottish Rally Championship as he won the prize for the first time in his lengthy service in the sport. The confirmation came when he took the final place on the podium at the Ayr-based stages – the last event on that year's calendar. It was a tense affair as Gillanders and Edinburgh counterpart John Baird ended tied on points after eight rallies, with the competition's countback system used to declare the man from the north as the eventual winner.

He joined illustrious company as king of the Scottish stages, with the late great Colin McRae and Jimmy Girvan among the household names to have had their names engraved on the trophy before Gillanders. Andrew Cowan, who went on to found the incredibly successful Mitsubishi Ralliart team, is another to proudly list the SRC prize on his resumé.

Having taken part in his first rally in the 1960s, it was a long but worthwhile wait for Gillanders to scoop the Scottish trophy. Satisfied he had accomplished everything he had set out to achieve, with both the national and British titles listed on his CV, it was the perfect time for Gillanders to retire from top-level motorsport and he bowed out on a high at the end of that victorious 1995 season.

The lure of the Granite City Rally, his home event and one he first won in 1986, tempted him to make a brief return to the fold in 1996, but his competitive outings were handpicked in the years that followed. Since then he has gone on to assist Land Rover UK with development projects and has turned his hand to motoring journalism as a road tester for various publications as well as maintaining his life-long link to the car trade as a partner in the company B2B Vehicle Solutions.

His achievements in winning the Scottish Rally Championship have since been matched by Brian Lyall, who claimed the crown in 1997, and fellow city driver Dave Weston in 2006.

BOXING

Lee McAllister

The Aberdeen Beach Ballroom has played host to some huge acts in the seaside venue's illustrious history, but none, not even The Beatles, has ever received the type of raucous reception reserved for the Granite City's most famous boxing son: Lee McAllister.

The self-styled Aberdeen Assassin has performed in front of crowds at arenas up and down the country, from the Robin Park in Wigan to the Aberdeen Exhibition and Conference Centre on his home patch, but his greatest displays have been reserved for his spiritual home in the Art Deco surroundings of the distinctive dance hall. Built with more sedate pursuits in mind, the 1920s design has become an unlikely setting for some momentous fight nights that have had the ballroom shaking to its foundations as McAllister's legion of followers roared on their hero in his quest for national recognition.

With his entertaining style and love of the media spotlight, the Silver City performer is adept at drumming up interest in his shows. Then there are his close links to Aberdeen Football Club, as a high-profile Dons fan who has adopted club colours to the extent of dying his hair red for his fights. In between bouts McAllister can often be found at Pittodrie, where he is a welcome visitor at the training and treatment facilities at the ground, and he has often been held up as an inspiration to the squad by managers Jimmy Calderwood and Mark McGhee.

Lee McAllister has carved out a reputation as a flamboyant and confident fighter (Picture by Raymond Besant).

McAllister and the Dons share their support and the football chants ringing around the crowd at his fights bear testament to the close bonds, making for a colourful and noisy spectacle. Three nights in particular brought the fans flocking through the doors to fill the compact Beach Ballroom to capacity and on each occasion the home boxer left the ring with a belt to parade to the assembled crowd.

The first was in October 2007 when former Commonwealth champion Craig Docherty ventured north from his Glasgow base to tackle McAllister in his own backyard. The WBU lightweight title was on the line and the experienced campaigner from the west coast proved a tough nut for the young challenger to crack. With an expectant home audience up on its feet as the pair locked horns, a telling blow from McAllister left the visitor nursing a burst eardrum and allowed the Aberdonian to try on the belt for size.

The roar which greeted McAllister's lap of honour was lost on the Glaswegian, but slowly the wider boxing public was being forced to take note of the boy from what had traditionally been classed as a boxing backwater by those with their focus on the Central Belt beat.

McAllister went on to add the WBU light welterweight prize after defeating Romanian opponent Mihaita Mutu at the AECC, but those titles were always going to be a stepping stone for the single-minded and extrovert showman. The fighter parted company with Brendan Ingle, the manager who had guided the bulk of his career following his move into the professional arena in 2002, and teamed up with Glasgow promoter Tommy Gilmour in 2008. The wily Gilmour promised a bigger platform and greater exposure, two vows which were instantly delivered in one fell swoop when McAllister was paired with highly-rated Manchester battler John Murray in a British lightweight showdown in Wigan.

The Beach Ballroom has become a home from home for Aberdeen favourite Lee McAllister, pictured landing a knockout punch against Charlie King (Picture by Kenny Elrick).

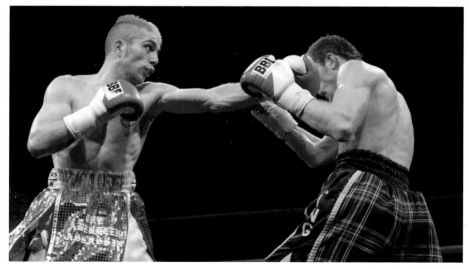

The fight, televised live on ITV as the Aberdonian finally got the national audience he had long craved, ended in victory for the Englishman, but McAllister's confident display in and outside of the ring served to highlight his credentials. Murray was the overwhelming favourite going into the match, but McAllister toyed with him in stages of an exciting contest before being felled by a perfect body blow in the eighth round. He was beaten but far from disgraced by the toughest opponent he had ever faced.

It was a case of one step back to go two forward as Gilmour switched tack in the wake of what was only the second defeat for McAllister in a 29-fight run up to that point, sending McAllister back to the familiar surroundings of the Aberdeen Beach Ballroom for a shot at the Commonwealth lightweight belt in June 2009.

This time it was the turn of African competitor Godfred Sowah to sample the intimidating welcome whipped up by the north-east fanatics for every big fight night in the city. The Ghanaian had no answer to the fast-moving Scotsman with his deceptive feints and lightning speed across the canvas, and the referee stopped the fight in the third round to hand McAllister a coveted Commonwealth title and create a second piece of boxing history at the Ballroom.

The third big night followed soon after when the more familiar name of Charlie King was put to the sword on the North Sea shore in October 2009 as the belt was defended in style, with McAllister winning in the seventh round.

A mandatory defence in Glasgow early in 2010 against Ghana's Samuel Amoako followed as McAllister set his sights on building towards further British and European title bouts on his way to the ultimate goal of a world prize prior to his well-planned retirement.

McAllister, a sharp-witted and switched-on young boxer who has already formed his own promotions company to add another string to his bow, had already stated his intention to pack away his gloves at a decent age. The plan is to bow out on a high and settle into family life with his wife and young daughter. Family has always been a major influence on McAllister's career, with his wife, parents and brothers ringside at every fight to spur him on. The clan connection extends far beyond cheerleading though, with his development in the ring led by his father David and brother David junior.

Both are respected trainers in their own right and have been with McAllister every step of the way as he has climbed from the youth and amateur sport to the upper echelons of pro boxing. David McAllister senior has helped a generation of talented young city fighters reach their potential as founder of the Granite City Boxing Club in the 1990s, working from the gym tucked away off Clifton Road. David McAllister junior has continued the tradition and his abilities were recognised in 2006 when he was named as one of the coaches for the Scottish team at the Commonwealth Games in Manchester.

Many from the club have gone on to compete at national level as amateurs and a group have also entered the paid ranks, including James Ancliff from Fettercairn. The next batch of professionals to hail from the Granite City stable could well carry the McAllister moniker, with Lee's younger brother Steven already a Commonwealth Games veteran following his involvement in the Manchester games and Matthew,

Lee McAllister training at the Aberdeen Sports Village (Picture by Kevin Emslie).

another brother in the city's best-known boxing family, also making waves in the ring. The siblings are following in medal-winning footsteps, with uncle James McAllister having claimed silver at the 1986 Commonwealth Games in Edinburgh.

Lee is the trailblazer for the emerging youngsters, having turned pro at the age of 20 in 2002 when he launched his career with a bout against Baz Carey at the Braehead Arena in Glasgow. The debut contest ended in a points victory and over the next year he racked up an impressive run of nine further wins. The only blot was a defeat against Dean Hickman, a fight taken at short notice and a decision McAllister was left to rue. That was late in 2003 and it was not until Murray's victory in 2009 that the Aberdeen Assassin sampled the bitter taste of defeat again. In between he continued to cut his teeth home and away, recording his first stoppage in 2005 when Karl Taylor was his victim at the Beach Ballroom and going on to record TKOs against Jackson Williams and Stuart Green at his favourite venue before the pulsating and bruising encounter against Docherty in 2007.

The switch from the Ingle camp to Gilmour's stewardship in 2008 also brought a change of trainer, with Dave Coldwell picking up the reins and adding fresh impetus to the quest for perfection. Coldwell, with a reputation as one of the sport's most ambitious young coaches, knows his way around the ring as a former boxer of great repute and is determined to add to McAllister's repertoire as the new look team moves towards fulfilling Gilmour's masterplan for an all-out assault on further major titles.

MARTIAL ARTS

Bill Berry

When Bill Berry was awarded an MBE in the New Year honours in 1994 it recognised almost four decades of devotion to promoting judo in his home city. The retired Aberdeen policeman, who celebrated his 70th birthday in 2006, has played a major role in the sport's growth as a competitor, coach and administrator.

In time Berry's influence has extended beyond his own sport, with a role championing all local sportsmen and women as part of the Aberdeen Sports Council, and he was one of the first 21 individuals to be awarded a place in the city's sporting hall of fame when the list was announced in 2006. Berry was included alongside football legend Denis Law, golf's Open champion Paul Lawrie and Scotland rugby captain Chris Cusiter – a measure of the regard in which he is held by those who have watched at first hand the energy he has devoted to sport in the Granite City. The accolades and plaudits are a far cry from his beginnings in judo, when he was one of the few to embrace a sport that had yet to win the popularity which makes it a staple of major sporting events today.

Berry joined Aberdeen City Police as a constable in the late 1950s. A quiet and mild-mannered officer off the judo mat, he displayed a ruthless streak once he was in full judo regalia and established a reputation for his skill and instinct. He had his appetite whetted for the sport while serving overseas with the Scots Guards and maintained that interest

Bill Berry MBE, Chairman of Aberdeen Sports Council (Picture by Kami Thomson).

Bill Berry in action in 1971.

when he returned to home soil, joining the Aberdeen Judo Club and also founding a section dedicated to the pursuit with the force early in his police career.

The Aberdeen club, located a stone's throw from Woolmanhill Hospital in those early days, had been formed in 1952 to cater for a growing interest in a sport which had been intriguing British exponents since the 1920s. The popularity grew in the post-war years when greater television and film exposure developed and the merits of judo as a form of self-defence also became clear.

As a traditional form of Japanese wrestling, the key is yielding to an opponent's strength to overcome them rather than attempting to defeat them by force. Judo was developed from the older schools of jujitsu and in the 19th century various schools began to develop the new techniques. Dr Jigoro Kano, who died in 1938, combined the features of the various schools of the sport and codified the rules, opening the first school, or dojo, in 1882. Kano was a member of the International Olympic Committee and a respected figure in the sporting world, giving added credence to the new concept.

Outside of Japan, judo developed slowly. The first international match took place in 1926 between the Japanese Budokwai School and a German national team, but there was swifter growth around the corner and that stretched to the north-east. Whereas boxing had been the traditional combative sport of choice, the lure of a new and more exotic pursuit proved tempting to a number of men and women.

George Aspinall became Aberdeen's first ever black belt, although his injuries made a mockery of the English translation of judo: 'gentle way'. Aspinall once broke his neck during a contest, but recovered to become New Zealand's national champion following his emigration to the southern hemisphere. He represented New Zealand at the 1972 Olympics in Munich to confirm his place as Aberdeen's most successful judo export. The Japanese and Dutch dominated the German event, with judo returning to the programme after being left out for the 1968 games in Mexico.

The club Aspinall left behind flitted between various homes, including a Nissen hut in Hayton, a back room at the Bon Accord Baths and Smithfield Hall before finally finding a permanent base at the purpose-built Beach Leisure Centre. The more comfortable modern surroundings have been vital in bringing through the next batch of talented Aberdonians, who will benefit from the groundworks laid by the veterans. Sessions are held three nights a week to keep up with demand, but the principles of the sport have not changed during the lifespan of the club. By the 1970s, with Berry installed as club secretary, the city's black belt count had risen to seven. He was part of that number, having climbed to the top grade and risen to the status of first dan by that point.

There were more than 130 regular members of the judo club as people flocked to try something new. The throws, arm locks and holds take years to perfect and Berry had the patience and perseverance to become an expert. He also had the stamina required, once losing five pounds in weight during a single gruelling training session. He demonstrated his ability when he won the British Police Championship five times to add to the collection of local and Scottish honours to his credit.

While renowned as a competitor, Berry also developed into an accomplished administrator and coach, instrumental in taking the British Championship to the Butchart centre at Aberdeen University in 1971. He had twice reached the Final of the event and hoped to go one step further in front of a home crowd, but he struggled to make an impact and, after a series of painful and persistent injuries, retired from competition later that year.

The temptation to return and pull on the judogi once more was too strong, however, and in 1972 the familiar figure was back on the mat after being invited to captain the Scottish police judo team for an Auld Enemy meeting with England in Coventry.

Ronnie Watt is another of Aberdeen's leading lights in martial arts.

By that point he had qualified as a referee, joining a select group able to officiate at national level, and that expertise has taken him around the world in the decades since then as he climbed the ladder. By 1977 he was a third dan and in great demand as a referee and within two decades had become one of the country's few seventh dans.

In 1993 Berry was appointed chairman of the Aberdeen Sports Council and he has worked tirelessly on behalf of all sports in the city to win a fairer deal, knowing from first-hand experience how difficult it can be for clubs in the minority sports to thrive.

In judo, Berry was appointed as a member of the Scottish Judo Federation executive committee as far back as 1972 and has remained an influential figure in the sport at national level. His duties have included a spell as chairman of JudoScotland and other executive positions within the governing body. The organisation of the sport has moved with the times and a national training centre has ben established at Ratho, near Edinburgh, to meet demand for top-class facilities.

Berry has been a major part of a martial arts explosion in Scotland and the Granite City, with his own efforts in judo mirrored by those of Ronnie Watt in karate. Watt, who became Aberdeen's best-qualified instructor when he became a black belt second dan in 1983, has gone on to excel in his field and the Aberdeen Shotokan Karate Club he founded in 1966 has grown year on year during more than three decades in existence. He has risen to the status of eighth dan and serves as World Karate Confederation director of Shotokan as well as sitting on the organisation's technical board. In 2001 he brought the World Championships to the Aberdeen Exhibition and Conference Centre, attracting more than 800 competitors to a championship in which he had been a bronze medal-winner on 13 occasions. The event was designed to attract thousands of spectators and put the north-east on the map as a capable host for major martial arts meetings.

Like Berry, Watt has travelled the world learning his art and serving as an official. Both have become key figures in the north-east martial arts scene and helped to create wave after wave of interest among generations of enthusiastic youngsters.

The 1994 trip to Buckingham Palace for his investiture ceremony was a proud moment for a man who had served his country during national service. It was Berry's services to judo which were noted at the time, but the nomination also recognised the proud Aberdonian had a far wider influence than that as a true ambassador for his home city.